Wrist Assured

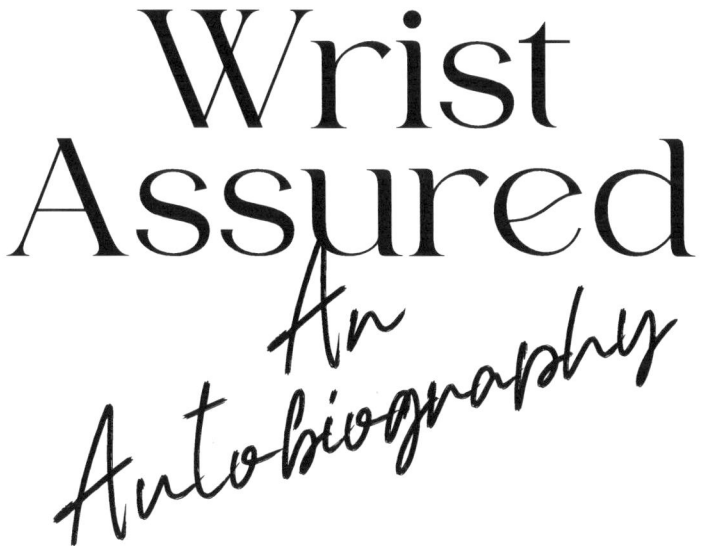

Wrist Assured
An Autobiography

GUNDAPPA VISHWANATH
with R. Kaushik

RUPA

First published by
Rupa Publications India Pvt. Ltd 2022
7/16, Ansari Road, Daryaganj
New Delhi 110002

Sales Centres:

Allahabad Bengaluru Chennai
Hyderabad Jaipur Kathmandu
Kolkata Mumbai

Copyright © Gundappa Vishwanath 2022

All rights reserved.
No part of this publication may be reproduced, transmitted,
or stored in a retrieval system, in any form or by any means,
electronic, mechanical, photocopying, recording or otherwise,
without the prior permission of the publisher.

The views and opinions expressed in this book are the author's own and the facts are as reported by him which have been verified to the extent possible, and the publishers are not in any way liable for the same.

ISBN: 978-93-5520-314-4

Second impression 2022

10 9 8 7 6 5 4 3 2

The moral right of the author has been asserted.

Printed at Manipal Technologies Limited

This book is sold subject to the condition that it shall not,
by way of trade or otherwise, be lent, resold, hired out, or otherwise
circulated, without the publisher's prior consent, in any form of binding
or cover other than that in which it is published.

*For all my well-wishers,
whose love and support encouraged me
to become the best version of myself.*

CONTENTS

1. An Evening Like No Other — 1
2. Bitten by the Cricket Bug — 8
3. This Is Spartans! — 15
4. The Making of G.R. Vishwanath — 20
5. First-Class Apprenticeship — 26
6. Nightmarish Initiation — 34
7. 137 Reasons to Smile — 42
8. Fitness, or Something Like That! — 50
9. The Caribbean Conquest — 58
10. The Sun Sets on England — 71
11. Monkey off My Back — 82
12. On Tiger's Trail — 93
13. Signature Stroke, Not My Only Stroke — 101
14. Scaling the Ranji Summit — 108
15. Summer of 42 — 118
16. A Shot at Redemption — 124
17. When 97 Trumped a Hundred — 132
18. The 'Other' Cricket — 139
19. At Home in Record Chase — 151
20. Romance Rekindled — 161
21. Captain's Log — 174
22. Playing Cricket, My Way — 184
23. My Pride and Joy — 195

24. Cross-Border Blues	207
25. Golf, and Other Ball Games	216
26. A Pack Full of Aces	227
27. Later-Day Titans	242
28. Human Being First, Cricketer Next	262
Acknowledgements	269

1
AN EVENING LIKE NO OTHER

My eyes fluttered open a little before 9.00 a.m., to the fuzzy memory of Kavita and Daivik wishing me at midnight. It brought an immediate smile to my face, enveloping me in a blanket of warmth and gratitude. I knew today would be a good day.

As is my wont, I lolled around in bed for a few more minutes, then picked up my phone. I'd be lying if I said I didn't expect a few messages. To my amazement, there were already dozens and dozens of them. I lay back again and closed my eyes. Now I was sure today would be a *very* good day.

It was a Tuesday morning like any other, yet this wasn't just another Tuesday morning. It was 12 February 2019. I had turned 70. Not a great achievement as such, I agree, but it was a milestone moment. Seventy has a nice, full ring to it.

I padded out of the bedroom and got my day going, catching up with my wife and son a few minutes later at breakfast. Another round of birthday wishes followed, accompanied by broad grins and plenty of hugs. All the while, the phone kept pinging or ringing. *Hey, what's going on? This isn't my first birthday, right? Oh wait, you only turn 70 once!*

I tried to reply to as many messages as I could in between fielding calls from family and close friends. I also received calls from people I had never met. I was so grateful to the Almighty for facilitating this. What can be better than to receive the good wishes of so many people? I was blessed.

Busy as I was on my phone, it didn't escape my attention that Kavi was in hush-hush conversations on her phone. Every time I put my device down, she would clam up with a 'you-won't-catch-me' look on her face.

I knew she was up to something; she usually is on such occasions and while I was curious what plans she had for the day, she was generically vague. *Hmm*, I thought. *Let's go with the flow.*

I am not a big fan of celebrating my birthdays in a grand manner. It's not that I don't like going out or socializing, but on such occasions, I'd rather spend a quiet evening at home, with Kavita and Daivik and a very few, very close friends. I am not particularly fascinated by the prospect of blowing on candles and having people sing 'Happy Birthday' to me. But I am also not fussy. *If Kavita and Daivik want to go out in the evening, I am happy to play ball.*

As the afternoon wore on and the frequency of phone usage—mine and hers—increased, my curiosity mounted. *What are you up to?* I thought to myself, looking at Kavita. As if reading my mind, she shrugged, grinned and then left the room. *Ok*, I told myself, *time to brace for what's ahead.*

Post lunch, she and Daivik announced that we would be going to a restaurant adjacent to the Karnataka Golf Association (KGA) for a celebratory dinner.

'Why not KGA itself?' I countered. 'It's a lovely setting, very cool and green, pleasant breeze... And we can have our privacy, too.'

'Nah,' they chimed in unison. 'We have been there so many times, let's go to a different place.' No scope for a discussion there.

I got ready for the evening, coming down the steps sporting a pair of jeans and a tee-shirt, as I normally do. The conspiring duo took one look at me and sent me scurrying upstairs to 'wear something nice'. So I did, diving into the 'formals' freshly procured for my Star Sports Kannada commentary stints. As mother and son finally cluck-clucked their approval, the doorbell rang and a close family friend sauntered in.

Pradeep is an old pal, our families go back a long time. We are part of three–four very closely knit families who meet quite regularly in each other's houses. He had left Bengaluru for Australia in pursuance of his career but returned to settle down in the city of his birth, and I was so happy to see him.

'Let's go,' he told us, then looked at me and said, 'I've got my car, so you don't have to drive.' He knew that driving during peak-hour traffic in our bustling city was an exercise that drove me up the wall. 'You just sit back and relax.'

I rode shotgun, with Kavita and Daivik at the back. By then, it was past seven in the evening and the traffic was unyielding, like on most weekdays.

'We are getting late, aren't we?' Pradeep looked at Kavita in the rearview mirror. *Late for what?* I wondered. *We are only going to dinner, a few minutes this way or that shouldn't really matter.* I half-turned to see Kavita shushing Pradeep. I allowed myself a quiet smile, the suspense would end soon in any case.

After braving multiple traffic jams, we eventually wended our way to Royal Orchid, next to KGA, as promised, around 8.30 p.m. By now, I must confess, I was a little caught up in the excitement. The furtive glances and Kavita's texting from the back seat had piqued my interest, and I had an inkling this was no ordinary celebratory dinner.

We took the elevator and I was admiring myself in the full-length mirror when the doors opened with a whoosh at the rooftop open-air restaurant. I thought I had caught a glimpse of him in the mirror, but I told myself my eyes were playing tricks. As I turned around, I realized I hadn't been imagining things.

The first person I saw amidst a small group waiting on the other side of the elevator was my brother-in-law, Sunil Gavaskar. Finally, the penny dropped!

Sunil embraced me in a warm hug and led me by my hand once I had regained poise. His unexpected presence had already knocked my breath out. Further jolts of pleasant shock coursed through my body as I saw the small but significant gathering. It was to be the start of the most memorable and unforgettable evening of my life. So, this was what the brother and the sister had been plotting all this while.

◆

As my eyes scanned the terrace, beautifully lit up and tastefully decorated with the shimmering, still water of the swimming pool occasionally stirred by gusts of wind, I took in the people who had assembled—old friends, some of them cricketers, others not so yet, all very dear to me.

People with whom I had played in my formative years. Those with whom I had shared a dressing room for Karnataka, South Zone and India as well as my friends from the media with whom I joust mentally quite often. And, of course, my family. I was particularly thrilled and moved by the presence of Kavita's older sister Nutan, her daughter Salonie, son-in-law Gaurav and grandkid, little Agastya, who had flown in from Mumbai especially for this occasion. You could have knocked me over with a feather.

Had I suspected anything of this magnitude? Of course not, no way. Just the previous week, I had been in Mumbai for the wedding of Sunil and Pammi's (Marshneil) niece. Sunil and I as well as our close friends Kishan and Pappu had spent a lot of time together at the wedding, and they were insistent that since 70 was round the corner, I stay on in Mumbai and celebrate the occasion there. They seemed genuinely disappointed when I had turned down their invitation, knowing all along what lay ahead. I wonder in hindsight how they were able to keep a straight face, an Oscar-worthy performance indeed! After all, this wasn't an 'event' stitched together overnight, it wasn't just a coming together of a motley bunch. Every invitee was hand-picked and personally invited by Sunil. To get them all under one roof—or no roof, in this instance—would have taken a lot of planning and coordination. Some of them had come from other parts of the country, a few from overseas. I was numbed briefly, then spent the rest of the evening with a song in my heart.

The stalwarts with whom I played were all there. The dapper Syed Kirmani, B. Raghunath, Brijesh Patel, Roger Binny, Sudhakar Rao and Sanjay Desai. We were to be joined later in the evening by my good friend B.S. Chandrasekhar (Chandra). Then, there was Bharath Reddy and his wife Geeta, who had come down from Chennai, and my old pal Aunshuman Gaekwad, who was here with his wife Jyoti. There was Anil Kumble and Venkatesh Prasad, both much younger but with whom I share a special bond. There were Kishan and Pappu, with wicked smiles on their faces. Yeah, yeah, you all got me! I would be remiss if I didn't mention warm congratulatory calls from Kapil Dev, Rahul Dravid and Javagal Srinath, who could not be there in person but whose wishes meant a lot.

My mind automatically went back to the time Aunshu made his Test debut, against West Indies in Kolkata in late 1974. When he came out to bat, it was to replace our captain Tiger Pataudi, who hadn't just been dismissed, but also taken a blow to his chin off Andy Roberts that necessitated stitches. There was blood on the pitch, and I sensed that Aunshu must be a little nervous. I spoke to him for a long time in a bid to calm him down and he showed the steel he is made of with a composed 36 as we added 75. It was the start of a wonderful friendship that has just grown and grown over time. We have roomed together several times, and apart from Sunil, with whom I played for India since 1971, Aunshu is the one I am closest to. Our families have gone abroad on holidays, and to see him and Jyoti that evening was one of the many high points.

I also reflected on Sunil Gavaskar the person. The whole world knows the kind of batsman he was, easily the best opener I have played with or, against or have seen in my life. Sunil the human being is equally special. He is thoughtful and sensitive, but very understated and quiet in the way he goes about things. He is totally devoted to his family and will go to any length to make sure we are all comfortable. He's not a man with a lot of time on his hands but was still able to put all this together with typical grace and selflessness. It wasn't just that he got so many people to come over, it was also in his choice of guests. Having known him for nearly 50 years now, I feel there's little he can do that will surprise me. But he had clearly surprised me yet again with the same meticulousness as when we played international cricket together.

I thought back to the time some four years back when I wasn't in great health. Sunil had called me and I could see that he was very emotional. All these years, he hadn't said a word about my drinking, but that night at the hospital, he told me, 'Vishy, you have fought it out for India on the cricket field so many times, you have come out with flying colours in a crisis and won so many games for India. For you, this is nothing. You can easily stop this and win the fight for your family.'

His words shook me, they touched a nerve. Sunil had never asked me for anything all these years. I spent a couple of sleepless nights; I couldn't get his words off my mind. In the past, several doctors had told me that it was time to kick the habit. Obviously, Kavita and Daivik had requested me to do the same innumerable times. I would give in for a few days, but only for a few days. There was, however, a different kind of impact in what Sunil had said and how he had said it. I decided that was it. I haven't had a drop of alcohol since.

It just goes to show that you don't necessarily have to talk to each other regularly if you have the kind of connect Sunil and I have. I know we didn't have more than a couple of 100-plus partnerships in international cricket, but even during those associations, we hardly discussed tactics or techniques mid-pitch, between overs. There was always a comfortable understanding as we communicated with our minds, not words. Our running between the wickets revolved around eye contact, not loud screams of 'yes' or 'no'. Over the years, little has changed. To this date, our interactions don't require the liberal use of the spoken word.

I hauled myself back to the present, once again awestruck by the presence of my nearest and dearest ones. Everybody had a kind word to say, but it was also one of those get-togethers where nothing much needed to be said. I felt a thrill being among the legends of the game, I must admit. I have heard of and read about 'love being in the air', but that night I felt it. There was hardly any talk of cricket, even though it was cricket that in so many ways bound every single person present.

It was an evening that melted away in the bat of an eyelid. I know we were all together for the better part of four hours, but it didn't feel like that. Time raced by; no one was looking at their watches, myself included. There was a soothing tone to the evening, and I felt blessed to be the recipient of so much love, goodwill and affection. From time to time, I go back to that evening in my mind, and invariably end up with a fond yet goofy smile.

There weren't more than a few brief moments on that terrace when I was alone, with my thoughts. During one of those rare phases, as the night wound to a close, I tightly shut my eyes and allowed my life to run through my head. I also reflected on the influence of Dr K.S. Satish, who has been with me through thick and thin, guiding and motivating me during my pre- and post-hospitalization years.

Whatever I am today is because of cricket. Our great game that we love and respect so much has brought me name, fame and the status of a celebrity; something I never really yearned for, but for which I am yet grateful. Had I not played cricket, had I done something else, this evening would not have been possible. Whatever happened was only because of cricket, it reiterated to me that the game is paramount.

Yet, it hadn't escaped my attention that everyone who was there loves Vishwanath the cricketer just as much as they love Vishwanath the person. That made me very proud, that I belong somewhere. It was a privilege to spend a special day with some of the most special people in my life. I couldn't have asked for more.

2
BITTEN BY THE CRICKET BUG

It wasn't until a couple of years after we moved to Bengaluru that I was hooked to cricket. Intricately and irrevocably.

I was born in Bhadravati, an industrial town in Shivamogga district, some 250 km from Bengaluru. My father, a stenographer with Mysore State Electricity Board, was transferred to the state capital when I was four years old, a move that would chart the course of my life in subsequent years.

Bang in the middle of seven children—we are four brothers and three sisters—I was brought up in a bustling home full of noise and action, but also plenty of love and warmth. We lived in a rented house in Visweswarapuram, very close to Minerva Circle and right next to the house of renowned poet A.N. Krishna Rao, aka Anakru, for 13 years. I attended primary and middle school there before moving to Fort High School for my high school education. This would be my comprehensive academic career. I got a job with the State Bank of India (SBI) a little after passing out of high school, by which time cricket had taken over my life. There was, of course, no question of going to college thereafter, not that I had the need for it.

From the time I can remember, cricket was all I wanted to play. Sure, I did kick a football around with the boys in our locality when it rained or when we couldn't rustle up enough numbers for a tennis-ball contest, but I was never really what you would call a keen footballer. Don't get me wrong, I love watching football and I am particularly excited when the World Cup comes around every four years. The artistry of Brazil has captivated me over the years, and I would spend hours admiring the craft of such maestros as Zico and Sócrates. I became a more committed follower of the sport on my first tour of England in 1971, when we watched matches live on colour television. But growing up, football was always a distant second to cricket. Actually, everything else was.

I am not exactly sure when I first picked up a bat, but I couldn't have been more than seven or eight. All we needed to get going was a bat—a glorified stick of wood, to be honest—of any dimension and a tennis ball.

Tennis-ball cricket made G.R. Vishwanath the batsman, of that I have no doubt. The challenges of facing up to a tennis ball are unique, as anyone who has played with it will agree. The bounce the ball gathers on pitching was considerable, and therefore you had to bring your wrists into play to keep it down. You had to loosen your grip on the wood to soften your hands and make sure the ball didn't go up in the air.

As I grew a little older and started playing tennis-ball matches, people noticed me, talked about me. I wasn't very tall—not that I am now, either—and I suppose that made me stand out a little more. A short, young lad keeping ball after ball down, out of reach of the hovering silly mid off and silly mid on fielders, seemed to catch their fancy.

My teeth sinking deeper into cricket had initially to do with two influential figures, one within our house and the other right next door. Our oldest brother, G.R. Jagannath, was a very good all-round sportsman who was also a successful club cricketer with Bangalore Cricketers, and represented the state junior side. He would wake up early in the morning to listen to radio commentary of Test matches in Australia, and would make detailed, meticulous notes of proceedings thousands of kilometres away—how many runs the batsmen scored, how they got out, how many fours were hit, stuff like that. I was too young and impatient to listen to commentary, but I would pore over his score cards. Very quickly, I realized that there was one name that seemed to score heavily every single time. Neil Harvey. Almost immediately, though I knew not how he looked or batted, he became my hero. I was told he was a left-hander and that he was a great batsman. That was enough for me to build an image in my head. Harvey was my hero and my inspiration; as destiny would dictate, not only did I get to meet him subsequently, but I also earned high praise from him, words I treasure to this day.

It was January 1960, and I was a month shy of my eleventh birthday, when the touring Australians came to Bengaluru for a first-class game against Indian Universities during their tour of India. The three-day match was to be played at the Central College Ground and it was too good an opportunity for me to pass up, especially with the ground not far from our house. I went over on the second day when I knew Harvey would come out to bat. He was leading the side with regular skipper Richie Benaud resting, and I felt a thrill run through my body when he strode out to bat. He didn't make many, 30-odd if memory serves me right, but it was enough. I didn't know a great deal about cricket, but he looked so lovely at the crease. I really enjoyed watching him bat. When he stormed my imagination and became my hero, I had no idea what this batsman was like. Not only was I privileged to have seen him live, I was also absolutely delighted.

I went to the ground the next day too, hoping I would come face to face with him. I didn't want to talk to him or get his autograph, I just wanted to touch him. Maybe to reassure myself that I wasn't in a prolonged dream, that this really was Neil Harvey in the flesh. At the ground, I came to know that the two teams had been invited to the University Visvesvaraya College of Engineering (UVCE) for evening tea. So, as soon as the match ended in a draw, I scooted across Nrupathunga Road and positioned myself outside the UVCE gates.

The University team's bus came first, around 6.30 p.m., and I didn't so much as glance at it, even though my friend in later years, P.R. Ashokanand, and one of my future influencers, M.L. Jaisimha, were both in it. I had eyes only for one person when the Australian bus arrived. I scanned each face with mounting anxiety until I spotted Harvey climbing down the steps. I edged closer to him, reached out with my small hand and touched him. I had actually touched Neil Harvey! I then took off, not turning back to see what his reaction was, what anyone's reaction was. UVCE was some distance away from my house, maybe a 45-minute walk for a kid my age, but I wasn't walking, was I? I ran and ran like the wind, I did. Thrilled at the close encounter, my legs flying across the road. I was home in 10 minutes, panting and out of breath but feeling very special.

One look at me, and my mother knew something was up.

'I just met my hero,' I told her.

'Fine, now go and have a wash,' she was practical, instantly sobering me up. 'You have been out the whole day, look at your state. Come back after a bath and I will get you something to eat.'

Bath? Not for two days, at least, no way. Not that I told her, of course.

Years later, on our 1977–78 trip to Australia, I told Harvey of that January 1960 evening. He chuckled, 'You must have been crazy. I am sure you must be meeting a few of those yourself, now that you have become famous and have been playing for India for a number of years. Must be exhilarating?'

It was. But only because I was sitting next to Neil Harvey, chatting with him and having a drink.

◆

In the immediacy of the UVCE tryst, I couldn't stop talking about Harvey. My brother Jagannath then recalled a story involving Harvey and Shubash Gupte, the great Indian leg spinner. By the time Australia came to India in 1956, Gupte had established himself as a pre-eminent bowler in the world of international cricket and was considered the biggest threat to the Aussies, marginally ahead of Vinoo Mankad. Harvey hadn't ever seen Gupte in action previously, let alone face him. And here he was, on day two of the first Test in Chennai, walking out at No. 3 after Gupte had gotten rid of Jim Burke cheaply.

My brother considered himself a master storyteller, though I wasn't a big fan of his long, dramatic pauses. With a smile, he revealed how, to the first delivery of Gupte's, Harvey skipped down the track and drove through the covers for four; against the turn, mind you, as well as along the ground. This was not only Harvey's first ball of the Test series, but it was also against a feared and skilful bowler. It was a statement of intent. I was entranced. Subconsciously, it seeped into my mind that, like my hero, I must disrupt the rhythm of the best bowlers in the opposition, that I must dictate terms, that I must entertain those who come to watch and that I should play my shots without hesitation. By now, I was convinced I would play for India, as most innocent, ignorant kids of 10 and 11 are. I didn't know how I would get there, what the intermediate steps were, I just knew I would represent my country. It's not meant to be a boast and am not saying it in retrospect. We all know the basis of the convictions of 11-year-olds—hopes and dreams.

So that's what I did in the tennis-ball games thereafter. It was no longer about survival, I started to play strokes too. Not desperate, manufactured shots but ones that came almost instinctively. I was fortunate that, in that period, I had the complete support and encouragement of the entire tennis-ball gang in our locality. You know how it can get with young kids sometimes, you want to be the centre of attention, but no one grudged me my runs. Everyone was so eager to win that they were happy for me to get runs. Thus, I was an opening batsman for a majority of my career-shaping tennis-ball adventures.

I have often thought about why I batted the way I did, but whenever I have tried to find out how, I have come up short. No answers. I am not sure anyone taught me how to bat in my early years. It just happened, that's all I can say. I first started to keep the ball down using my wrists because I didn't want to get out, caught close-in. Something told me, I guess, that when I am playing defensively off the back foot, I must loosen my grip. But that's about it. I didn't consciously think about batting. When I graduated to higher grades, the ball was harder, the pace was quicker, but apart from adapting to situations, I didn't bat any differently from what I did as an early teen. The early grounding in tennis-ball cricket was the bedrock of my batting journey, it helped me tremendously, as I am sure it has helped many others of that period.

◆

Harvey was an unwitting inspiration. However, apart from my elder brother, the other willing, physical influence on my cricket when I was in middle school, answered to the name of S. Krishna, our next-door neighbour. He had captained his college team and gone on to make a century on his Ranji Trophy debut for Mysore state. He was employed with the SBI and turned up to watch, sometimes play, our tennis-ball matches. He saw a spark in me and started to take a keen interest in not just my cricket but my life too. When I was in high school, he told me that he would get me a job in his bank so long as I passed out of school successfully. That was the spur for me to immerse myself, briefly, in studies. I wanted to get the 'pass' out of the way so that I could get a job and focus on cricket, not worry about having to go to college.

A bank job, and that too in the SBI, was a secure posting, much coveted, but clearly, my parents weren't thrilled. They wanted me to go on and get a decent education, like my older siblings. But I was having none of it, so eventually they gave in and that was that.

By this time, I had graduated from tennis to leather-ball cricket with my elder brother and Krishna charting my progress, acting as friends and mentors. I had also changed schools and joined Kotte High School, where I met the man who facilitated the realization of my dreams.

Chandra Shetty was not a serious cricketer himself, but he was a great cricket enthusiast who owned the Spartans Cricket Club in the Mysore state league. He would watch and umpire school matches, and I suppose he liked what he saw in this short 15-year-old who played with neither fear nor discomfort against older, stronger boys. I say this only because in the past, my height was held against me when I wasn't picked for the State Schools' side. Chandra was the one who took me to the selection trials, attended by thousands of school kids from across the city. I was in the very long shortlist of 150 and was convinced my selection to the final 15 was a mere formality. After all, everyone had been speaking in hushed tones of wonderment about how good I looked as a batsman, how easily I played my strokes. Ah, how little I knew!

The following day, when 150 was further pruned, I recoiled in physical shock. I wasn't going to be in the State Schools' side. My head was spinning, and my immediate reaction was that I should stop playing cricket altogether. *What's the point, after all?* I was informed that the chairman of the selection committee, Dr K. Thimmappaiah, was wary of picking me because I was so short and so young. 'What will I tell his parents if something happens to him?' the good doctor is said to have asked his friends. At 15, I was finished as a cricketer.

As it turned out, that was the only disappointment of my cricketing career. The only time I was not selected. From the time I made my debut for Mysore state in Vijayawada in November 1967 to the time I played my last Test in February 1983, I wasn't dropped even once. Someone above had always looked out for me, and for that, I am eternally grateful.

I moped for a while, but how long can you sulk when you are 15? How can you resist the pull of this great sport? And how can you ignore the enthusiasm and constant prodding of Chandra, who immediately exploded my disappointment by signing me up for his club Spartans, then in Division III of the Mysore state league. Now, my destiny awaited me.

3

THIS IS SPARTANS!

Chandra Shetty knew he could pull rank. And he knew how to do it, too.

I must say I wasn't a popular choice when I joined Spartans. It had nothing to do with whether I was a decent batsman or not. My age and my height were considered the big no-nos. I was 15 years old, I stood five-feet-two in my boots. Everyone felt I was vulnerable and that I could so easily get hit by the hard cricket ball. My counter always was, 'Anyone can get hit, by anyone. Age and height don't matter.' Those were prophetic words; later in my career, I would get hit on my temple during nets by my Karnataka and SBI teammate Raghuram Bhat, the left-arm spinner.

Fortunately, Chandra Shetty was not among those who feared for my physical well-being. He had seen enough of my batting to understand I was perfectly capable of looking after myself. He summoned the Spartans captain and informed him that I would be playing in the next league game, against Hindustan Aeronautics Limited (HAL), who had a fairly quick bowler in S. Balakrishna. Taking one good look at me, the captain told Chandra, 'No way am I playing him. What's wrong with you? You want this boy to play against this fast bowler? I am scared for him, I can't include him in the side.'

The boss in Chandra revealed himself. 'This is my club, I am the owner, the boss. I know you are the captain, but I made you the captain, don't forget it,' he admonished the skipper. 'If I tell you that you have to play him, you have no option but to do so. I have promised him that he will play, and I intend to keep that promise. He has suffered enough because of his age and height, it won't happen again. Not on my watch.'

Reluctantly, the captain included me in the XI and slotted me in at No. 6. I faced Balakrishna without incident, I think I remained unbeaten on 25 or thereabouts. The captain was impressed enough to push me up the order, admitting that he had misjudged me, but that he had only been worried for me. I knew his intentions were good, I had no issues with his point of view. I welcomed the promotion by making runs in almost every game. I wasn't a 100-hitter at the time, but I made lots of 70s and 80s. My consistency over a period of time emboldened Chandra Shetty enough for him to go the state cricket association office at the Central College Ground and speak to Mr M. Chinnaswamy, the then secretary of the Mysore State Cricket Association.

I was subsequently picked for the Pentangulars, and then the Quadrangulars, where I had my first taste of B.S. Chandrasekhar. I was playing for City XI against the genius who was representing College XI. Already mortified at being asked to bat at No. 11, my embarrassment and anger grew when I couldn't lay bat to the first three or four balls from Chandra which just thudded into my pads. All I remember was that he was very quick. Far too quick! Somehow, I managed to stay unbeaten, which earned me a promotion to No. 9 for the next game. Not long thereafter, I moved up to No. 4, a position where I batted for the rest of my league career with the Spartans.

I didn't play league cricket for any other club until I joined SBI after my first-class debut. Spartans, or to be more specific, Chandra Shetty facilitated my growth, giving me a platform to express my skills and catch the attention of the men who mattered. Chandra was a wonderful mentor who walked every step of the way with me. He couldn't help me a great deal from a coaching perspective, but he made sure I got the right breaks, that I wasn't wanting for anything. I would say that, if you take coaching out of the equation, he was to me what Ramakant Achrekar was to Sachin Tendulkar.

It was thanks to Chandra Shetty that I had my first taste of formal coaching. Spartans didn't have a ground of their own, so there were no practice sessions as such. Chandra was always on the lookout for venues where I could net, and one day asked me to accompany him to the Sree Kanteerava Stadium in Bengaluru. Upon reaching, I realized that the state sports council was conducting coaching classes in all disciplines, including cricket, which alone would be held outside the stadium in deference to its unique requirements.

There were two sets of nets in operation: one under P.S. Vishwanath and the other run by Salus Nazareth. Both were big names in Mysore cricket, with a great deal of practical and theoretical knowledge. Mr Vishwanath was the grandson of Sir K.P. Puttanna Chetty, the philanthropist and former president of Bangalore City municipality after whom the town hall is named. They had a huge property in Chamarajpet, and Chandra was one of Mr Vishwanath's tenants, which is how he got me into the coaching camp.

I learnt a fair bit from the camp, as did all other cricketers including some of my old tennis-ball colleagues who had also joined Spartans. Unlike most of the others, I would attend sessions in the mornings and the evenings. There would be a bottle of milk for each of us, which became an incentive to not miss a single session. At the time, milk was the secret of my energy.

During this phase, I never needed to ask my parents to get me a bat or any other cricketing equipment. Chandra would take care of my every requirement. Chandra would get me everything I needed—new bats, new pairs of pads, gloves and even shoes. I was thrilled to bits when I received my first pair of buckskin shoes, very classy and very prestigious. They used to be hand-stitched by a gentleman called Seetaram in a very small shop in front of Victoria Hospital, and there would be a beeline from south Bengaluru, primarily, to lay hands on these shoes. To the best of my knowledge, Seetaram made only cricket shoes and was a much-in-demand shoemaker. When Chandra handed over my first pair of buckskin shoes, I was almost afraid to try them on, they looked way too beautiful to be marred by dust and dirt. The shoes fitted me beautifully; of course, there were no spikes or nails because all our cricket was on matting pitches. It was a prized possession for a youngster like me. Chandra did things like that, without being asked, and without making it look like he was doing me a favour. I am not sure how my life would have panned out had he not been in it in those early years. I considered Chandra my guru, the man who fuelled the fire in me.

It wasn't easy to run private clubs in the 1950s and '60s, but there were a host of individuals who did so selflessly and to whom we owe a massive debt of gratitude. Apart from Chandra Shetty, there was Yagna Narayan, who ran City Cricketers, which produced such gems as E.A.S. Prasanna and B.S. Chandrasekhar. N. Doraiswamy oversaw Friends Union Cricket Club (FUCC), Dr H.C. Keshavdas was in charge of Jawahars. All these giants did a tremendous job for their clubs and for cricket as a whole, paving the way for a generation of cricketers who would go on to represent not just Mysore state but also the country.

♦

My three years at Spartans had been a great experience, and as much as I would have loved to continue there, I knew I had to take the next step forward. I was biding time, waiting to pass out of high school, waiting to turn 18, waiting for the time I would join SBI.

My mother especially was extremely unhappy that I was willing to forsake college education to join a bank and play cricket. She would constantly point to the academic conquests of my siblings and cousins, while my father largely stayed away from these discussions, thereby neither backing nor discouraging either his wife or his son.

'Look at them, how well they are studying and how many marks they are scoring,' she would chide me towards my final days in high school.

'Yes,' I would agree, infuriating her further with, 'because they are studying, they are getting good marks. I don't study, so how will I get marks? I do get runs, though.'

Mother would huff and puff and tell me that runs would not help me in the future. I had visions of playing for India, so I knew runs would help me. Had I known that initial payments would be in the range of ₹30 per game, I wouldn't have been so sure of myself, I suspect!

By the time Krishna fulfilled his promise and I joined SBI, I had already played for the Mysore State Juniors for a couple of seasons, and made my Ranji Trophy debut as well. By now, the bitter taste left by non-selection to the State Schools' side had evaporated, and I enjoyed my stint with the State Juniors, making runs aplenty against traditionally strong sides such as Hyderabad and Tamil Nadu. The hundreds didn't come at the junior level, but I still had the numbers to back me up.

When I did finally make a strong start to league cricket in SBI colours, my big regret was that I didn't play alongside Krishna. A very dependable batsman, Krishna had a brief first-class career, averaging 38.18 from eight games. He would and should have played more, but for a showdown with a non-cricketing official of the state association during a Ranji Trophy game against Kerala at the Central College Ground in November 1963. On an uncovered pitch drying up from heavy rain and thus making batting impossible, he was out to a spinner fending a ball that exploded from a length. As he was walking back, the official panned his batting and said that was no way to play cricket. Krishna offered him the bat and told him to go show him how to bat. He only played two more matches for the state after that.

He continued to play on for SBI, but once he got me over to the bank, he told the authorities that as far as he was concerned, it was mission accomplished and that he was done with playing. I would have loved to bat alongside him, but that was not to be.

A string of good performances in the league for Spartans first, and then the State Juniors, pitchforked me into the State Senior side. There was a touch of fortune to my selection, because during the 1967–68 domestic season, the Indian team was touring Australia for a Test series. V. Subramanya, the dynamic Mysore captain, Budhi Kunderan, E.A.S. Prasanna and B.S. Chandrasekhar were all in the Test squad, which meant places had opened up and the selectors were looking for fresh faces. Mine was one of those faces on which their eyes settled. The breaks were coming thick and fast. But would I continue to make the most of them?

4

THE MAKING OF G.R. VISHWANATH

Having been in the reserves for the previous Ranji Trophy match against Madras at the Central College Ground in Bengaluru, I fancied my chances of a debut when we reached Vijayawada in early November of 1967 for our final game of the season, against Andhra. Mysore had not even a mathematical chance of qualifying for the knockout stages as the lone representative from South Zone; additionally, several of our established players had left for Australia with the Test squad. With Subramanya, Budhi, Pras and Chandra all unavailable, the selectors chose to invest in youth, so it was a young side that travelled to Vijayawada under Y.B. Patel.

My hope turned to reality when, a day before the game, Y.B. and C. Nagaraj, the long-serving team manager who would subsequently go on to become a sterling administrator, confirmed my presence in the XI. It didn't come as a great shock; after all, I had been in the squad for the previous game and among the newcomers, I had reasonable experience, having already represented the State Juniors side. But what did jolt me into an adrenaline rush on match-day, 11 November, was being informed that I would be batting at No. 4.

I had endured a sleepless night on the eve of the match. I kept telling myself that this was my opportunity, I had to get a big score if I aspired to climb the next rung. I had worked myself into a state of nervous anticipation, and that reached fever pitch once Y.B. won the toss and informed us that we would be batting first.

In the protective *shamiana* (ceremonial tent) housing our otherwise structure-less 'dressing room', the captain read out the batting order and triggered a flurry of activity. I quickly dug into my gear and padded up when I was told of my two-drop position, which was just as well because in no time, we had lost our openers to N. Venkat Rao and slumped to 15 for two.

Among those dismissed was V.S. Vijay Kumar, one of four debutants alongside myself, V. Ramdas and V. Anantharam. Ramdas, Anantharam and Nataraj had all been regulars in the state 'A' division league while I was still with Spartans, which was why I was a little surprised when I was slotted in at No. 4. But I wasn't complaining.

By the time I joined, Syed Kirmani, who had made his debut in our previous encounter, in the middle, the butterflies had grabbed hold of the insides of my stomach and were performing a violent dance. But as I took guard, an eerie calm descended on me. It was as if someone had flicked a switch; the nerves had vanished, it was just the ball and me. Nothing else mattered. Andhra had two good new-ball bowlers in Venkat and R.P. Gupta, a feared duo though not so much for their bowling; it was more face-wise than pace-wise, I would tell my teammates afterwards.

Almost 30 years later, when I went to Vijayawada in my capacity as national selector, I was invited by the Andhra Cricket Association for a function to felicitate some of the stalwarts of Andhra cricket. There were customary speeches, one of which referenced my debut.

The speaker was Professor Prasanna Kumar, a well-known commentator who was closely involved with Andhra cricket. We met a fair few times at Sri Sathya Sai Baba's Ashram in Puttaparthi, and had become very good friends. His talk was revealing and hilarious, laced with humour and wit.

Apparently, within Andhra circles, Venkat and Gupta were celebrated as Wesley Hall and Charlie Griffith after the great fast-bowling pair which had toured India with West Indies the previous year. They were considered dangerously ferocious, but when they saw me come out to bat, their hearts kind of melted.

Looking sympathetically at the slight figure of the 18-year-old, they decided to go easy on me.

'He is so small, let him enjoy his debut,' one of them said.

'Of course,' the other concurred. 'Let's give him 10 runs, then we will get down to business.'

In no time, I had raced away to 25, and they had had enough. 'Let's bowl seriously, he's had his fun.'

The good professor went on to talk less about my innings and more about the mounting consternation and frustration of Venkat and Gupta as I kept piling on the runs. After a point, they stopped looking at Mysore's tally, focusing solely on my score.

'This boy isn't getting out at all. First 50, then 100, on to 150 and now 200!' they griped. 'Maybe we shouldn't have given him those easy runs early on.'

As I heard this story narrated with such gusto, I enjoyed myself enormously. It was great fun, though I also secretly thanked my stars that I hadn't had to face the original Wes Hall and Charlie Griffith ever.

◆

I remember that innings so clearly that I could have played it yesterday, not 50 years back. Once the tension dissipated, I started to take control. Uncharacteristically, I played a lot of sweep shots; it's not like I haven't swept the ball subsequently, but I feel that stroke should be the last resort, you should only play it if you don't have any other options.

That particular day, I was forced to employ the sweep because of the line Andhra adopted. They had a top leg spinner in Mahendra Kumar, who also played in a strong Hyderabad side that included Tiger Pataudi and M.L. Jaisimha. I did play all around the wicket, but it's the slant towards the sweep that distinctly stands out.

An appreciative fair-sized crowd egged me on as I passed one landmark after another. By close of play on day one, I was unbeaten on 209, out of 392 for five.

For the second night in a row, sleep eluded me, but this was a different kind of sleepless night. Both nights were lessons in themselves. Twenty-four hours earlier, I was close to a nervous wreck. Now, I had made a double-hundred on first-class debut. Me! G.R. Vishwanath, 18 years old, a double-centurion. I replayed the entire innings in my head, and when I finally nodded off with the sun threatening to appear on the horizon, I suspect I had a satisfied smile on my lips.

The next morning, I was dismissed for 230, trapped leg before by the medium-pace of K. Chandrasekhar Rao. It wasn't until the evening that Nagaraj informed me that I was now the owner of the record for the highest individual score on Ranji Trophy debut. George Abell, the Worcester-born Englishman, had made 210 for Northern India in the 1934–35 season, Nagaraj told me. I had broken a record that had survived 33 years.

All through my career, I never played for numbers and statistics; averages and centuries never really mattered that much. I'd be lying if I said I wasn't happy to hear of my achievement on debut, but more than the record, it was the innings as a whole that completely changed my life. Two hundred and thirty was a means, not the end in itself.

On its own, it was an impressive effort by a teenager. That was as far as the outside world was concerned. To me, it was to catalyse a change in thinking, attitude and mindset. It suggested to me that I was closer to realizing my ambition of playing for India than two days previously. It proved to me that I was not mistaken in trusting my skills and my ability to score runs at every higher grade.

It's not as if I haven't scored big runs subsequently, but the satisfaction I derived at the end of that innings was never matched by anything I did even in the Test arena. I have several cherished memories of my performances for India, don't get me wrong, but this is one innings I will always take with me. It will forever remain No. 1 in my eyes.

Not only do I consider it my career-best knock, but it was also a career-changing innings. I started dreaming bigger, but paradoxically, my dreams also appeared more realistic and achievable. When I look back, I marvel at the breaks that came my way, and my good fortune at being able to capitalize on those opportunities. This break came at absolutely the right time; cricket assumed a whole new significance in a life that already revolved around it.

It was after this knock that young Vishy realized what G.R. Vishwanath was made of, if you know what I mean. That's why the first-class debut will remain my favourite cricketing memory.

◆

I thoroughly enjoyed the process of making runs, and making them on *my* terms. The knock was vindication of the effort I had put in during the preceding years, and it was to completely as well as irrevocably chart the path my career would take. All of a sudden, people recognized me, they talked about me and kept an eye on me. It pleased me that no one thought it was a fluke, a one-off. That innings made it so much easier for me to graduate to the next level, it was the backbone of my career.

It was that effort on debut which gave me the confidence to score a second-innings hundred on Test debut after being dismissed without scoring in the first, almost two years later. Not many fans or pundits had been in Vijayawada to watch my 230 first-hand, but because of what I did there, they had read and learnt everything about me by the time I debuted in Kanpur against Australia.

What stunned me was that even after my hundred on Test debut, people were talking about the 230. It went to show how much of an impact the magnitude of that effort had made. Had I scored just a century, people might have felt, 'Big deal, so many have done that.' But because of the sheer size of my first hit in first-class cricket, there was a general feeling that my first Test hundred wouldn't be my last. Until then, no Indian who had heralded his first appearance with a ton had made another century for the country. If there was no mention whatsoever of the hoodoo after my 137, it was thanks to how I had handled 'Hall' and 'Griffith', among others, in the Andhra city.

I was transported to another world after the Vijayawada match, it was just an amazing time for me—simply amazing! It was very kind of Nagaraj to present me with a bat autographed by players from both teams to mark the achievement. I clung on to that bat for a long time before finally parting with it for a charity auction.

◆

During my second visit to Vijayawada, which I have alluded to earlier, a gentleman serving as local liaison stopped our car at a bare, gravelly ground with a small, concrete building inconspicuously positioned on one side. As I turned to face him, he had a knowing but very sincere grin.

'What, boss?' I asked him, genuinely perplexed.

'Sir, you know...' he kept smiling.

'Know what, boss? Enough now, tell me.'

'Sir, you don't remember? This is the ground where you made your debut.'

To be perfectly honest, that did nothing to jog my memory. Yes, the outfield was as grassless as it had been in 1967; the pitch was different in that it was turf and didn't need to be covered by a mat anymore. But I couldn't believe this was where I had taken my first steps as a senior representative cricketer.

'Are you sure, boss?' I asked him, sceptically.

'Hundred per cent, sir,' he replied without hesitation, 'I watched every ball of that game.'

No wonder then, I chuckled to myself, that I got 230. It was such a small ground, I should have scored more. But then again, 21 others had played in the same match, in the same conditions, and no one else had touched three-figures. I felt a sense of pride, peppered with humility, as I reminisced that innings.

5

FIRST-CLASS APPRENTICESHIP

People who matter had taken note of my roaring Ranji debut, this became apparent even during the Vijayawada game. I had received a telegram from P.R. Man Singh, who ran Hyderabad Blues, to come over to the City of Nawabs and play for his team in the Moin-ud-Dowlah Gold Cup, a prestigious tournament which enjoyed first-class status. Man Singh would go on to become a successful administrator and long-serving secretary of the Hyderabad Cricket Association, apart from managing the Indian team both at the 1983 World Cup, when they created history, and again at home, in 1987.

I was thrilled to bits to be invited to play in the Moin-ud-Dowlah, even if it meant going straight from Vijayawada. I had watched a fair bit of cricket in Bengaluru, and because I was so invested in the game, I respected the platform such competitions provided. I prided myself on knowing the history of the game, on the significance of tournaments like the YS Ramaswamy Trophy, from which many have emerged, who went on to represent first Mysore and later the country. I might not have always been able to put faces to names because most of my knowledge had come either from newspapers and magazines or from listening to other influencers who spoke with such passion about the game.

I knew, for instance, that Pankaj Roy and Vinoo Mankad held the record for the highest first-wicket partnership in Test cricket. I could readily rattle off the names of everyone who had played Test cricket for India, I was aware of who all had made a hundred on debut. I found all this fascinating. To read and hear about their stories was an inspiration, tales which further fuelled the fire in me and made me look forward to the time when I would don the India cap.

As brilliant as my Ranji debut had been, I knew that a Test call-up wouldn't materialize suddenly and dramatically, out of thin air. India had a wonderful batting line-up and if I wanted to gatecrash the party, I needed to be patient and consistent. I strongly believed it was just a matter of time before I played for the country; I wasn't sure when that would be, but I didn't really waste too much time fretting over it.

Upon return from Hyderabad, it was back to league cricket and practice. I would 'net' with the SBI team even though I was still representing Spartans. The wheels had been set in motion for me to join the bank now that I had played for the state at the senior level. Finally, in October 1968, I was recruited by SBI primarily to play cricket. I was thrilled that I would have my good friend B. Raghunath for company as colleague and teammate. Raghu and I had played a lot of tennis-ball cricket against each other from before our teens, and our bond strengthened once I joined him at SBI. Over the last five and a half decades, our friendship has blossomed. Raghu is one of my dearest mates, and when I first got into the bank, he was always at hand to help me out with my cricket as well as banking responsibilities.

From playing against each other in by-lanes, we were colleagues in the first division league, and then for several years for the state. Meticulous and organized, Raghu has been by my side every step of the way for more than 57 years. I have great memories of us playing together, and we are still going strong as friends.

Similar is the case with Sudhakar Rao. Since we were from the same neighbourhood, we grew up playing tennis-ball cricket for the same side. Our careers overlapped and progressed along similar lines. We turned out together for the state and the zone, and I was delighted to have him for company on the Indian team's twin tours of New Zealand and the West Indies in 1976. I was filled with pride when he climbed administratively to become the secretary of the Karnataka State Cricket Association (KSCA), a prestigious seat occupied by several stalwarts in the past. That's one of the greatest gifts cricket has bestowed upon me—numerous friendships that have strengthened with the passage of time.

◆

The 1968–69 domestic season was my first full season for Mysore; it would also be the last season for Subramanya, who was to settle down in Australia.

After modest outings against Kerala and Andhra, we ran into a formidable, popular and stylish Hyderabad side in our third match, at the Central College Ground in our backyard, in the first week of December. I must confess I was overawed at the thought of playing against Tiger Pataudi, the Indian captain, and M.L. Jaisimha (Jai), under whom Tiger played for their state side.

I had a feeling that Pras had told them about me the previous year in Australia, for I sensed that both were observing me closely. I was nervous, yes, but focussed on what I needed to do. In a low-scoring draw on a tricky surface, I made 39 in the first innings and 69 in the second. It was the only half-century in a match graced not just by Tiger and Jai, but also Abbas Ali Baig, Abid Ali, Budhi and Subramanya.

Had I scored heavily in a tall-scoring game, I might not have impressed Tiger and Jai so much, of this I am sure. Having been tipped off by Pras, they followed my every move, and I think they liked what they saw. I was still very small and barely managed power in my strokes against the spinners, off whom you have to make your own pace. In my head, I would have hit the ball really, really hard; in reality, if I did score a four off a spinner, it was because the fielder was so slow that he couldn't get to the ball that was struggling to reach the rope.

At the end of the game, as Tiger walked towards me, I was certain I was dreaming. The Indian captain, Tiger Pataudi, wanted to talk to little G.R. Vishwanath.

Tiger said he had enjoyed watching me bat, adding that I needed to get stronger. 'Do you work out in the gym?' he asked.

Gym? Me? No way! 'No, I don't,' I mumbled, softly.

'Okay, so you don't lift weights, or work with dumb-bells. Never mind. I am sure you must have buckets at home?'

The change of tack caught me unawares. All I could do was nod, warily, in the affirmative.

'This is what you do. Fill up two buckets with water and lift one with each hand 20 times in a row. Do this three to four times a day, regularly.'

Right. Buckets. I wore a nervous smile as I looked up at him. I had heard that he was a great prankster who loved playing practical jokes, and this would just be another of those instances when he would pull someone's leg with a straight face. Could you have blamed me, really, for not being able to picture him lifting buckets of water to strengthen his forearm and wrist?

I realized embarrassedly that he was dead serious, he was actually offering me a solution to a problem which could have hampered my progress to the next level.

Grateful for his advice, I diligently followed the routine he had suggested. I could make out a visible difference within a month, which was motivation enough to keep at it. In no time, the ball was speeding off the bat even against the slowest of slow bowlers. My wrists had become stronger but not stiffer. I am not sure what might have happened had Tiger not taken the trouble of talking to me. What I do know is that the Vishwanath wrists that were to become such a talking point owe everything to Tiger's inputs and encouragement.

When you look back all these years later, it might not seem like a big deal but believe me, it certainly was. That little interaction taught me that no matter how young and raw or seasoned one might be, if you want to learn and if you are a good listener, sky's the limit. Suggestions will come from various quarters. It's not that you must implement all of them, but you can't disregard them entirely, either. Listen, think, attempt and see if it works for you. Unless you try, you won't fail. And unless you fail, you won't succeed, either.

◆

I struggle to find words to express the emotions that run through me even today when I first meet someone who has represented India globally, be it a cricketer or someone from any other discipline. It isn't just a feeling of kinship, because from even before I played for the country, I would be fascinated to meet a Test player, for instance.

The Moin-ud-Dowlah Gold Cup was a fertile ground from that perspective. The prestigious tournament attracted several Ranji Trophy teams as well as such star-studded sides as All India State Bank of

India and Vazir Sultan Tobacco (VST). Automatically, it also brought the legends of Indian cricket to watch matches in various capacities. It was at the Moin-ud-Dowlah that I first met Lala Amarnath ji, such a giant. I got to interact with Vijay Merchant and Polly Umrigar, who left me star-struck and wide-eyed. It was in my nature, I guess. Cricket was more deeply entrenched in my system than I had imagined.

I particularly enjoyed travelling to Hyderabad with the Mysore team. Both sides had stalwarts who had played together for the country and got along famously. We would stay at the Fateh Maidan Club within the Lal Bahadur Shastri Stadium premises, and every evening, these superstars would meet up on the outfield for a few drinks and a lively chat. For a young lad, it was the education of a lifetime. I would hang on to their every word, relish the tales they exchanged, imbibe the wisdom they shared. They were warm, welcoming and happy to feed my inquisitiveness. Effortlessly, they created an atmosphere of affection and inclusivity, that's the beautiful thing about my seniors. Encouraged by their attitude, I opened up slowly, not once feeling out of place or as if I had intruded on their private space. I can't stress how crucial that was to my development as a cricketer and as a person.

Tiger and Jai were pillars of great strength and support. They were thick friends whose ideas and ideologies were invariably in sync, and they were always on the lookout for talent that would strengthen the Indian team. I consider myself fortunate that I was among the runs in my early matches against and with them, and that they felt I was a talent worth investing in.

Even though I didn't make a hundred in the Central College Ground encounter, the quality of my batting seemed to have impressed Tiger, with whom I first shared a dressing room on my Duleep Trophy debut, in the semi-final against East Zone at the Eden Gardens in January 1969. Under Jai, South Zone had a cracking batting line-up, which meant I could only come in at No. 7. On another of those difficult surfaces that seemed to be the norm at the time, I made 36 in the first innings; only Jai, with 69, contributed more to our tally of 188. Making the most of my promotion to No. 3 in the second innings of the final, I scored an unbeaten 76 against West Zone in Hyderabad to finish my season on a high, even though I hadn't touched three-figures even once.

◆

Another Duleep Trophy semi-final brightened my India prospects considerably as I began the 1969–70 season confident that this would be my breakthrough year. We were playing North Zone at Chepauk on a very uneven surface exploited masterfully by Bishan Bedi, who was at his peak and bowled superbly; he didn't really need assistance from the surface as such but when he did get some help, he was doubly dangerous.

Chandra took five wickets on day one to send North tumbling to 100 all out, but we didn't fare much better, either. Down at No. 8, I made 20 before becoming one of Bishan's seven victims as we folded for 111. North put up an improved batting display a second time around and left us needing 245 for victory, all but impossible given how spectacularly the surface had deteriorated.

The pitch had become so up-and-down that by the time Bishan came on to bowl, Samir Chakrabarti, the medium-pacer, had done substantial damage. We were tottering at 60 for four when I joined skipper Jai in the middle. We had a small partnership but after that, the wickets tumbled again and we were bowled out for 146, Chakrabarti picking up six. Again, I didn't have a huge score against my name, but my unbeaten 51 had impressed teammate and opponent alike. One of those was the Indian captain; thrice in the last year and a half, he had watched me produce good innings in difficult conditions against top attacks, first-hand. That was to hasten my entry into the Test team.

◆

Graham Dowling's New Zealand came to India for a three-Test series in September–October 1969 and were to play the Indian Board President's (BP) XI in a three-day game in Indore between the second and third Tests. The selectors felt I had done enough to merit a serious look, so I was picked in a relatively young side led by the seasoned Chandu Borde.

I felt blessed. Until I was named in the Indian team, I had watched just one Test match, against West Indies in Chennai in January 1967. My oldest brother-in-law, who worked for the Food Corporation of India, was posted in Chennai, excuse enough for a bunch of 10, including my brother and his friends, to land up at his house. We would take turns waking up at 4.00 a.m. so that we could go early to queue up in the quest for good gallery seats.

I watched every ball of that Test. Farokh Engineer got a 100, Sir Garry Sobers made 90-plus, several others topped 50, but the innings that stayed with me was Borde's 125. Armed with my limited cricketing knowledge, I arrived at the conclusion that it was a brilliant innings, so good to watch and so meticulously compiled. When I came to know that he would be captaining the BP XI, I could feel the stars aligning favourably.

Borde and I were involved in a decent partnership after we had lost three quick wickets. He guided me through a tough initiation against Richard Collinge, the tall and strong left-arm paceman with a big in-swinger. Instinctively, I started playing my flick and glance until Borde suggested that I would be more balanced and risk-free were I to move across to my off stump and play with the swing, which would give me greater control over my leg-side play.

Borde was a massive name in Indian cricket, a veteran of so many battles and the second highest run-getter for the country. When you are batting with someone of that stature, in the middle of a good partnership, and he volunteers a nugget, it's simply amazing for a youngster. I ended up with 68, run-out. A day later, on 13 October 1969, I earned my first Test call-up.

The series was tied 1-1 as India and New Zealand squared off at the Lal Bahadur Shastri Stadium in Hyderabad from 15 October. I had no illusions that I would be picked in the XI for such a vital contest, so there was no disappointment when it was confirmed that I would be in the reserves. Just being in the Indian dressing room, soaking in the atmosphere of a Test match, was an experience of a lifetime. We were housed at the stadium, with Eknath Solkar (Ekki), Ashok Gandotra and I sharing a room. No, before you jump to conclusions, we newcomers weren't thrown into a cramped space. It was a huge room which I had shared previously with at least six others when I played for Mysore or for the State Juniors. Ekki, with whom I already had a strong relationship, and Gandotra were making their debut.

Ekki was dismissed without scoring in the first innings. Understandably, he was distraught and almost in tears. I would come to know, in a month's time, what it felt like to fail to get off the mark in your first Test innings, but here I was, trying my best to pacify him and telling him that it was all part of the game.

I rattled off names that had scored zero on debut but had gone on to greater things. They just flowed off my tongue: Bradman, Harvey, Sobers, Kanhai. I knew I wasn't being truthful, but I just wanted to soften the blow for my friend. Not sure if it worked, though he did make an unbeaten 13 in the second innings.

The game ended in dramatic fashion with India on the ropes at 76 for seven, after scoring a mere 89 in the first. Providence smiled benevolently upon us; the road just outside the stadium was bone dry, but it pelted at the venue relentlessly. When the rain eased up, several members of the New Zealand side, including their captain, tried to help the ground staff with the mopping up operations because they knew they were on the cusp of a series win in India, but their endeavours bore no fruit. My first experience of Test cricket from the dressing room had been memorable.

6
NIGHTMARISH INITIATION

After the Hyderabad stalemate against New Zealand, the entire contingent travelled to Bombay (now Mumbai) ahead of the Test series against Australia, a fortnight away. We were to have a few days of practice, not a training camp as such, while Bill Lawry's men would ease into the tour with a three-day game against West Zone in Pune.

At the time, my older brother Jagannath was employed in Hyderabad, so naturally he came to watch the New Zealand Test. He and Pras were good friends, having known each other from before their Bangalore Cricketers days, and we had a few nice evenings together.

Pras then invited my brother over to Bombay for the first Test against Australia, throwing in the clincher by saying I would definitely make my debut. My brother wasn't as confident, but agreed after much cajoling, with a caveat. 'If he doesn't play,' he told Pras, 'you will have to get me a ticket for the match.'

'Don't think it will be necessary,' Pras chuckled, knowing that players were entitled to complimentary tickets, 'but if it comes to that, I will sort it out.'

After a couple of days in Hyderabad, we landed in Bombay for our training stint at the Brabourne Stadium. The 20 of us from whom the final 15 was to be chosen stayed at the Cricket Club of India (CCI) Chambers, across the road from the CCCI, which housed Brabourne.

When the 15 was named two days before the Test, my name was missing. By this time, my brother had already boarded the train in Hyderabad, and it wasn't until he reached Bombay a day before the game that he realized the young one wouldn't be playing, after all.

'What now?' he mock-defiantly asked Pras. 'You now have to sort out two match tickets, not just one.'

That wasn't a big deal for Pras, well connected as he was, but we had a more immediate problem to address. Where would we stay? Again, enter Pras.

Over the years, he had made friends in all parts of the country, and it was no different in Bombay. Pras got in touch with one Mr Rao, a fellow-Bangalorean who readily agreed to house my brother and myself. His younger brother, Kishore, was a good cricketer who had played alongside Sunil Gavaskar at the intercollegiate level, and then for Tata's. If memory serves me right, the Raos stayed in Bhagirathi Building, where Sunil too spent his early years before moving to Dadar.

We travelled to the Brabourne every day to watch the action, and my brother and I met Pras in his room on the fourth evening. My brother was keen to return to Hyderabad at the earliest and suggested I should go back to Bangalore (now Bengaluru) too, though I didn't share his enthusiasm. But Pras was insistent that at least I should stay put in Bombay.

Team India was on the verge of losing the Test, and neither Dilip Sardesai nor Chandu Borde had made a significant contribution. Pras hinted at possible changes for the second Test. It was no secret that Pras was very close to Tiger, that he was one of the captain's confidants. But he couldn't, of course, come out and openly say that a few spots would open up. All he told me was, 'Don't book your ticket or rush back to Bangalore immediately. Until I say something, don't do anything.'

As it turned out, the squad for the second Test was announced on the last day of the Bombay game, and I was back in the 15. After all these years, I can finally say with a cheeky smile that I replaced Borde in the side, I slipped into his No. 4 position. These were big shoes to fill, he was a big name in Indian cricket, and replacing someone of that stature is not easy, to say the least. But I didn't know any of these things at that stage, did I?

◆

There was nearly a week between the Bombay and the Kanpur Tests. As the Green Park showdown loomed, my excitement mounted. We flew from Bombay to Delhi and took a train to Kanpur, slowly easing into our routines. I immersed myself in practice, not losing sleep over whether I would get into the XI or not. For most of my Test career, XIs weren't named until just before the toss—even today, I can't comprehend why—and I told myself there was no point in thinking about it this early.

Apparently, a couple of days before the match, there was a selection trials of sorts at nets. I didn't know about it, which I think is just as well. Vijay Merchant, the chairman of selectors, was watching the proceedings with an eagle eye, like he had on the rest day during the second Test against New Zealand in Nagpur in early October. Eknath Solkar, Ashok Gandotra and I, all knocking on the doors of selection, had been summoned then to have a hit so that Mr Merchant could see what we were made of. This was his second sighting of me, though I had no idea what he thought of my batting.

It wasn't until much later that I came to know that I owed my Test debut to Tiger's insistence. I believe when he met with the selectors during the Bombay Test to pick the side for Kanpur, he categorically stated that I must be picked in the 15 only if I was going to play. 'I don't want him to merely warm the bench,' Tiger was firm.

Mr Merchant is said to have countered, 'I know he made a double-hundred in his first Ranji game and I have watched him bat at nets, but I haven't seen him play in a match.'

Tiger, being Tiger, retorted, 'But I have seen him bat—at nets and in matches. Don't pick him in the squad for the sake of it. If he is in the 15, he's playing.'

If I repeatedly talk about the influence Tiger has had on my cricket, it's with good reason. He literally put his foot down and made sure I played in Kanpur. Who knows what might have happened had there been another captain who didn't have the stature and the conviction to stand up to Mr Merchant? Who knows how much longer I would have had to wait had Mr Merchant backed someone else and that batsman had delivered the goods? That's why I say that I made my debut when I did only because of Tiger.

Pras let it slip the night before the Test, informally, that I would become India's 124th Test cricketer the following day, on 15 November

1969. Not for a moment did I doubt him. But until the team was pasted on the notice board in the dressing room the next morning, I was a little bit on edge.

Usually, on the morning of the match after the toss, the captain or the manager used to put up the long, official-looking sheet of paper on the notice board, outlining the playing XI in batting order. Most of the players knew their positions, so there wasn't any great scramble. In keeping with the mood, I casually strolled across to see whether I would be batting at No. 6 or No. 7, like I had in Duleep Trophy for South Zone. I was understandably anxious, but not overly so.

That was only until my eyes scanned the sheet, frantically searching for my name. Initially convinced I had missed out again because I didn't figure in the second half of the page as I had expected, I felt my breath leave me in a 'whoosh' when I spotted my name below Farokh Engineer, Ashok Mankad and Ajit Wadekar. At No. 4. Oh my God! Number four? That's when the millions of butterflies started their unending sorties inside my churning stomach.

It was also then that the enormity of the situation hit me. I was too caught up in my anxiety to recognize that my captain had shown so much faith that, on my debut, he had penciled himself below me in the batting order. All I knew was that Borde had occupied that position previously, as recently as in the last Test. Now, I was India's No. 4!

It's not that I wasn't used to batting in that position. That was the slot I occupied in the Mysore Ranji team, where I had worked out a routine I was comfortable with. When the openers walked out, I would put on my thigh pad, abdomen guard—all the inner protective wear. I wouldn't put on my pads until the fall of the first wicket, and then go out to the viewing area to watch every ball before it was my time to take guard.

But with the butterflies dictating terms, I wore my legguards too, acutely aware that I hadn't a proper 'net' even on the first morning of my Test career. Never mind, that had become a routine too.

There are some batsmen who must have a few minutes in the nets every day of the Test match, no matter what. I was the exact opposite. Be it a Ranji game or a Test match, I never ever hit the nets during the game. I would pat away a few throwdowns, at the most, but I never wore pads and batted in the nets at any stage of my career when I was playing a match.

In simple terms, I didn't want to waste energy. I have always been a profuse sweater and even today, when I hit the golf course on a sunny day, my tee-shirt is drenched in a jiffy. Early on, when I used my sleeve to wipe the sweat off the eyes, I often got blurry eyed. My only counter to the sweat when I was batting was to take off one glove and rub my fingers on my eyebrows, but never the eyes themselves.

This being the case, I asked myself why I should bat in the nets on matchdays. Wouldn't it be more prudent to save my energy for when I am actually batting, out in the middle?

◆

As Farokh and Ashok walked into the middle, I plonked myself in one of the chairs in the front row of the viewing area, on ground level and just outside the dressing room. Once I took that position, I watched every ball and wouldn't budge an inch until there was a break in play for drinks, or one of the more extended intervals.

The openers added more than 100, after which Mankad and Wadekar were involved in another useful partnership. My mind was blank; I was taking in the bowling but not so much the atmosphere because I was completely engrossed in the contest between bat and ball. At any moment, I could be needed to go out and extend the good work of the top order.

I had been immersed in every ball for nearly four hours when Wadekar was dismissed by Alan Connolly, the right-arm, fast-medium bowler. I played that over out without incident, a little later I negotiated a full over from Ashley Mallett, the off spinner. Then, soon after Mankad fell to Mallett, I was up against Connolly, again.

I defended the first two deliveries comfortably, but the third one had my number on it. Perhaps I am exaggerating, but it was possibly the only ball that turned in the entire Test. And this, from a fast bowler!

Connolly bowled a slower one, an off-break that gripped and turned. I eased forward in defence, loosening my grip on the bat, but the bounce meant that the ball smacked into my glove and then brushed my pad on its way to short leg, where Ian Redpath took a fairly comfortable catch at a good height. I didn't even look at the umpire; I was so disappointed that I immediately left the crease, crestfallen that my first Test foray hadn't so much as troubled the scorers.

Perhaps, that was how it was destined to start, but I wasn't looking for logic at the moment. As the match progressed, I found that even Pras and Bedi were struggling to turn the ball on that flat deck, yet I had been dismissed by a paceman who had bowled an offbreak. I mean, what are the chances?

As if to make up for that unkind cut, Green Park was extremely generous to me in subsequent outings. I have three hundreds and four fifties from 12 innings there, averaging 86.22 in seven Tests. Over time, my colleagues used to refer to Green Park as 'Vishy's green'.

So here I was, trudging back disconsolately without a run to my name, when the Kanpur crowd began to express its disappointment. Obviously, they had all come to cheer for India and to catch a glimpse of this new guy, and felt let down when I was dismissed for zero. During my walk back to the dressing room, I was the object of the ire of the fans, who hurled matkas (earthen cups) in which tea used to be served at the ground. They didn't come too close to me; like my strokeplay in my formative years, the fans' efforts also didn't have much power behind them. But while I wasn't injured physically, there was plenty of mental scarring.

The next four days were the most miserable of my life. I was starting to get the feeling that this could be the end of my career. I didn't know if I would play for India again.

I will eternally be grateful for the support I received from my teammates. Pras and Chandra, seniors and elders from the same state, took care of me like a younger brother, with words of comfort and assurance designed to ensure I didn't get overwhelmed by negativity. Tiger, a man of not many words, kept a close watch but didn't embark on a discourse or a lecture. All he told me was, 'Boy, don't worry. It will be okay.' To hear those words from the captain, from a man of his stature, was very reassuring.

However, as we retired for the night, the demons would start to resurface. Fortunately for me, even then, I had a fabulous voice of warmth and empathy in the shape of my roommate, Ekki.

The night of my debut, I was beside myself with grief, but Ekki would have none of it. When Ekki had been dismissed without scoring in his first Test in Hyderabad the previous month, I had reeled out (some made-up) names of great batsmen who had suffered a similar fate at the start. Ekki repeated all those names and then said, 'You can add Eknath Solkar too to that list.' I couldn't help but crack up.

Ekki knew how to lift my spirits. There was an immediate connect from the first time we met, and we became extremely good friends, apart from sharing rooms on numerous occasions when we played in the same team. He was an excellent cricketer, but more importantly, he is one of the nicest guys I have come across. I shudder to think how events would have unfolded in Kanpur had he not been my roomie.

◆

But as towering a pillar of strength as Ekki was, I couldn't shake off the gremlins of self-doubt gnawing at me. Surrounded by teammates during the day, I was reasonably distracted from my predicament, but the moment we switched off the light at night, the apprehensions returned all over again. For four nights in a row, I didn't sleep a wink. I kept replaying my brief stay at the crease, much as I tried not to, and I grew despondent by the minute.

My concerns didn't revolve around my skills, to be honest. All I felt was that I had missed my chance to make an impact, I had fluffed my lines on my first day on the big stage. Would the decision-makers give me another chance to showcase my abilities? Would they continue to show the same faith in me as my captain had? Those four nights, I so badly wished I had made a 20 or a 30. Later in my career, I was accused of being dismissed in the 20s and 30s far too often, the experts and critics pointed to things such as lapses in concentration. But lying in bed at the allegedly haunted Berkley Guest House those nights, I would have so gladly taken a 30. It was the big, fat zero that was killing me.

The rest of our first innings after my dismissal was a bit of a blur, and once we posted 320, Australia replied in kind. Doug Walters and Ian Ritchie Redpath made half-centuries; despite my agony, I couldn't help but admire a wonderful hundred by Paul Sheahan. Very stylish and full of strokes, he tackled our spinners exceedingly well and made 114, but we took their last six wickets cheaply on the third evening to keep their lead down to 28.

The third day's play ended with John Gleeson's dismissal. Our openers would take guard first thing the next morning, and at some stage, over the next two days, I'd be out there, batting again. As I left the field, I braced myself for another sleepless night. At the very least.

7
137 REASONS TO SMILE

The Berkley Guest House came with the 'haunted' tag. No one knew the origin of the label, and there was no indication that anything was amiss—no creepy sounds, no strange sightings, no unexplained movement of inanimate objects—but you know how it is in these situations. And how an unsettled, anxious mind can start imagining things.

Some of the other members of the team who had stayed here previously alluded to its haunted nature more than once, and always very casually. But for a 20-year-old who had got out for zero on debut, there was nothing casual about it. Already, my nerves were shot; nights became even worse with my short-term future and the thought of residing alongside 'ghosts' competing to keep me wide awake.

If I were to say that I was cool as ice when we reached the ground on the fourth morning, I'd be well short of being truthful. The butterflies in the first innings seemed insignificant compared to the swarm gorging itself on the insides of my stomach this time around.

Like I had in the first innings, I was kitted out for battle by the time the openers took guard, and had settled into my seat in the front row of the viewing area. I was lost in my own thoughts though I watched the proceedings carefully. I was so caught up in my own world that the crowd barely registered on me, but once Farokh and Ashok hit a couple of boundaries, I could no longer ignore the loud cheers.

Without warning, the image of the matkas being hurled after my first-innings dismissal floated in my mind. Already on edge, that was the last thing I needed. And the longer the openers batted, the more my anxiety started to grow.

I could feel my entire body tightening up, an inescapable sense of foreboding growing with every minute. An hour or so into the day's play, I sensed someone standing behind me. As if in confirmation, I felt a tap on my right shoulder. I didn't whirl back to see who it was, half-turning in my seat and trying to figure out from the corner of my right eye even as I stayed focussed on the action unfurling in front of me.

'Relax, boy, don't worry,' were the first words. It was the captain's distinctive, familiar voice. 'You will get a hundred. Don't be tense.'

Tiger's reassurance hit home at once. Even while he was talking, I knew that it's not as if he were certain I would get a hundred, or that he even expected me to do so. Just because he had said that didn't mean I would automatically get there. But my tension dissipated in a jiffy and I was overcome by a sense of calmness. Tiger's confidence was a soothing balm. But only for a few deliveries. It didn't take long for the nerves to resurface, not helped by the fact that once Farokh got out, Mankad and Wadekar put on more than 50 for the second wicket. Eventually, when Wadekar was dismissed, it was my time of reckoning.

I have no idea what the spectators' reaction was when I crossed the boundary line and entered the arena. There might have been resounding boos or claps of encouragement, but to me, there was just the sound of silence. My legs were like jelly, threatening to give way any second, but my face gave nothing away. I thought it was ominous, though, that the first ball I would face in the second innings would be from the same bowler who had got me out in the first—Connolly.

◆

That ball is still fresh in my memory, on a good length and defended off the middle of the blade. It felt good, but it wasn't enough.

A week ago, it would have been a different story. Till then, middle of the bat on first ball was practically the trigger on which I thrived. Not anymore. I know there are tons of high-quality batsmen who love that feeling, but the first-innings duck involuntarily transformed my mindset. For the rest of my career, I would only start breathing after I got off the dreaded 'nought'. Maybe that explains why I have only 10 zeroes in 155 Test innings, or that I picked up just one career 'pair', in the Ranji Trophy.

The jitters eased somewhat when, maybe 10 minutes into my innings, I glanced Graham McKenzie to fine leg for a single. I had my first Test run. No big deal, you say. An improvement on my first innings, I raise.

Once the first-run 'monkey' was off the back, I settled down. One of my few regrets is that there is no video footage of that innings, a knock I consider one of my best hundreds even without the attendant self-imposed pressure. It was a very clean innings; the shots were perfect in that they went exactly where I wanted them to go. It was an effort built on fours— I had 25 of them. Later on, every time Sunil referred to me as 'the boundary man', I would immediately reflect on my first Test hundred.

There was a minicollapse not too long after my entrance, with Mankad, Tiger and Ashok dismissed for the addition of just 25 runs. I had been looking forward to having a partnership with the skipper, but he was trapped leg before by a McKenzie ball that came in for a duck. At 147 for five and so much time left in the game, we were in trouble.

Out came my roomie, at No. 7, to join me. There was a general view that, not unlike Abid Ali, Ekki was a utility cricketer. A fluent left-hand bat, he could bowl both left-arm medium-pace and spin in addition to being an outstanding fielder whether in the deep where his anticipation was incredible, or in close where he pulled catches out of thin air. The way he moved in the outfield was an awesome sight, and once he eased into short leg with the spinners in operation, you always felt a moment of magic was around the corner. In my book, Ekki is much, much more than a utility cricketer.

I was delighted that, having spent so much time together off the park, Ekki and I had a chance to bat side by side. Over the last few days, we had discussed batting together and talked about how much fun that would be. This was our chance to extend our friendship to a meaningful on-field association, especially with the team needing us to deliver.

Ekki played his strokes freely while I breezed past my 50, and we were unseparated at stumps. We had put on 57, I was batting on 69. What a day it bad been! I knew, though, that the night would be no different to the previous four.

◆

Neither of us generally slept long hours, so much of that night was spent reliving our partnership. The anxiety and tension of the past had disappeared, the adrenaline had taken over. At one level, we couldn't believe what we had done; at another, it was so satisfying that I had brought up the first mini-milestone of my Test career in the company of one of my best friends.

Ekki pointed out that I had a great chance to get to three-figures. Overnight, he was 20, but he had batted really well and I told him that he must make the most of good touch, too. We kept chatting until we forced ourselves to get some sleep, well aware that there was unfinished business and that we needed to be fresh when play started the next morning.

I would have loved for Ekki to be the first to congratulate me when I got to 100, but unfortunately, he fell to McKenzie for 35, stopping our stand at 110. I was disappointed for him but also aware of the job on hand, consciously ensuring that I didn't do anything silly.

With new man S. Venkataraghavan, I stitched together another useful stand as we gradually wended our way towards safety. I eased into the 90s, but the journey from thereon was anything but swift. It took me 44 minutes to go from 92 to three-figures. Bill Lawry did what Bill Lawry does best—pack the infield and cut off singles. Lawry made me work really hard for those eight runs, but as I was to learn later, that was typical Lawry. He never gave an inch, nor did he seek any. It was a tough learning for me, but it was also a good lesson very early on in my career.

Strangely, I felt no nerves during that phase. I knew it was only a matter of time before the runs came, I was willing to wait patiently and stick to my natural game. That approach had brought me into the Indian team, it had taken me to 92 in this innings. Why change it just because a century beckoned?

The wait was over when I square drove Gleeson for four. The first emotion was great relief. Then, a tsunami of delight and satisfaction swept me away.

I had never expected to get a century in Test cricket and most certainly not on debut. I had been forced to earn that privilege, and I was fortunate that my colleagues had backed me to the hilt after the first-innings debacle. But at the same time, I was conscious that there still was a game to save. We knew there was no way we were going to win the Test, so it was imperative that we didn't do anything daft and lose it.

I say it with all respect that in that era, our first thought didn't necessarily revolve around winning. Yes, we won the odd Test match, maybe even the occasional series in India, but not as frequently as Indian teams subsequently did. For many of us, a draw was as good as a victory. Every time I went out to bat, my principal objective was to ensure we didn't lose a game.

You can't score a hundred every innings, not even the great Sir Don Bradman could do that. But I felt you must never come away thinking the team lost because of you. I may not have got 100 runs all the time, but I gave my 100 per cent every time I stepped on the cricket field. As luck would have it, I came to know long after I played my last game that India never lost a Test when I made a century. That's very satisfying. Would I have loved to score more than 14 hundreds? Of course. But when I look back at my career, I pause at the games where I made runs and the team won or fought with its back to the wall and came away with a draw.

◆

During the slow march through the 90s, I kept telling myself that this was a golden opportunity to get to three-figures. And it pleased me even more that though my 137 had 25 fours, I had patiently worked my way through the 'nervous nineties', not raced through it with the milestone in sight.

With the match totally secure, I was trapped leg before by Mallett. The crowd rose as one, the flying matkas a distant memory, as they clapped me all the way back to the dressing room. Another lesson: if you want them on your side, keep performing. For some reason, fans in India took to me and backed me to the hilt for the entirety of my career. There was the odd blip, such as the orange-throwing incident in Kolkata when I failed in both innings against Keith Fletcher's England team in 1982, but they were few and far between. In any case, the Green Park crowd had already prepared me for any eventuality.

In the dressing room, as I sat after a shower and soaked in the congratulations of my mates, Tiger walked up with a twinkle and said,

'What did I tell you? Right?'

'Yes, I remember that Skip,' I smiled shyly. 'I will never forget that, not for a moment in my life.'

I loved the word 'Skip'. I had heard all the Hyderabad lads—all except Tiger and Abbas Ali Baig—refer to Jai as Skip or Skipper, but in Mysore, we didn't have that culture. To me, Skip wasn't a word, it was a title well-earned and deserved. This was the first time I had called Tiger 'Skip', and his indulgent smile told me that he knew it, too.

My interest in cricket history had made me aware that previously, Lala Amarnath (Lalaji), Deepak Shodhan, A.G. Kripal Singh, Abbas and Hanumant Singh had all made hundreds in their first Test. But I didn't know about the hoodoo, I wasn't aware that none of these batsmen scored another Test ton. The media made sure I was properly educated, with repeated references to this soon after I brought up the hundred.

Tiger got a fair bit of stick for delaying the declaration and not making even a token attempt at victory though the surface was still excellent for batting. In his characteristic deadpan fashion, he told me that all the criticism directed at him was of my making.

'Me?' I stammered, mortified. 'What did *I* do?'

Sensing my growing trepidation, Tiger sought to calm me down. 'Just kidding, I know you played your normal game. It's just that I wanted you to get a 150. No Indian has made a 150 on debut, and with this hoodoo hanging over everyone's necks, I thought I'd be buying you some more time if you could get past 150.'

I couldn't believe my good fortune, I wondered what I had done to deserve this. Tiger knew he would be pilloried for not declaring earlier even though victory wasn't a realistic proposition, yet he put me first.

It took me more than three years to double my tally of Test hundreds, but I did break the jinx. More of that later.

◆

I rode an emotional rollercoaster for six days at Green Park. There was a dream-like ending all right, but this had not been an easy Test. I never experienced the anxiety that gripped me in that game ever again in my career. I did face challenges. I did worry about a Test match, about my future. You have to go through this, otherwise there is no fun—the rigours of playing express pacemen, the thought of tackling top-quality spinners on a turner. But no other game was as emotionally draining as the first one. It pushed me to the lowest of depths, then elevated me to the highest of peaks. From chief villain, I quickly became the hero in the eyes of the crowds. I learnt more in those six days than I had in my previous 20 years.

The day after the game, I got a telegram from the legendary actor Raj Kapoor. It said, 'Congratulations, young man.' I was over the moon. I hadn't met him, but I knew he was a great cricket enthusiast. Everyone knows the relationship Chandra and playback singer Mukeshji enjoyed; less talked about is how much respect and affection Chandra and Raj Kapoor had for each other.

To get a telegram from such a towering personality sent me into raptures. I kept that piece of paper with me for a long, long time in our old home in Rajajinagar, but when we shifted to our current residence, it got misplaced. I wish I had kept it with me, pasted it on my scrapbook like I had pasted newspaper clippings of the exploits of Sobers and Kanhai and Harvey. How I really wish!

Even today, I am grateful to Raj Kapoor for the sweet gesture which meant the world to me. It's a pity I never got to meet him, but thanks to Chandra, I have spent a lot of time with Mukeshji. And later in life, I came to know Rishi and Randhir Kapoor, Raj Kapoor's sons and themselves great followers of cricket.

The telegram reinforced my belief that I had arrived in Test cricket, that I belonged at this grade. After the first-innings failure, I was petrified at the prospect of not playing another Test. The 100 gave me some breathing space, a cushion of sorts. I knew I wouldn't be dropped for at least the rest of the series—three more matches remained to be played.

I know of so many gifted players who vanished without a trace after their first failure. If, somehow, they got a couple of more chances again and still failed to deliver, it worsened their case. They were unfortunate to get off to bad starts and encounter a confidence-crisis. My 100 had made sure I didn't fall into the same trap.

More than 50 years on, I still can't find the words to describe how much security and confidence the 137 instilled in me. Just like the 230 on Ranji debut had swept away most of the thorns in my path, this debut performance was the catalyst for what I consider a smooth ride in international cricket.

Kanpur was an unforgettable experience. Four days of anxiety and uncertainty, followed by two outlook-altering, path-charting days of unfettered joy. I wasn't just a Test cricketer now, I was a Test centurion too.

8
FITNESS, OR SOMETHING LIKE THAT!

One look at cricketers of today, and you can't help but marvel at how fit they look and, in most cases, how fit they are. It's no secret that they spend almost as much time at the gym, or on working at their bodies, as they do honing their skillsets. There is a scientific temper to their approach which is inevitable, given how high the stakes involved are and how many more matches there are to play. Great care is given to diet and nutrition, to workload management, to injury prevention and treatment, to fitness drills specific to each player and to each discipline. Organic as these developments are, they are wonderful additions that have made our sport so much more exciting as a spectacle.

In the pre-professional era, however, fitness held a totally different connotation. We were cricket-fit, if you like. We were fit enough to bat long periods, fit enough to bowl 30 overs or more in a day. We might not have resembled the magnificently chiselled athletes of today, but those were different times, when the concept of fitness as it is viewed today had not taken concrete shape, and where awareness of what to eat and what not to eat wasn't even in the realm of our imagination.

These days, players work out on their own when they are not playing as a team. Several of them have gyms of some shape or form in their homes. I didn't see the inside of a gym until much after my last first-class game in 1988, yet that didn't stop me from playing 87 Tests on the trot. And it does say something that two of the three players to have played the most successive Tests for India belong to our generation, Sunil topping the list with 106 appearances in a row until his retirement in 1987.

My early memories of fitness routines in structured cricket revolve around a couple of laps of whichever ground we were practising at. Once we were picked to the State Junior side or the Ranji Trophy squad, we were asked to assemble at a specified time for nets.

Keki Tarapore was invariably who we'd report to. He would make us run two or three laps of the ground, followed by a few stretching and loosening-up drills. Then came short sprints, maybe 60–70 metres with five repetitions. And, before we hit the nets, he would give us catches.

The coach, or the equivalent in those times of the coach, used to identify five or six of us for close-in catching, while the captain or a senior player would take charge of providing outfield catching and putting the rest through ground-fielding sessions.

Keki was unbelievably committed to whatever he did. No matter how many catches you wanted, he would never say he was tired, he'd never turn you down. The routine involved the five or six of us in a ring taking around 25 catches each, after which he would give us individual attention, summoning us for 25 more catches designed to simulate the kind of catches you would get in a match, depending on where you fielded close in. If, after this, someone wanted extra attention, Keki would uncomplainingly, indeed happily, oblige. It was thus that I ended up taking 100 catches at the minimum during each training session. That being said, there were some players who, even for a Ranji game, would only arrive at the ground half an hour before the start of play, have a knock or send down a few balls, and were ready to go. Hard to comprehend, I know, but believe me, that wasn't the exception in the 1960s and '70s.

The somewhat laid-back attitude changed when you got into the Indian team, where the same routines took on a more formal look. The intensity might not have been that much more, but there was a religious adherence to the drills.

◆

Again, contrary to now, we once used to have long offseasons when you were on your own, and therefore had to find creative methods to keep yourself occupied. I was a compulsive runner; I loved running on my own, I loved running with my friends. I'd run anywhere, at any ground, be it the Central College Ground or at some school close to my house. It wasn't so much of a conscious choice to get fitter or to lose weight; I had time on my hands, I enjoyed running, so why not spend that time doing something I liked doing in any case?

Before I played representative cricket regularly, I'd often watch Bangalore Cricketers practise in the evenings, their ground very close to my school. I was drawn not just by all the big names in their side—G. Kasturirangan, L.T. Subbu, Deepak Dasgupta, L.P. Shyam—but also because my brother Jagannath played for them. I was so regular that one day, Shyam called me into the nets at the end of their session. 'Why just sit outside and watch us, come and have a hit,' he said, under-arming the ball at me. He'd make me play the cover drive, the on drive and the straight drive over and over again. When I look back, this was one of the key reasons for my becoming a strong driver of the cricket ball.

Slowly, I started to run with them, both slow laps of the ground and the shorter sprints. Without my realizing, it became an everyday occurrence—running, taking catches and knocking at the nets.

◆

To provide some perspective on what place fitness occupied in those times, the Indian team didn't have its first genuine 'camp' until before the 1977–78 tour of Australia. And I had made my Test debut in 1969.

This 15-day camp in Chennai was a game-changer for a lot of us. The Board of Control for Cricket in India (BCCI) had put one Major Tandon in charge of the camp, and he was a wonderful tutor—pleasant and amiable. He had a way of making us do what he wanted, and we were all so taken in by his charm and personality that for the first couple of days, we did everything he asked of us.

However, clearly, we were not used to such strenuous, sustained workouts. Soon, we had numerous cases of muscles becoming tight and of a couple of the players not being able to even walk. Everyone was aching and sore all over, and to some, the journey from the bed to the washroom wasn't unlike attempting to scale Mount Everest.

When we brought this to Major Tandon's notice, he was immediately sympathetic to our plight. He had joined us in all our routines, and even though he was well past 50, he went about his drills effortlessly, in stark contrast to men half his age who were struggling and gasping for breath.

He soon switched his methods, easing up on the workload and seeking feedback all the time. Once he realized that we didn't require the same level of fitness as those in the Army did, the camp blossomed. Like I said, he was amazing in how he conducted the camp. He wasn't a strict disciplinarian who tried to force you into sticking to a rigid pattern. Like us, he bought into the cricket-fitness concept, and allowed us to customize segments essential to our chosen disciplines.

For example, I told him that I couldn't run 10 laps around the ground, but I was game for doing several short sprints which would help me both chase down balls aggressively and eat up ground quickly while running between the wickets. He saw where I was coming from and encouraged me to stick to what worked best for me. But he could sense an excuse very astutely, and if you were trying to cut corners, he would quickly be in your ear, politely but firmly. He is easily the sweetest Major I have come across, and largely because of him, the camp became both enjoyable and immensely beneficial. After 15 days, we were fitter than we had ever been, and we looked forward to subsequent camps under Major Tandon and then Major Dogra.

I don't need to tell you how completely different the scenario is today, not just at the international level but even in club and age-group categories. Fitness is both non-negotiable and mandatory, as integral as bowling, batting and fielding. Teams travel with specialists in strength and conditioning, in physiotherapy, even sports science. The professionalism is admirable, and I enjoy watching them go about their business. Would I have enjoyed doing all this if I had had the opportunity 50 years back? Hmmm...

◆

When Sunil was appointed the Indian skipper, he entrusted training responsibilities to Chetan Chauhan, his opening partner. Chetan was the equivalent of the training captain, organizing sessions diligently and making it an inclusive process. By now, we were all well-versed in the drills taught by Major Tandon, and Chetan would kick off the stint by being in the centre and doing exercises that the rest of us would emulate.

One by one, he would then invite each of us to go to the centre and lead the way by adopting our individual favourites. That way, none of us felt we were doing 14–15 exercises in a mundane, disinterested manner. Because each one of us was given a responsibility, these sessions lasting 40 minutes became fun and enjoyable. They also instilled a sense of team spirit and togetherness, which, in turn, made a big difference when we took the field as a unit.

We were, however, less regimented when it came to diet. We could eat whatever we wanted, but we all knew what we were doing and therefore seldom did we over-indulge. Each of us had our own ways of embracing food during a match. When I was batting, for instance, I would have nothing more than a bowl of soup or a glass of juice at lunch or tea. Some others didn't have even that, especially the bowlers who obviously can't be expected to operate on full stomachs. A couple of players didn't mind a hearty meal whether they were still batting or bowling. By then, we had played enough to understand what worked for us individually.

The one area in which I made no compromises was catching. I have mentioned previously about the sessions with Keki, and as I started playing more, I continued to work on my catching. Early on, I fielded at gully, and manned the infield—covers, mid off, places like that. I was a good fielder, but I wanted to be brilliant, which I couldn't become. I was however well above average, and even if I say so myself, I had a very good arm for up to 50 metres. Syed Kirmani (Kiri) sometimes used to marvel at the power behind my throws.

'How come, *baap*?' he used to ask. 'I have seen some brilliant throwers, you are no less than them.'

Grinning wickedly, I'd reply, 'From my dumb-bells, you know.' My 'dumb-bells', of course, were the buckets of water I used to lift to strengthen my wrists. That had made my forearms strong too, and it's from there, the forearm and the wrist, that I was able to generate substantial power behind my throws.

Once I moved regularly to first slip, I was very happy to be there. Some people might think slip is a very relaxed position, hardly any long chases, but I beg to disagree. It's a position that calls for great powers of concentration for long stretches of time. You might go through an entire day with not a ball coming your way, and in the last five minutes, you could so easily be confronted with a thick edge flying towards you. If you are even a touch off the boil, down goes the chance and out come the critics, their sharp knives at the ready.

More than the criticism, though, I was mindful of not letting the bowlers down. Bowling in general, and fast bowling especially, is a physically demanding task, and the last thing you want as a bowler is to create a chance and see it not being taken. That's why I concentrated a little more when I was in the slips. I didn't want the bowler to suffer on my account. It's not as if I took all the catches that came my way, but any spills were neither due to want of effort nor loss of focus. I always gave that one per cent extra to my catching and fielding compared to my batting. I was a fielder, not a bowler. It was my duty to stay fully committed for those six hours, never mind whether I was at slip, the infield or the outfield.

◆

Full disclosure. I was a reasonably regular part-time bowler in my early days, a budding leg spinner with fantastic drift, sudden dip and ripping turn—at least that's how I saw it. After all, I do have 15 first-class wickets, and my only Test wicket was that of a specialist leg spinner. Jim Higgs, the Australian No. 11, just can't live it down. Perhaps television recordings might suggest otherwise, but I did him in the flight, lured him with loop and fooled him with turn to have him caught by Dilip Vengsarkar, who was keeping wicket during the final stages of the Delhi Test in 1979. Oh, what a ball that was!

I had started off bowling regularly for Spartans, and boasted more than one five-wicket haul, though when I joined SBI, I hardly bowled because we had senior leg spinner S. Mahendra in our ranks.

I had to put my bowling aspirations on hold owing to an accident not long after my Test debut. From my house in Rajajinagar, I'd go to Malleswaram on my scooter to pick up my friend and colleague Arun Kumar. After breakfast at his place, we'd get going to our bank. This routine continued even after he purchased a two-wheeler of his own.

One day, as we left his house on our respective scooters, I told him that I needed to stop at the gas station near Bashyam Circle. The petrol pump was to our right, and while I put my hand out and took that half-turn, Arun was lost in his own world. Oblivious to what I was doing, he kept going straight, and rammed into my scooter from behind. As I went down in a heap, the front wheel of his vehicle ran over my right knee.

Sprawled on the road, I was in considerable pain. Amidst all the commotion, a car stopped by our side. Providentially, Dr Thimmappaiah got out of the car, and was shocked when he discovered that I was the injured party. He requisitioned ice and strapped up the knee, and after a while, I started to feel better.

I was categorically told to stop bowling even in the nets, and I managed to follow those instructions for almost an entire year. But you know how it is with batsmen who fancy themselves as bowlers. One not so fine day, the itch got the better of me, but within four or five deliveries, I twisted the knee again.

That was the worry those days when you bowled on matting pitches. Not all the groundsmen did an efficient job of laying the mat. The nails are hammered haphazardly, and sometimes the mat puffs up when it isn't nailed in properly. That's what happened; my foot got stuck and as I was forced to drag it, the right knee gave way.

I rushed to Dr T.D. Ram, the state association and Dr Chinnaswamy's go-to man, when any of the state players got injured. I had consulted him previously too at the Jubilee Nursing Home behind the Central College Ground, adjacent to the old Central Jail. Sufficiently annoyed, he told me in no uncertain terms that if I entertained hopes of a long international career, I must resist the temptation to bowl again.

All was well until the final of the Duleep Trophy against East Zone in January 1971. The tour of the West Indies wasn't far away. From my position at slip, I gave chase to a ball heading towards the third man boundary at Mumbai's Brabourne Stadium. I couldn't stop the ball from crossing over, but in the process of trying to do so, I tripped over the rope and jarred my knee.

It was thus, with that troublesome knee, that I left for the Caribbean. I didn't play the first two Tests because I was still carrying the injury, and at least one person asked if I had been 'smuggled in' despite being unfit. Since returning for the third Test in March 1971, however, I played

87 successive games until my last match against Pakistan in Karachi in February 1983. That's something I take great pride in.

Sunil loves the fact that he has 106 straight Test appearances to his credit. Like me, he wasn't obsessed with fitness, he was not a fitness freak. He built up reserves of stamina that could help him spend an entire day at the batting crease without losing concentration even towards the very end of a long six hours. Not only did he do that, but he did so brilliantly throughout his career, without ever going to the gym.

Fitness is viewed through various prisms; ours revolved around cricket, and I am proud to say that while I might not have looked the fittest, I must have done something right to play 87 Tests in a row. And 91 in all.

9

THE CARIBBEAN CONQUEST

When we left for the Caribbean towards the end of January 1971, my excitement was at a fever pitch. My four previous Test appearances had all been at home, the last of them in December 1969 against Australia in Madras. For the whole of 1970, India didn't play a single Test, so when we left Bombay, I couldn't wait for us to touch down in Kingston.

Between the home series against Australia and the tour of the West Indies, I had made my first foray outside the country. Pleased by how I had started my Test career, Raj Singh Dungarpur invited me to be a guest player for CCI on their tour of East Africa in July–August 1970. I was thrilled. The CCI was a respected entity, would be led by Hanumant Singh, and included stalwarts such as Vijay Manjrekar and Salim Durani.

There were plenty of youngsters too including Milind Rege, who went on to captain Mumbai in the Ranji Trophy, and Atul Mankad, Ashok's younger brother who represented Saurashtra in first-class cricket. To me, the tour represented a great opportunity to further my cricketing education; by the end, I had picked up several valuable lessons.

Even though he was closing in on 40, Manjrekar was still an active first-class player. Age had done little to blunt his expertise, and to my good fortune, we were involved in several partnerships during the dozen matches in Kenya, Uganda and Tanzania. I made plenty of runs, which did my confidence no harm, and while the quality of the opposition might not have been of the highest order, it was a very good experience for someone like me who had just made his international debut.

Manjrekar's influence on my career extended beyond watching and learning from him. In my early days, I had my fair share of problems against left-arm spin. I had been dismissed numerous times by the ball coming in with the arm, bowled or leg before as I went back to cut. I suppose that was an instinctive fall-out of playing exclusively on matting pitches until my first-class debut.

Watching me in the nets and from close quarters in matches a few times, Manjrekar had a ready fix. 'You only go back to a spinner if the ball is really short and merits back foot play,' he said. 'Otherwise, against any spinner, your first plan must be to get forward. In other words, try and get to the pitch so you don't allow the ball to turn.'

I lapped up his words gratefully and tried to put his advice into practice in the nets. Soon, I began to encounter fewer and fewer problems against left-arm spin. To receive such a valuable tip from a legend so early in my career was to have positive spin-offs as I played more top-flight cricket.

It was a thrill to watch Manjrekar bat, he was a master technician. Hanumant was a beautiful strokemaker, also very good technically and an attacking batsman, which immediately struck a chord with me. Apart from cricketing lessons, I also learnt life lessons. It was my first time away from the comfort of my home, my country, and I fell in love with Kenya and its wildlife. That was the start of a beautiful relationship; in subsequent years, I made several trips to Kenya, playing cricket and making great friends who have walked the journey with me. To date, Kenya remains one of my favourite destinations.

◆

Memories of the Kenya visit came flooding back when, sitting in the aircraft in Bombay, I reflected on the fact that my first overseas Test tour would be to the land of Garry Sobers and Rohan Kanhai, my heroes and two of the greatest cricketers ever to have played the game. And that at some stage over the next couple of games, I would be figuring in the same Test match as them.

I knew the knee injury wouldn't allow me to be an active participant at the start of the five-Test series, but that didn't dampen my enthusiasm. It was a matter of time before I would share the same playing arena with the mighty West Indies—a team that had captured the imagination of cricket lovers with its uninhibited style of play and gentlemanly conduct.

It wasn't an easy first month. The knee didn't heal as swiftly as expected, so I ended up missing three practice games and the first two Tests. With each passing day, my frustration mounted just that bit and I was desperate to get back on the park, but I also knew that if I rushed back, I ran the risk of aggravating the injury and spending even more time on the sidelines.

Both I and the newest entrant into the Indian team, a certain Sunil Gavaskar, were unavailable for the first Test, in Kingston. Sunil was suffering from whitlow, a painful infection on the middle finger of his left hand, which forced him to sit out the Sabina Park game; by the time the five-Test series ended, he had established himself as a household name in India and made the cricketing world sit up and take notice.

If I didn't go completely nuts watching from the sidelines, it was largely due to M.L. Jaisimha. Jai wasn't just a calming influence, he was a great reservoir of experience and wisdom which he readily allowed you to tap into. If anything, he didn't wait for you to go to him. Despite his seniority, he would seek out youngsters and share his knowledge with them, which I knew was a luxury I had to make the most of. He made me sit by his side for the entire duration of the second Test, and for the concluding stages of the first Test when he came off the field, breaking things down and patiently explaining the finer points without making it sound like he was lecturing me.

The opening day of the series was washed out, so essentially the first Test was a four-day affair. We were put in by Sir Garry when play got underway on day two, and were immediately in trouble at 75 for five, quick bowlers Grayson Shillingford and Vanburn Holder picking up two wickets apiece.

Dilip Sardesai then batted like the champion he is, and like he would bat throughout the series. He had already played 21 Tests in 10 years, including in the Caribbean nine years previously. Piece by small piece, he stitched the innings together in the company of my great pal Ekki, in whose success I rejoiced. Jai had been dismissed for three, but soon after he shed his pads and had his shower, he called me over so we could watch Dilip and Ekki rescue the innings.

It was the small things Jai told me—knowing when and which bowler to pay greater attention to, figuring out what are the safe scoring options, and finding a way to manoeuvre and manipulate the field—which stayed with me. It was too good an opportunity for a youngster like me to pass up, and like an obedient student, I listened attentively and soaked up every word that left his mouth.

Dilip and Ekki put on 137, and even when the latter fell for 61, the former retained fierce focus. He batted nearly 10 hours in making 212, hauling us to 387. The nerves of 75 for five had long disappeared, and with only a little over two days left in the game, we knew we had achieved our first objective—of not losing the game.

What happened thereafter was extraordinary as the West Indies top order showcased their vast skills. I particularly enjoyed Rohan's 56 and Sir Garry's 44; I noticed how beautifully, but in contrasting styles, the two legends used their feet against our three world-class spinners—Chandra was not part of the touring party.

Not for nothing, though, are Bishan, Pras and Venkat rated so highly. Once they sensed an opening, they were all over the opposition. From 183 for three, there was a spectacular procession once Venkat got rid of Rohan. We picked up their last seven wickets for just 34, Pras taking four and Venkat returning three. West Indies were bowled out for 217, around tea on day four, our lead was 170.

At the changeover, Ajit Wadekar, our captain, darted over to the Windies dressing room and told Sir Garry that he had decided to enforce the follow-on. The West Indian skipper laughed and said, 'I hope you are only joking.'

'No, not joking,' Ajit replied, explaining that since this was now a four-day Test, a lead of 150 was enough to stick the opposition back in.

If Sir Garry was fazed, he didn't show it. He threw his head back and laughed again, 'Alright, maan, so we will bat again.'

Realistically, our shot at victory was an outside one at best, but Ajit had fired an unexpected salvo. We feared retaliation of some sort and sure enough, Rohan and Sir Garry did not disappoint.

Batting with flair and authority, and almost as if they were slighted at being asked to bat again, the two virtuosos put on an exhibition on the last day. Jai was by my side for a majority of that partnership, insisting that I not take my eyes off the action. He had played against these batsmen previously and had seen it all before, yet he said modestly, 'Just to watch them bat is a great lesson for all of us.'

The general impression around that time was that West Indian batting was all about power, about how hard they hit the ball and tore bowling attacks apart. That certainly wasn't the case with either Rohan or Sir Garry. Because of the proximity from which I watched them tackle our three spinners for the second time in the match, I picked up things that not even a thousand net sessions would have allowed me to.

They were completely different in all aspects imaginable. Rohan was right-handed, Sir Garry was left-handed; Rohan was short, Sir Garry tall and lithe. The latter played with the bat always in front of his pad, not adjacent to it, to eliminate the possibility of bat-pad catches, but possessed a rich array of strokes that he unleashed at the slightest hint of error from the bowler. Rohan played the ball late, was light on his feet, and a master of the 'falling sweep'. Their footwork was assured, and I was captivated by the softness of their hands. I knew we were at the receiving end, but sitting on the bench, I thoroughly enjoyed their 173-run stand.

I was perhaps more disappointed than Sir Garry when he was out for 93; Rohan had reached 158 when the teams shook hands and agreed to a draw. Despite not playing the game, I had come out richer for the experience. Jai's encouragement, masterpieces from Sir Garry and Rohan, and 0-0 with four to play after we had shocked them by asking them to follow-on. Now, if only my knee would cooperate.

◆

A glimmer of opportunity opened up when I played in the four-day game against Trinidad and Tobago at Pointe-à-Pierre just days before the second Test in Port of Spain, but it wasn't a particularly pleasant outing. I made one and 16, but more than the lack of runs, it was the knee that troubled me. I knew there was no way I would be ready for the second Test, starting a mere two days after the conclusion of that match.

Sunil, now fully recovered, warmed up for his maiden Test with 125 in the first innings and 63 in the second. Our confidence already high after we had the better of the exchanges in Kingston, we were further buoyed by the availability of our first-choice opener as we headed to Queen's Park Oval, little knowing that history was in store.

Bishan and Pras did the damage on the first day to bowl out West Indies for 214, and we got our first glimpse of Sunil the Test opener that same evening. In the short passage to stumps, he had reached eight, and everybody could see that this wasn't just another Test opener. Here was an extraordinary batsman who would go on to achieve extraordinary things. I didn't have any specific numbers in mind, but I knew right then that by the time Sunil was done with the game, he would have gone where few before him had.

What a debut Test Sunil had! Indeed, what a debut series my future brother-in-law would have! Right in his first innings at the Test level, the message was loud and clear: I belong here, I am cut out for exactly this. The way he acquitted himself in his first game, and the intensity and hunger he carried right through the series, was unbelievable.

He had no prior experience of playing Test cricket, though, unlike me, he must have seen a few matches previously because he was from Bombay. But he showed neither nerves nor anxiety while making 65 in the first innings. Dilip got 112 and Ekki came up with another half-century to take us to 352, a big lead of 138 on a track helping the spinners. When Venkat's five for 95 sent West Indies tumbling to 261 in their second knock, we required 124 for our first victory in the West Indies. There was a slight sense of disbelief. Was this really happening? And would we hold our nerve?

Yes, as it turned out, and yes again. For the second time in the game, Sunil got into the 60s, this time reaching 67 when he and Abid Ali closed out a seven-wicket victory. We were over the moon, but not for one second did we think it was a flash in the pan. Over the first two Tests, we had played the better cricket consistently, and 1-0 was no more than what we deserved.

Ajit was a phenomenal leader who played a big part in our emergence as a strong Test force. He was an excellent batsman in his own right, and his man-management skills were exemplary. He had a host of established players to feed off—Jai, Dilip, Pras, Salim—as well as a young group that included Sunil, Ekki and myself. Ajit didn't impose himself, nor was he insecure when surrounded by such giants as Jai. It spoke of the spirit that existed within the group that everyone pulled in the same direction, and that Ajit was actually happy for Jai to take over captaincy duties whenever he came on to the field as a substitute.

I remember the Port of Spain Test fondly not just for the result, not just for Sunil's career-defining half-centuries or for Dilip's second successive 100. I also fondly recall, with a big smile, the genius that Salim Durani is.

West Indies had reached 150 for one in their second innings on the third evening. That night, Salim bhai, as I called him, told Ajit that if he was thrown the ball, he would guarantee his skipper two wickets. Not just that, Salim bhai also nominated the batsmen—nothing special, just two big left-handers named Clive Lloyd and Sir Garry Sobers.

Ajit was too shrewd to pass up this dare, so early on day four, he summoned Salim bhai's left-arm spin, after Roy Fredericks was run-out for 80. True to his word, Salim bhai bowled Sir Garry neck and crop for a duck with a ball that turned in sharply; a few overs later, he forced Lloyd to chip to Ajit at short mid on. Between them, the two batsmen had contributed just 15.

At the end of the over in which he got rid of Lloyd, Salim bhai tossed the ball to Ajit and told him, 'I have done my job, no more bowling.'

Salim bhai was an absolute genius of a cricketer. He was so laid-back that to the casual observer, he might have bordered on the lazy, but to watch him in action was exhilarating. I never fancied myself against his left-arm spin, he was a killer. His biggest threat was being bored to distraction due to the lack of a challenge, but if he made up his mind, he was something else. If he wanted to trouble you, he would torture you endlessly. He had a beautiful, easy action, all languid grace and total control, and he could turn the ball on any surface, anywhere in the world. As a batsman, he was attacking and imposing, and didn't turn a deaf ear to demands for sixes from the crowd. In the 1960s and '70s, he had 15 sixes in 29 Tests. Need I say more?

◆

While Salim bhai showcased his awesome skills, the high-quality spinners put on an exhibition and Dilip reiterated his credentials, the one who had stood taller than the rest during the Port of Spain win was Sunil. As he was going about his business with characteristic meticulousness, there was stunned admiration within the dressing room. Straightaway, he had showed us what he was capable of, what he would do in a career that eventually lasted more than 16 years. To finish with 774 runs in just four Tests in your debut series was unimaginable. As much as the quantum of runs, the manner in which he got them was equally impressive.

More than 30 years after our careers ended, I have no hesitation in calling Sunil technically the best batsman I have played with and against, and seen before or subsequently. An opener's job is, at the best of times, not the easiest. If you are batting on the first day of a Test, which Sunil often did during his 125-match career, you are up against well-rested bowlers itching to let it rip on a fresh pitch. The quality of pacemen he was up against was of the highest order, but the felicity with which Sunil tackled them at a time when protective gear was basic and the helmet hadn't made an appearance was magnificent.

Throughout his career, he assiduously avoided the helmet—not out of ego but because he felt it might affect the stillness of his head and carried the danger of lulling him into a false sense of security—though that didn't prevent him from becoming the first batsman to reach 10,000 runs or finish up with 34 centuries and an average of 51.12. Not once did he flinch in the face of express pace; I should know, because I have batted alongside him several times, though it is a little unfortunate that we didn't have as many long partnerships as I would have liked.

I consider myself fortunate to have played alongside him even if technically speaking, I am senior to him, having made my Test debut nearly a year and a half before him. Just spending time with him in the middle helped me learn a lot—innings by innings, Test by Test—and I have no hesitation in admitting that it facilitated my maturing as a batsman and a cricketer much earlier than I had expected.

His famed concentration transfixed me, and I marvelled at how he was able to pick up the length of a ball so much quicker than most other batsmen. That's not a skill which can be worked on and honed; it's instinctive, it comes from within, a gift if you would like. Even though he had not faced balls hurled at 85 mph before setting foot in the Caribbean, he was seldom hustled by pace. He was always in position, he adjusted so quickly. That was one of his greatest attributes.

Rarely did he go 'fishing'. He played so close to his body that he was in control right throughout, whether as a 20-year-old in his first Test or as a 37-year-old in his last, when he produced a memorable 96 on a M. Chinnaswamy Stadium minefield against Pakistan in 1987.

In my book, Vivian Richards is the greatest batsman I have had the privilege of watching. I say this because I watched him on his Test debut during the tour of India in 1974 and followed his career closely till he finished up nearly two decades later. From the first game till the last, he remained the master of strokeplay. He was 'The Boss', and he let you know it. He had swagger and strut, but he wasn't just style. There was so much substance to him, such nonchalance with which he decimated bowling attacks. It was as if he felt insulted that a bowler had the temerity to even bowl at him. He retained his domineering, attacking, intimidating essence throughout his playing days.

Sunil will forever be the greatest technician, a champion of discipline and self-denial. In his early days in international cricket, he was a compulsive hooker. He loved taking on the short ball, but within his first four Tests, he came to the realization that it was better for him to put that stroke in cold storage. For one thing, it isn't a shot you can be in control of all the time. More significantly from his standpoint, the team would be better served if he eschewed the hook because of the accompanying risks.

By the end of his first series, Sunil had established himself as the best batsman in the team, the backbone of the Indian batting. The middle order wasn't the most solid or sound, so from the team's point of view, Sunil had to bat for as long as he could. If that meant putting away a prolific scoring option, then so be it, he decided. I know it sounds simple: don't play the hook shot. But it's a stroke he had played all through his adult life, so one can well imagine how strong he must have been mentally when still so young to completely ignore that run-scoring option. It was as if Sunil put the hook in a box, locked it up and threw the key away.

Until, dramatically, he rediscovered the key in 1983, at the Kotla, against the same team that had facilitated his memorable debut. Batting like a man possessed against Malcolm Marshall, Michael Holding, Winston Davis and Wayne Daniel, he played his most bruising Test innings. I remember Marshall's wry smile when Sunil played his first hook shot in forever in Test cricket. For the rest of his innings, the West Indies fielders were merely retrieving the ball from the fence. Sunil reached his 100 off just 94 balls, and when he was dismissed for 121 off 128 deliveries, he had smashed 15 fours and two sixes. It was as if someone had flipped a switch on somewhere. Truth be told, he couldn't have played a better innings to draw abreast of the great Don Bradman's record of 29 Test centuries. A couple of matches down the road, in that same series, he came in at No. 4 with the score reading zero for two and batted nearly 11 hours to make his highest score, 236 not out. What is this man made of?

♦

As we left Port of Spain, in high spirits, we sensed we were on to something special. Sunil had set stall, Ashok Mankad wasn't doing too badly, Dilip was shoring up the middle order, Ekki was among the runs and the bowlers were on top of their game. The team was well-knit and well-led, and we knew we had rattled West Indies. At the end of the game, Ajit told us that we had a golden opportunity to win the series but took pains to point out that there still were three Tests to go. That if we slackened even a little bit, we would have to pay the price. Any complacency quickly went out of the window.

I was delighted to finally make my Caribbean debut in the third Test, in Georgetown, Guyana. We had a decent platform when I walked in on the first afternoon, 116 for two, and watched a Sunil special from the best seat in the ground. Having missed out on a 100 in Port of Spain, he wasn't to be denied here, and I was the first to congratulate him when he reached three-figures for the first time in his Test career. From experience, I knew the significance of that milestone; I was happy for him, happy that we put on 112, and personally thrilled when I made a half-century myself.

Dilip was again primed for a big score when was run-out for 45.

In all, Dilip was to stack up 642 runs at 80.25, a huge influence on the outcome of the series. I have held Dilip very highly as a technician. He started off in the middle order, opened the batting for a long time and then returned to the middle order in time for this series, a move that paid a handsome dividend. The confidence he gave the batsmen around him was immense. For us, as a team, it was wonderful to see a youngster on his first tour and an established name join hands to showcase the ability of Indian batsmen to score big and tackle pace in alien conditions.

Just how dependent we had come to be on Sunil and Dilip was evident in the fourth Test in Bridgetown, where West Indies amassed 501 for five. Sunil had his only failure of the tour, dismissed by Uton Dowe for one, and we found ourselves in a deep hole at 70 for six. Dilip produced a masterclass for the next six hours, treating the bowling with the respect it deserved but not allowing it to dictate terms. Ekki and he put on 186, but when Venkat was the ninth man out, we were at only 285 and needed 17 more to avoid the follow-on. There was so much time left in the game that we feared the worst.

We shouldn't have, really, not with Dilip in such glorious touch. Alongside Bishan, Dilip steered us to safety with a last-wicket stand of 62. We had still conceded a huge lead, 154 runs, but West Indies would now have to set us a target. All thanks to Dilip's magnificent 150.

On the final day, we were asked to chase down 335 in a little over 100 overs, not enough time to force the issue but sufficient for Sunil to make an unbeaten 117. We were beginning to get the message: if Dilip doesn't get a 100, Sunil will!

We returned to Port of Spain for the final Test with our lead intact, and knew we had to avoid doing anything silly to keep our tryst with history. Sunil made his third successive 100 and, after we conceded a lead of 166, knuckled down to produce another epic. For nearly nine hours, he was unshakable, making light of a wearing track to bring up his first double 100. Apart from one in the first innings in Bridgetown, his sequence of scores read 65, 67 not out, 116, 64 not out, 117 not out, 124 and 220. Not only did he like going big, but he also hated getting out! Really, who was this guy?

Once again, I couldn't help but admire his hunger, his stamina, his concentration and his ambition. Not only had he done everything and more than what had been asked of him over the series, he had also saved the *coup de grâce* for the finale. If I wasn't already, that's when I became a die-hard Sunil Gavaskar fan.

West Indies survived a top-order collapse to escape with a draw on the final day, and while we were a little disappointed that we couldn't round off a 2-0 scoreline, that paled in comparison with the elation at a rare but very well-deserved series victory away from home. That it came in the Caribbean was the icing on the cake.

From our standpoint, it had been a fabulous tour. Our world-class spinners had done a wonderful job throughout; Venkat finished with 22 wickets, Bishan took 15 and Pras 11 though he only played in three matches. To watch them bowl in tandem against Sir Garry and Rohan, as well as Charlie Davis, was quite an experience.

Davis sat out the first Test but was excellent against the spinners, subsequently, making more than 500 runs. Sir Garry was even more productive, amassing 597 runs and making hundreds for fun as if compensating for being dismissed for 93 in the first Test. He insisted on playing the four-day game too for Barbados and made his customary 100 there as well.

Sir Garry is easily the greatest cricketer I have played with and against, no two ways about it. At various stages during that tour, I had to pinch myself as a reminder that I wasn't actually dreaming of being on the same ground as him and Rohan. I had conjured larger-than-life mental images of these two gentlemen from my early teens; in real life, they were even more likeable and friendly. Rohan made it a habit of talking to me every time I batted, little tips about how to go about building an innings. Sunil has spoken of similar guidance from the great man. I couldn't believe that a member of the opposition, that too someone of Rohan's stature, would voluntarily assume the role of mentoring young batsmen trying to score runs against his own team. Really, they don't make them like Sobers and Kanhai anymore.

I must confess that I was pleasantly surprised at the quality of the West Indian fast-bowling group. I mean no disrespect, but the red-hot pace we had expected was conspicuously absent. Wes Hall and Charlie Griffith were no longer around. West Indies were in the process of rebuilding their attack and trying out options; it was still the fastest bowling I had faced till then, but not of West Indian standard, if you know what I mean. Apart from Sir Garry, no one else played all five Tests, which testifies to their inconsistency and waywardness. But hey, don't think I am complaining. It was still the quickest bowling I had come across until then; thankfully, it wasn't too hot to handle.

10

THE SUN SETS ON ENGLAND

Within two months of our triumphant return from the West Indies, we were on our way to England, in late June 1971. From the time I can remember, the prospect of playing in England had fascinated me. I had heard tales of how the ball swung around corners or jagged off damp, grass-laden surfaces, and I was keen to test my abilities against nuances of bowling I hadn't previously encountered. Our confidence was high after the series win in the Caribbean, and we saw no reason why we couldn't back that up in England, even though they had defeated Australia 2-0 in the seven-Test Ashes Down Under only a few months back.

We had a new manager in Col. Hemu Adhikari, a strict disciplinarian who unsurprisingly, because he had been in the Army, placed a lot of emphasis on discipline and fitness training. We had a short camp of sorts in Mumbai; it wasn't as structured as Major Tandon's six years later, but we were brimming with energy by the end.

Vijay Merchant, the chairman of selectors, met the team at the CCI, enlightening us on what to expect in England. A majority of the batsmen were on our first tour of England and the chairman had played there during his time, so we tried to get as much out of him during that talk as possible. Merchant also told the team that Chandra's selection was a 'calculated risk', a choice of words that didn't amuse my good friend one bit.

Chandra was one of three inclusions for the England series and already determined to give a good account of himself. The chairman's words upset him, I could clearly make out; I also sensed that he wanted to prove a point. At the best of times, Chandra is a handful given his command over his craft. When he feels wronged, he can be doubly dangerous, as England found out to their detriment at The Oval.

While we were apprehensive about how the conditions would line up, there was an air of expectancy within the group. There is no greater confidence-builder than an overseas series win, and we were keen to carry the momentum over to England. There was a subtle change in mindset; we were no longer talking about not losing, we were actually discussing winning. That's what confidence does. They say cricket is a mind game. What happens between two ears is at least as important as what you do on the field. You have to apply your mind and more importantly, you must do so at the right time.

We are living in times when teams practically get off flights and plunge into action. I simply can't overstate the benefits of easing into tours, a luxury we enjoyed throughout my playing career. In England, for instance, we played eight three-day games before the first of the three Tests. That's right, eight matches to get used to the conditions, to find your feet, to recognize what works for you and what doesn't, to acclimatize to the weather. When we landed in June, we were told England was in the middle of a glorious summer. Summer? I asked. Really? Maybe it was for them, maybe their definition of summer was when it didn't rain. But their hottest day was still colder than the coldest many of us had endured in India. Even in the sun, blustery winds sent us diving for our sweaters. It was an experience like no other.

◆

Those eight warm-up games served their purpose. We did travel every fifth or sixth day, but all of them were road trips lasting no more than three hours. Given the weather, tiredness wasn't a factor. Hearteningly, from my point of view, I had at least eight innings, possibly twice as many, to make the adjustments I needed to succeed in England.

What practice games before and between Tests do is allow players going through a lean patch to rediscover form. Because of the crammed nature of tours these days, and because teams seldom play more than three Tests in a series, changes to playing personnel are minimal, often dictated by injuries. If, say, you are unfortunate to be dropped after a couple of failures, there is no way of working your way back into runs and wickets; it's one Test match to another. But we had the opportunity of addressing technical chinks, or recovering from the odd niggle, owing to the plethora of warm-up and practice games. On this tour of England alone, we played 16 first-class games in addition to the three Tests. Remarkably, four of them were after the Test series had been won! We had a glorious run during the two-and-a-half-month tour, winning six first-class games and losing just one, by six wickets to Essex. That was our second match since landing in England. Just goes to show that there is no better learning ground than the cauldron of competitive match-play.

The county sides we ran into offered us a multitude of challenges, each different from the other. It's one thing to be aware of what you are likely to face when you go to an alien land, quite another when you are actually out in the middle. The bowlers weren't the quickest, but so much seemed to happen in the air and off the pitch that you had to constantly be on guard. Even the slightest mental relaxation would come with a heavy price.

We were riding the crest of a wave after convincing wins on the trot against Leicestershire, Warwickshire, Glamorgan and Hampshire when we lined up at Lord's for the first Test. Our first match of the tour had been against Middlesex at the same venue, which was my first sighting of the celebrated Lord's. I felt happy that my first Test in England would be at this revered venue.

It's a ground I have always enjoyed playing in. True, there are better, bigger grounds in the world, but because of the traditions they have kept going at the headquarters of the Marylebone Cricket Club (MCC), there is a special feel to playing at Lord's. There's an Honours Board that you can only get on if you make a century or take five wickets in an innings. I watched with pride when my name went up in 1979 after I made 113 in the second Test. I had become part of the history of Lord's; to find myself bracketed with so many greats of the game was surreal.

Our spinners quickly hit their stride—the benefits of eight first-class games, anyone?—to reduce England to 71 for five on the first morning after Ray Illingworth chose to bat. Alan Knott and John Snow rallied them to 304, and we quickly lost Ashok Mankad and Sunil before Ajit

Wadekar and Dilip Sardesai settled our nerves by putting on 79.

I walked out at 108 for three and received the shock of my life. The bowlers in the Caribbean were the quickest I had faced until then, but the two Johns (John Price and John Snow) were something else. It was my first taste, I realized with a start, of genuine fast bowling. Snow was coming off an excellent Ashes campaign, which he finished with nearly twice as many scalps as the next highest wicket-taker. My initial shock quickly gave way to excitement as I looked forward to the challenge, to see how my game measured up against these two frightfully quick bowlers.

England was then considered the ultimate cricketing destination. For you to be recognized as a quality player, you had to score in England, in front of their fans and pundits and former players. I didn't necessarily subscribe to that theory, but that was the accepted norm, so I too wanted to give a good account of myself.

I won't say I liked fast bowling—anyone who says so isn't being entirely honest—but I was up for the task of pitting my skills against Price and Snow. That's the beauty of international cricket; you are confronted with unfamiliar situations each time. How well and quickly you adapt will determine how successful you are. I am glad to say that against Price and Snow, I didn't take too much time to make the necessary adjustments.

I loved the sound of bat hitting ball when I negotiated the two pacers. There was a lot of pressure, but at the same time, there was a lot of pleasure too, if you know what I mean. Whether in defence or while playing my strokes, I was very assured. And it helped that I had a lovely piece of wood in my hands. One of the perks of playing in England was that sports good manufacturers would flock practice sessions and first-class matches of visiting teams to push their products. There was no financial consideration, but following a formal contract or an informal agreement, the manufacturer would ply you with all the gear: bats, leg-guards, thigh-pads, gloves and sometimes even shoes. You had to mandatorily use the brand for the duration of the tour, though nothing stopped you from doing so once you left for home. But if you returned to England for a subsequent tour, you were not obligated to stick to the same manufacturer.

Feeling like royalty as I worked out an arrangement with Gray-Nicolls,

I was delighted with the bats I got. All through my career, I used bats with a super-short handle. Back home, I would manually slice off the top of normal-sized handles to suit my requirement, but thanks to Gray-Nicolls, I had a willow with a perfect, factory-made, super-short handle as per my specifications. I always went with a light bat, generally 2.3 pounds; the weight remained more or less constant throughout my career. It was ideal for my kind of game, back footed and punctuated by horizontal-blade strokes like the square cut and the hook. This particular Gray-Nicolls bat felt beautiful, an extension of my arms.

Armed with this lovely stick, I enjoyed my first Test innings in England. It wasn't particularly flamboyant or strokeful, but I ground it out for four and a half hours while making 68. Having warded off Price and Snow, I fell to the medium-pace of Richard Hutton. I did derive immense satisfaction in having added 92 with Ekki and helped the team take a feel-good of miniscule lead of nine runs.

◆

With our spinners on song again, we bowled out England for 191 on the final morning, leaving ourselves needing 183 for victory. A glance at the score card will suggest we just about managed to scramble to safety, but the scoreboard seldom tells the full tale, does it?

Our first-choice wicketkeeper was a bit of a local himself, playing as he was in the county championship for Lancashire. Farokh Engineer, larger-than-life, was only available for the Test matches and, using his familiarity with local conditions, told us that rain was in the air, that we might have no more than 50-odd overs of batting left. He also usefully informed us that the forecasters seldom got the prediction wrong. I thought to myself, 'Beautiful, these English guys even know when the rain's going to come.'

Farokh suggested we go for the target, pointing out that if we did lose a few quick wickets, we could always batten down the hatches. Ajit and Dilip, the two senior statesmen, readily agreed. That's how Farokh was pushed up to No. 4 when we lost two quick wickets.

Sunil had batted nearly an hour to make four in the first innings but was purring along nicely in the second. He and Farokh added 66 attractive runs while running aggressively between the wickets to bolster our victory hopes. Perhaps, England were feeling the heat too, I am not sure.

Whatever the reason, Snow allowed his emotions to get the better of him. The ball had ricocheted close on the onside off Farokh's pad, and he and Sunil set off for a quick single. On his follow-through, Snow was made to run for the ball, and found Sunil by his side, chugging along towards the striker's end. The towering Snow shoulder-charged little Sunil and sent him sprawling to the turf. It was a no-contest; in other circumstances, it might have been funny, but this was serious business, so we had to struggle to control ourselves in the dressing room.

No damage done, thankfully. Sunil made his ground, Snow picked up the bat lying on the ground and tossed it over. In the evening, he also apologized to Sunil for his actions, and all of us, Sunil included, understood that it was just one of those things, Snow hadn't intended malice. But the English board took a dim view of his antics and suspended him for the next Test.

Back to our chase. After the Farokh-Sunil stand, we suffered a mini-collapse of three for 13, including yours truly for nine and Sunil for an excellent 53. We were 114 for six with the cream of the batting gone, but there was no panic. Ekki was solidity personified, and Abid and Venkat kept him company for long enough so that Bishan had spent less than 10 minutes at the crease when the rains arrived on cue. My admiration for British forecasting skills went up a notch. After all, at 143 for eight, it was touch and go.

◆

I am not sure if, even four months earlier, we would have so much as thought about victory, but as I have mentioned previously, West Indies changed our way of thinking. We weren't willing to lose in trying to win—it seems to be a modern-day concept that makes no sense to me—but we were happy to give it a shot and revisit our options.

We were slightly fortunate to escape with a draw at Old Trafford, but that was no more than we deserved, given the brand of cricket we had showcased. Sunil and Ekki both made half-centuries to prevent the follow-on after England amassed 386, but when they declared at 235 for three on the fourth evening, we had our work cut out. This time, there was no talk of mounting an assault on the 420-run target. Our aim was to bat out time and walk away with our heads held high, though at stumps, we had lost Ashok, Sunil and Ajit with only 65 on the board. Dilip and I were in the middle, and I spent a troubled night playing out the various scenarios in my mind. Completely unfounded, as it turned out. The notorious Manchester weather proved our ally, with not a ball bowled on the final day.

When we made our way back to London after further first-class matches in Leeds and Nottingham, the series was wide open. Pre-match talk at The Oval revolved around playing it by the ear, seeing where we were in the game at the end of each day, and taking it from there. Victory would be sweet, no doubt, but we weren't going to fritter away our labours of the previous two months on a whim.

England did the early running after Ajit lost his third successive toss and piled up 355 on the first day. The second day's play was washed out, and by the third evening, we were in trouble at 234 for seven. We somehow scrambled to 284, but it was advantage England, armed as they were with a 71-run lead.

Chandra had taken seven wickets in the first five innings of the series, and knowing him as I did, I was aware he wasn't a happy chappy. Merchant's words had stung him to the quick and he had unfinished business to attend to. From our perspective, he chose the perfect time to fire his riposte.

Brought on early, Chandra was unplayable. The ball leapt off his hand, propelled by strong wrists, and fizzed off the surface. I recognized that something magical was happening, but I didn't grasp the true significance of his genius until much later. So caught up was I with the breakneck pace at which the game was progressing that I failed to appreciate the beauty of that spell then and there. I do remember that it was a spell of the likes I had never previously witnessed in my fledgling Test career.

A couple of spectacular catches at short leg by Ekki and a Chandra special that bamboozled John Edrich, feels like they happened yesterday. Chandra had already played a part in the first wicket, getting a hand to a firm drive from Brian Luckhurst that disturbed the stumps at the bowler's end with John Jameson out of his ground. In walked Edrich, a picture of consistency through the series. Just as Chandra was about to bound in to have a go at him, Dilip shouted to him, '*Isko Mill Reef daalo* (Bowl him Mill Reef).'

The horse Mill Reef had been having an excellent British summer, pocketing all the prestigious races, and dominated newspaper headlines. So taken in by the name was Dilip that he started referring to Chandra's faster one as Mill Reef. Chandra took Dilip's suggestion on board and sent down a quicker one. Edrich's bat was still on the way up when his stump went cartwheeling.

From then on, Chandra scythed through the batting. In 18.1 probing overs, he sent England plummeting to 101 all out, finishing with six for 38. Like the champion that he is, he smiled shyly as he led us off the field; I was so happy that Merchant's 'calculated risk' had paid off handsomely. In the space of two hours, he had turned the Test on its head.

Chandra was that kind of bowler. When he got it right, which was often, the batsman stood no chance. I regard him as the biggest match-winner India has produced, across eras and generations. Each of the four spinners was great, collectively they were a mesmerizing combine of guile and cunning. Each of them had a different way of operating, and I am not in minority when I say that had even one of them played for any other country, or in another time, all four would have finished with a lot more wickets. Like the fast bowlers of the great West Indian teams, they had to share the wickets, though if there was any competition, it was only of the healthy kind. It boggles the mind to imagine what numbers they might have achieved had, say, only two of them been around simultaneously.

Time was not a factor—we had nearly four sessions available to us—when we set off in quest of 173, and our maiden Test and series win in England. It wasn't the kind of total to give you sleepless nights, but it wasn't as small as it seemed either. Illingworth made us work for every single run; there were no great alarms during our chase, but the runs had to be earned diligently. In true Test match tradition, there were no freebies.

Ajit and Dilip provided the foundation by adding 39 for the third wicket, and when I joined Dilip in the first over of the last morning, we needed less than 100. Dilip continued his purple patch with a fluent 40, while I thoroughly enjoyed myself during our partnership of 48. Mine wasn't a free-flowing, indulgent innings studded with glorious strokes; instead, I had to graft and fight and nudge and nurdle. I batted nearly three hours to make 31, not a single boundary to my name. It's one of my least talked-about knocks, but for as long as it lasted, I soaked in the ebbs and flows that only a last-day chase in Test cricket can throw up.

Even today, I cringe when I reflect on how I was dismissed with just three required for victory. How I dismissed myself, to be more accurate.

When Illingworth turned to part-time left-arm spinner Luckhurst, I didn't need Farokh to walk down the track and tell me that England had waved the white flag in surrender. Farokh and I had weathered the dismissals in rapid succession of Dilip and Ekki by putting on 36, the finish line was tantalizingly close.

I decided to go for the glory shot, naively believing that it was my due to be the hero. Luckhurst sent down the rankest of longhops, short and outside off. My eyes lit up, but I ended up playing the most atrocious cross-batted slog, wanting to seal victory in a blaze. My heart sank when all I managed was a feather through to Knott. It was like a body blow, a sickening feeling in the pit of my stomach accompanying me on my walk of shame to the pavilion.

It's a moment I will never live down. I wasn't upset that I hadn't nailed the winning blow, but you just can't get out like that in Test cricket. All the hard work done, victory within sight and I had tossed everything away carelessly. To a non-regular bowler. No one said anything, but I was already so ashamed that even the harshest of words would not have registered. It was another important lesson: Test wickets must be earned, not gifted away. Oh, and for the record, I was Luckhurst's only Test victim.

I keep watching the footage of that match from time to time, more to relive and enjoy Chandra's magical spell than anything else. And to see the winning runs being scored. Every time I see myself getting out, I shudder involuntarily. I have often reached for the object closest to me to hit myself with; fortunately, all of them have been too heavy for me to lift.

Abid walked out and slammed his fourth ball for four, allowing us to bask in the afterglow of a second overseas Test victory in the space of a few months. As the ball sped across the turf, I set the disappointment at the manner of my dismissal aside and joined in the celebrations. The Indian fans who had invaded The Oval to cheer us on charged to the middle, even managing to smuggle an elephant on to the outfield to symbolize our historic four-wicket victory on Ganesh Chaturthi. For all but a handful, it was the first tour of England. To emerge from that series on the right side of a 1-0 scoreline was overwhelming.

Like in the West Indies, this too was a victory for team effort and astute leadership. I have heard people refer uncharitably to Ajit as a lucky captain. Rubbish, I say. Luck had no role to play. Ajit was a more than competent batsman and a shrewd strategist as well as a tremendous motivator. Anyone who associates fortune with Ajit's accomplishments as captain ought to look himself in the mirror. To be at the helm during successive overseas series victories, and that too in the West Indies and England, was unprecedented in Indian cricket. Indeed, it would be 36 years before Rahul Dravid emulated Ajit by leading the team to series wins in the Caribbean in 2006 and in England in 2007.

These two twin successes were to shape the course Indian Test cricket would take, similar to what the 1983 World Cup triumph was to do to 50-over cricket. Post the glorious first half of 1971, we carried the belief that we could win anywhere in the world. Agreed, we didn't win as much as we would have liked, but that's another matter altogether. For the larger group, the greatest satisfaction lay in the fact that these results hadn't come about by accident. The year 1971 changed the way India looked at Test cricket, and how the world viewed Indian cricket. We were no longer the charming, endearing tourists who would lose with a smile and make you feel good about yourself. If you did beat us, you would know that you had been in a fight.

Not even the fact that we had to play on in England for two further weeks after The Oval coup dampened our enthusiasm as we emplaned for Mumbai. We had been mobbed on our return from the Caribbean, but that was nothing compared to what awaited us this time around. There was pandemonium at the airport, as though the whole of the city that never sleeps had congregated to welcome us back. The ride from the airport to the Brabourne Stadium seemed to last an eternity, but all of us were grateful for the love and support of the fans, whose good wishes and prayers have helped us tide over several difficult patches. The scenes on the streets were extraordinary as tears of joy and showers of flowers transported us to dreamland. To this day, I get goosebumps thinking of that journey.

11

MONKEY OFF MY BACK

We didn't play many Tests during the first few years of my international career. The gap between my first and second series was 13 months, and after our twin tours of the West Indies and England, there was a further wait of 16 months before our next encounter, also against England, but this time on our turf. We would have liked to play earlier, if only to build on the momentum generated by two series wins overseas, but there was nothing we could do.

There was a lot of first-class cricket in the interim. I played 18 matches between the two Test series against England: for SBI in the Moin-ud-Dowlah Gold Cup, for Mysore state in the Ranji Trophy, for South Zone in the Duleep Trophy, for Rest of India in the Irani Cup (earlier called Irani Trophy) and for an Indian XI in the Defence Fund matches.

With further matches for my employers in the Mysore state league, I was pumped up when England arrived in December 1972 for a five-Test series. I was looking forward to starting a five-match contest, for a change; against Australia, I had made my debut in the second Test and in the Caribbean, I had to sit out the first two matches due to my knee injury. There was no guarantee I would play all five Tests—that would depend on my performance—but for the first time, I had the opportunity of playing five Tests in one series and seeing where I stood.

I loved the concept of a five-match series, and I am speaking purely from a batsman's perspective. I am sure the bowlers have a different point of view, largely because of the workload they have to shoulder. The thrill of a five-Test, country-versus-country duel is unparalleled, particularly if the teams are evenly matched. Every match is an event, all of them together make for a spectacle.

It's been said that a five-Test series can expose specific technical inadequacies of batsmen and maybe that's true. Then again, therein lies the charm, doesn't it? You can't have a bad patch over five Tests, it just means you are not playing well. If you are getting out in the same manner, you must make adjustments. You have the time to do so, but for that, you must first accept there is a problem, then understand what has to be done to fix that issue and eventually hit the nets to iron out the kinks. The coach can tell you what to do, but it's like taking a horse to the water—just as one can't make the horse drink the water, the coach cannot go out and bat for you.

It amuses me a little when batsmen say they got runs because of the coach's inputs. I am not belittling the role of the coach but in the final analysis, it's the player who makes runs or takes wickets, who succeeds or fails. He has to be adaptable enough to make adjustments on the fly. From experience, I can say the chances of rectifying mistakes are greater in a five-match series. There will be the odd change in the bowling attack, but most of the time, you are facing the same three or four bowlers for five games in a row. Surely, you should be able to get a hang of things sooner than later?

These were not my foremost thoughts when we assembled in Delhi for the first Test, on 20 December 1972. I was excited at the prospect of playing in front of home crowds after three years; yes, we hadn't played in India since the Australia series in 1969.

I had had a reasonable look at the English bowling two weeks earlier, playing for the Indian Board President's XI. England had a new captain, Tony Lewis. Nothing out of the ordinary, except that he hadn't played a Test match previously. His first Test as skipper was also his first Test for his country, which amazed me because I had never imagined that England, of all teams, would entertain this unique yet intriguing possibility.

Lewis is a lovely man who later went on to become the president of the MCC, and had come with a very good, very balanced side. He had, by then, more than 15 years of county cricket experience and commanded the respect of his team, which had a generous sprinkling of high-quality batsmen and an excellent pace attack manned by Bob Cottam, Geoff Arnold and Chris Old. I couldn't help a giggle when I was told that Old was the youngest member of the touring party, though I knew better than to do so in front of the fearsome pacer. Old and Tony Greig were the fast-bowling all-rounders and they had four excellent spinners: Derek Underwood and Norman Gifford offered the left-arm option, Pat Pocock and Jack Birkenshaw were the acknowledged off spinners. All of them derived encouragement from the presence behind the stumps of Alan Knott, the best wicketkeeper in the world at the time.

We too had a pretty good team, so the stage was set for a cracking contest. Or so we thought, until Arnold destroyed us on the first morning at the Kotla by packing off the top four in next to no time. Chandra's eight-wicket burst gave us some hope as we restricted England's lead to 27, but when we managed just 233 in the second innings, the writing was on the wall. Lewis made a pleasing unbeaten 70 to take his side to a six-wicket victory, a fairy-tale start to his captaincy career.

For us, it was a rude awakening. After two wins abroad, we were full of confidence, but it didn't take England long to burst our bubble and in our conditions, at that. We were disappointed, the loss hurt, but we were determined to bounce back and show our fans what we were made of.

Towards that end, we were served brilliantly by our world-class spinners, Chandra embracing the lead role. He was practically unplayable, finishing the series with 35 wickets. We felt embarrassed that we had frittered away his great work in Delhi, where he returned Test-best figures of eight for 79. Bishan bowled just as well as Chandra and ended up with 25 wickets, while Pras was very effective in all of his three appearances. It was lovely to watch them go about their business, they all bowled like the world-class spinners that they are. More often than not, they came on very early when the ball was new and tough to grip because we hardly had any new-ball bowlers, but their control and command was something else.

It was a tremendous boost to Indian cricket. I must mention too that most of the pitches were good tracks, not dustbowls or a spinner's paradise. Then again, such was the class of these spinners that they didn't need any assistance; just the natural wear-and-tear of a five-day game was more than adequate, they were that good. No England batsman appeared fully in control, though there were some excellent batting performances, not least by Keith Fletcher in Madras (now Chennai) when he made a fluent unbeaten 97 on the first day.

Of their batsmen, Fletcher was the most comfortable, using his feet well and playing his strokes confidently even when our magicians were up to their tricks. He made more than 300 runs and scored a century in the last game in Bombay. But to me, that 97 not out in Madras was the best innings by an English batsman in that series.

After the Delhi defeat, we landed in Calcutta (now Kolkata) desperate to make amends. I enjoyed playing in front of huge crowds, and you didn't get them bigger than in the City of Joy. The Eden Gardens somehow manages to pack in close to 100,000 spectators. Such is the noise and energy reverberating around the stands that sometimes, it feels as if there is an equal number outside. I was always lifted by the atmosphere in Calcutta and in Madras, where the crowd wasn't as boisterous but very knowledgeable and appreciated good cricket, even from the opposition.

We felt we owed the Calcutta crowd the result they deserved, and even though we didn't make too many runs, we did have Chandra and Bishan. Between them, they took 16 wickets to fashion a thrilling 28-run win in a low-scoring game where our first-innings 210 was the only time either team passed 175. It was a great way to end 1972.

New Year celebrations out of the way, it was time to turn out for South Zone against the Englishmen in Bangalore. Before you wonder, I haven't got the timeline wrong. I know it's unthinkable now that a player involved in a series would also feature in a warm-up game against the visiting team between Tests, but that was a different era altogether. Not just I, Chandra and Abid Ali also were in the side to be led by Venkat.

I was coming off scores of 27, 3, 3 and 34 in the first two Tests, and needed time in the middle. Such are the luxuries accorded by a five-Test series, as I have mentioned earlier.

◆

The three-day game at the Chinnaswamy Stadium ended in a draw, but it was a game of great significance. Tiger had not been picked for the first two Tests but was in with a shout because the batting hadn't really clicked. A good outing in Bangalore, and he stood a great chance of returning for the Madras Test.

I was nervous for him, but the Nawab was unflustered. Then again, I can't say with any conviction that I have known him to be anything but composed. South Zone were in early trouble, and Tiger and I had a small partnership when I was dismissed for 42. As I trudged off the ground, another Bangalore hero walked in and played a fairly spectacular innings.

Brijesh Patel was a mighty fine batsman, especially against spin; he and Tiger put on an exhibition in front of an awed audience at a venue still under construction. Brijesh was the more adventurous, while Tiger purred along as they rallied us from 74 for four. Brijesh fell just short of a well-merited 100, but Venkat waited long enough for Tiger to reach three-figures before applying the closure.

The rest of the match was fairly unremarkable, except right at the very end when Tiger picked up a rare first-class wicket. Neither he nor I had batted in our second innings, but when he bowled Barry Wood in the dying stages of the match with his medium-pace, Tiger was more delighted than when he scored the 100. Understandable, I guess, when you have 33 hundreds but just 10 wickets in first-class cricket.

Tiger's reward was a recall for the third Test in Madras, with the series level 1-1. It was the traditional Pongal Test in the Tamil Nadu capital, and the festivities continued for the duration of the game. In a rerun of the first two encounters, Chandra packed off England for 242 on the first day, but this time, we replied strongly with consistency throughout the order.

I was batting at No. 6 and joined Tiger at 155 for four, nearly a hundred behind. The small association in Bangalore had whetted my appetite. Now, we had a more meaningful partnership. I had great fun from the best seat at the ground as Tiger took on the bowlers. It was a typical Pataudi knock in the sense that he hit the ball over the infield repeatedly, with a couple of sixes thrown in for good measure. I was very happy to see him among the runs for India, and to have added 65 runs in his company. Tiger made 73, I chipped in with 37, but somehow, the numbers didn't seem to matter.

Everyone weighed in—Pras at No. 9 entertained us with 37—and when the last wicket fell, we had opened up a lead of 72. Mike Denness played an outstanding knock of 76, but with Chandra taking the back seat for a change, Bishan and Pras spun England out for 159. We had more than a day to knock off 86 and snatch a 2-1 lead.

◆

We got there in the end, but it wasn't without artificial excitement. At close on day four, we were 32 for two with the recalled Chetan Chauhan and Salim bhai in the middle. There was plenty of batting to come: Tiger, Ekki, myself and Sunil. Sunil had suffered a hairline fracture on his thumb after being struck on his hand by Old while batting in the first innings, and would only come out if desperately required. With this array of talent and a target of 86, surely, he wouldn't be required to bat? Wrong, very wrong.

Let's face it, we were complacent, as anybody in our position would have been, I am sure. We needed 54 for victory on the final day with eight wickets in hand, and everyone including the England side felt it was a matter of when, not whether we would coast home. In fact, had there been another hour's play on the fourth evening, we would have won comfortably because momentum was on our side. But then again, what is Test cricket without a little drama?

Day five, and things began to unravel rapidly. Pocock, the crafty off spinner, was in the thick of things, turning it a bit, getting it to jump a little. Chetan was the first to go, and I didn't last long, dismissed for the fourth duck of my then brief career. There was no panic, though, and when Salim bhai carted a couple of sixes, we were home and dry. Well, almost.

Pocock trapped Salim bhai leg before for 38 and then packed off Ekki, which meant that with eight runs to get, Sunil had to come out to join Tiger. The two calmest members of the team took us home without further alarm, and I felt there was a bigger power at play there when Tiger scored the runs that brought us a four-wicket victory and the series lead. I do shudder when I think what might have happened had we been chasing 150 for victory. Perhaps we would have struggled even more, perhaps we wouldn't have switched off mentally. Glad we didn't have to find out, all told.

Over to Kanpur for the fourth Test, with our noses in front for the first time in the series. I reflected on the strides I had made since my last visit to Kanpur with the Indian team. This was a totally different experience; the scenario had changed completely. I had already played a few Tests, I was no longer the rookie of 1969. As soon as I reached the ground for practice, two days before the Test, I was seized by that feel-good factor which comes from having enjoyed the success there previously. The ambience of the Green Park gave me the confidence that I would make runs. Maybe not a 100 like on debut, but runs nevertheless.

By now, whispers had started to make the rounds about my lack of concentration when I got into the 20s and the 30s. I hadn't done myself any favours by being dismissed between 22 and 38 seven times in my last 16 Test innings, but how could the experts decide that it was because I had lost concentration? I found it strange that they seemed to know more about me than I did.

There has to be something wrong with you if you can't focus properly on getting to 30 in Test cricket. For a pure batsman, 30 is just the beginning. I did play the occasional bad shot, I admit, but the fault lay in shot selection and execution, nothing more sinister. I can understand that, if you have batted six to seven hours and got to 130 or 140, fatigue can induce a loss of concentration. But for a hungry 23-year-old to be prone to lapses in concentration on making 30? I don't think so.

Not that I did my cause any good by falling for 25. I had batted nearly two hours when the young Old ended my stay. I could picture the knowing looks floating around in the press box. 'Told you, no concentration.'

We lost wickets cheaply towards the end and were bowled out for 357 on the third morning, to which England replied with 397 with a maiden century from Lewis, and late resistance from Birkenshaw and Arnold. England batted 173 overs, and despite a deficit of 40, we were reasonably secure with less than a full day's play.

But not for long. Within two hours of our second innings, we were in deep trouble at 39 for four, bringing Ekki out to join me. Only Abid of the recognized batsmen was left, so we had a big job on our hands to keep a rampaging Underwood at bay. We had got through to tea, and Ekki and I had put on 64 when Birkenshaw struck, and Abid joined me to take the fight forward.

We weren't ahead by too many, maybe 70 or 80, when the twelfth man came out with water. Without provocation, he told me, 'Vishy bhai, you have been dropped for the Bombay Test. The selectors met during tea-time to pick the team. But so what if you are not there, *ladho, ladho* (fight, fight).'

For the life of me, I couldn't understand why he told me what he did at that instant. I was trying to save the match for the team alongside Abid and this was just the kind of information I could have done without. I casually told him, 'Still batting,' gave the water bottle back without having a sip. I told myself that he had only been joking, that the match was not over and that this wasn't about me. There was a job ahead, distractions could wait.

I continued to bat the way I normally do, I didn't change anything. I didn't become overcautious or too aggressive, merely treating each ball on its merit. Abid was in control and we batted ourselves out of trouble with a stand of 78. When Lewis put out his hand to signal the end of England's token push, I had batted four hours for 75 not out.

It would have been difficult to justify my exclusion after what I had just done. I still don't know if the selectors had met at tea and dropped me, only to be forced to sit again after the match and reselect me, or if the tea-time meeting didn't happen at all. What I do know for certain is that the selection panel assembled at the end of play. Whether it was the second time that day, who knows? Irrespective of, I left Green Park with fond memories. I had scored my first half-century in 13 innings. To Bombay now for the final Test, with the series ours to win.

◆

I had played at the Brabourne Stadium, but never in a Test match. I enjoyed the ball coming on to the bat, the bounce was even, and in the evening with the breeze wafting in from the magnificent Arabian Sea not far away, there was assistance for the bowlers too. All in all, it made playing and watching cricket a unique experience.

Another excellent track welcomed us, and a platform had been already set when I made my way to the middle at 221 for four. However, we had lost three wickets for just four runs, so Salim bhai and I needed to consolidate towards the closing stages of the first day against a rejuvenated England attack. Farokh Engineer had made a blazing 100 and Ajit delighted the home fans with 87, but the crowd spent an anxious half an hour as we carefully negotiated the passage to stumps.

The next morning, I felt really good. Clearly, the previous innings was a shot in the arm, and I played my strokes with freedom. The ball sped off my bat and across the fast, somewhat uneven outfield, and Salim bhai graciously allowed me to be the aggressor. Our stand had reached 150 when Pocock dismissed Salim bhai for 75, but I kept going.

At long last, after tea, I got to my second Test hundred. It was a milestone moment not just for me, but for Indian batting as a whole. The monkey was off my back! For the first time, a debutant Indian centurion made a second hundred. I am glad I wasn't the last.

I had gone 13 Tests without a century, which is a pretty long time for a specialist batsman, to be honest. I knew that before me there had been five centurions on debut: Lalaji, Deepak Shodhan, A.G. Kripal Singh, Abbas Ali Baig and Hanumant Singh. They were all extremely good batsmen who made lots of runs in Test cricket, but somehow another ton remained elusive. I had played against Abbas and Hanumant and knew their quality. For these men to not add to their tally of hundreds did play on my mind, I will be honest. I was beginning to think it was one of those things that happened for no reason.

So, when I did touch three-figures in Bombay, I was a relieved man. Subconsciously, I had started to believe I would never replicate my feat in Kanpur. I wasn't desperate for a hundred, no, but I was still looking to get over 'the hoodoo', as it was called in Indian cricket circles.

That being said, I am grateful no one put any pressure on me, no one kept pointing out this fact to my face. The selectors didn't demand a century, my teammates didn't refer to the jinx, and when the media referred to it, it was as a matter of fact and never suggestive that I would follow in the footsteps of my illustrious predecessors. If I was around a mate reading a newspaper article about 'the hoodoo', he would put an arm around me and tell me, 'Don't worry, just a matter of time.'

Any pressure was more internal and self-imposed. The second hundred didn't take over my mind to the point of desperation, because I was getting runs otherwise; I was not totally out of sorts. I had made good runs in the West Indies and England, I was far from a total failure, but that lacuna was there. It was only when I raised my bat at the Brabourne that I realized how much I had wanted hundred number 2.

Tony Greig was fielding close-in as I got into the 90s and forewarned me that he would be up to something when I got to a hundred. He didn't say 'if', which silently delighted me. I was curious to see what he would do, so I was both a little worried and a little excited as I worked my way through the 90s.

When I got there, Tony effortlessly picked me up off the ground and cuddled me like you would a baby. At six feet six inches tall and a body to match, he towered over me and I wasn't surprised at the ease with which he held me. It was a lovely gesture from a lovely man, and I appreciated the warning more than ever. I am not sure how I would have reacted had he, a grown man, suddenly chosen to cup me in his arms.

We amassed 448 to all but bat England out of the contest, and they replied with 480, underlined by hundreds from Fletcher and Tony. When Tony entered his 90s, Sunil whispered conspiratorially, 'Let's return the compliment.' Sunil and I gamely tried to lift Tony after he touched hundred. It was a no-contest, I am not even sure if his leg left the ground for even a second. But it was all good fun and you could see that the crowd absolutely loved this interplay. Tony was already a popular man in India, but once he cradled me, the adulation was more pronounced.

I made 48 in the second innings as the Test meandered to a dull draw. We didn't mind it one bit. Not only had we pulled off a come-from-behind 2–1 victory, but it was also our third successive series win. Not bad, not at all.

Throughout the series, with the adrenaline taking over and with several tight corners to negotiate, there was no let-down in intensity. But once the last ball was bowled, a certain fatigue set it. I hadn't bargained on how gruelling a five-Test series would be, especially with neither side willing to concede an inch. All of a sudden, there was an ache here, a niggle there. It had probably been there all along, but you were too engrossed in the battle to notice it. Now, my body was throwing up a more strident reminder. I needed a break, a little time away from the game I love.

12

ON TIGER'S TRAIL

My first five-Test series out of the way, it was time to recharge the batteries mentally and physically. What better way to begin that process than play a benefit game for one of India's greatest, Polly Umrigar?

Polly Kaka had played nearly 60 Tests and close to 250 first-class matches in a career spanning 18 years before retiring in 1962, and I considered it a great honour to be invited to be a part of the occasion. The match was in Kolhapur and included not just players who had defeated England in the just-concluded series but also several of his contemporaries. Among them were Chandu Borde, Bapu Nadkarni, Baloo Gupte and Sharad Diwadkar, apart from active Bombay Ranji Trophy players at the time.

My only visit thus far to Kolhapur was a wonderful experience, with a lot of leg-pulling and fun and games. Coming close on the heels of a draining Test series, this was a match devoid of any tension, the result immaterial and the focus on entertainment. Polly Kaka was delighted with the purse from that game.[1] Personally, I couldn't have been happier. We had won a third series on the trot, and I had played in the match put together in honour of one of our legends.

I was figuring out how to get back home from Kolhapur when Tiger came up to me and said, 'I am also headed to Bangalore, why don't you come with me? Let's go by car.'

My surprise grew when he told me that it would be just the two of us, apart from the driver of the air-conditioned Ambassador car. I had

---
[1]Meaning, with the money he made from that match. Since it was a benefit game, a share of the proceeds would go to the designated beneficiary.

the option of politely turning down the offer, of course, but why would I? Tiger might not have been the captain of the Indian team anymore, but I still called him 'Skip', and I considered his invitation captain's orders.

We settled down to a comfortable drive, most of it spent in pleasant silence. There were snatches of discussion about the England series, but as a rule, Tiger didn't really like talking about cricket off the field.

Our conversations were in English—to the extent that I could speak the language then—though I had started to also converse in my version of Hindi with some members of the Indian team. When I started playing for the country, I kind of knew I had to learn Hindi. Not necessarily chaste Hindi, but enough to talk to my colleagues. I gradually picked up a new language, though I knew that whenever I spoke in Hindi, it generated much mirth and amusement. Even today, some of my lovely former teammates make fun of my Hindi. It doesn't bother me, just as it didn't in those days. I was conveying what needed to be said, in my own way. Most of them understood the point I was trying to make; to those who didn't, all I'd say was, 'bad luck.'

◆

Our car pulled up outside the lobby of West End Hotel around 5.30 in the evening, and I got off, intending to pick up my gear and head home. I was looking forward to the break, to going back to my house after a long time, to being pampered by my mother and appreciated by my father.

Tiger put a hand on my shoulder and said, without explanation, 'We will be leaving in two hours.'

I wondered why he thought it fit to tell me when he'd be leaving. My face must have mirrored my confusion, for he pointed at me, then immediately at himself and emphasized, 'We.'

'We? You and me?' my voice went up a notch involuntarily. 'Where?'

'Ooty.' Like I said, Tiger wasn't a man of too many words.

I was in a tizzy. When we left Kolhapur, I was under the impression that after many months, I would get to sleep in my own bed. Now, this giant who had been such an influence on my career was inviting me to Ooty. On a vacation?! 'It's been a long series, I am sure you must be tired. Let's relax in Ooty for three or four days.'

'I haven't gone home in a long time.'

'Oh, go home by all means,' he replied. 'Of course, you should go and meet your parents. Have a shower, pack your clothes and be back here by 7.30, we shall leave as soon as you return to the hotel.'

I had never been to Ooty before, but I had obviously heard so much about the hill station which was a six-hour drive from Bangalore. I also knew that to get there, we had to travel through the Ghats. A night journey through the Ghat section? I wasn't sure how I felt about that.

'Go on,' he egged me. 'Say my hello to your folks, bring change of clothes for three to four days. I'll be ready by the time you are back.'

He bundled me back into the car and waved me away, and a few minutes later, I was home, talking to my parents. They were as happy to see me as I was to be with them, and I could sense their pride not just at my performances but those of the Indian team. We chatted away for nearly an hour before I excused myself to have a shower.

Afterwards, I began the process of unpacking, stowing away my cricket gear, separating the clothes that needed to be washed and picking up fresh clothes for my imminent road trip. As I pulled a small suitcase down, my mother walked in and asked me what was going on.

'I am off to Ooty for a couple of days, Tiger has invited me to join him there. He's waiting for me, we'll relax for three or four days, that's all.'

By then, my father too had joined the discussion. 'You have just come back...' he began, then, 'Who all are going?'

I told him that it would be just the two of us. He looked at me for a while and adopted the fatherly tone that always accompanied words of great seriousness, 'Be careful how you conduct yourself,' he said. 'You are going with a big man, be mindful of how you behave. Take it easy and relax, have fun. But mind your manners.'

He was just being my father, looking out for me, wanting me to give a good account of myself when in Tiger's esteemed company. I looked at him with grateful eyes, said my goodbyes and embarked on what would turn out to be the most memorable holiday of my bachelor life.

◆

As promised, Tiger was fresh and ready when the car pulled up at West End for the second time that evening. We settled into the back seat when he told me, 'You know, my wife is shooting for a film in Ooty, the shoot is in the final stages. Once she finishes up in a couple of days, we will all come back together.' I was nervous and excited; I had obviously seen Sharmila Tagore's movies and was a big fan, but I had never met a non-cricketing celebrity before. My father's words assumed even greater importance. By 9.30 p.m., we were in the thick forests of Bandipur. I was in a daze, not quite believing all this was real when we spotted a herd of elephants, a few metres ahead of us. The big boys and girls crossed the road in a disciplined manner; my heart was pounding so loudly I was sure even they could hear it from that far away. It was the first time I was seeing these majestic creatures from such close quarters, at night, in the natural setting of a thick forest. I had seen elephants in East Africa, but that was nothing compared to this spectacle. To say that I was awed would be an understatement.

Tiger gently instructed the driver to neither turn off the headlights nor switch off the engine. 'Just be yourself,' he said calmly, as much to settle the driver's nerves as mine. 'Like all other animals, they are docile by nature. If you don't do anything, they won't harm you. Only if you disturb them...' He didn't have to finish the sentence.

I don't know if it was the driver's first elephant-sighting, but clearly, Tiger had seen all this and more many times previously. It amazed me how quickly he sized up the mood in our car and effortlessly set about putting us at ease. It was ordained that Tiger would be just as calm and poised as his namesake.

The rest of the journey through the forests of Bandipur and Mudumalai passed without incident, though my eyes were peeled wide open in the hope of spotting more elephants and other animals. The fear had faded away, replaced by joyous anticipation, and though there was the disappointment of not encountering a few more four-legged friends, it was with a smile on my lips that I got off the car when we got to our destination by two in the morning.

I was shown to my room, massive and tastefully decorated, and after a quick wash, I joined Tiger for a drink when Sharmilaji joined us. Like

Tiger, she carried herself gracefully, and it was a great honour for me to be introduced to her.

It was only the next morning that I realized the size of the bungalow we were residing in. The drive from the gate to the porch alone was more than half a kilometre, and the building was called something or the other Palace, as I recall. Take it from me, it was palatial.

We fell into a routine from the next day. Wake up late, a leisurely breakfast, another nap. Then gin and lunch. Afternoon siesta. We'd wake up in the evening, play some table tennis, dive into a bottle of whiskey, finish up with a very late dinner. It was the ultimate definition of the word 'holiday'!

On our second day in Ooty, Rajesh Khanna came over to meet us. Unlike Rinkuji (as Sharmilaji is called), he wasn't there on work; instead, like us, he had chosen to get away from the hustle and bustle of city life. I rubbed my eyes in disbelief. I had only seen Rinkuji and Rajesh on the big screen, now here I was sitting across from them listening to stories, narrating some tales of my own. *Not bad, lad,* I told myself. Not bad at all.

◆

As our adventure ticked over to day four, I asked Tiger when we were going back. 'Fed up with my company already, are we?' he chuckled.

'No, no. Not like that,' I stammered. In all honesty, I was enjoying myself, having the time of my life. But I had to inform my parents that I wouldn't be back for a few more days.

We booked a trunk call and I waited by the side of the telephone, wondering what my parents' reaction would be. 'Everything okay?' my father asked when I broke the news. On hearing that all was well and I was having fun, he said, 'Good then, no issues. Hopefully, we will see you soon.'

'Soon' is a relative word. Just like 'a couple of days'. When we left Bangalore, Tiger had said we'd back in a couple of days. As it turned out, three days became 15. Yes, that was the length of our stay in Ooty—15 lovely, wonderful, memorable days in great company!

Don't get me wrong, I wasn't star-struck. I wasn't then, I never have been. But I love meeting successful people, across all disciplines. I respect and appreciate the effort and hard work they have put in, in order to reach the top. I admire their simplicity and humility, and the fact that they don't take themselves too seriously or think that they are better than anyone else. I have always admired the genius of Pele and John McEnroe, though I never got the chance to meet them in person. It's one of those strange coincidences that I have been to England so many times during the summer, often coinciding with the Wimbledon, yet I haven't seen a single match at SW19, let alone meet McEnroe.

The more I think about that Ooty trip, the more I realize what an absolutely brilliant fortnight it was. Rinkuji and Rajesh are among the loveliest people I have ever met (I don't think I need to say that about Tiger again and again). There was no talk of the film industry, no mention of their successes and their hits, nor of the adulation they got from the fans.

Rajesh would constantly ask about cricket, about my career. He did it out of genuine curiosity, not merely for show. Over time, we became good friends, he was such a friendly and down-to-earth person. A beautiful soul, one of the nicest superstars I have met. He came to my wedding in Bombay a few years later. Rinkuji is well, Rinkuji; she and Tiger completed each other. She and Kavita also enjoy a very pleasant relationship.

It wasn't until we left the bungalow on our way back to Bangalore that, I realized with a start, I hadn't stepped out of the building for 15 days. If my parents asked me what I had seen in Ooty, I'd have no answer. How could I explain to them that I never felt the need to go out? That everything one required was at hand? And that even if I needed something, there were so many people ready to go and get it for me? I was made to feel like royalty, thanks to Tiger's understated, unpretentious love and attention to detail.

Rinkuji was in Ooty for the shoot of a film with Dharmendra. I must confess I wasn't even tempted to go and watch the shooting. I'd have had to go alone, leaving Tiger behind, and I didn't like that idea. In fact, I still don't know the name of that movie, though I was a reasonably regular movie-goer in those days, and even watched *Aradhana* with Ekki during my debut Test in Kanpur. It was the only time I went to the cinema hall during a Test match.

I made the most of this unexpected holiday, which took my mind entirely off cricket. As I have mentioned previously, Tiger didn't like cricket talk in the evening when we were not in the middle of the match. I have never heard him say, 'X is a great batsman', or something to that effect. Jai, by contrast, would discuss cricket at length: what made Sobers the greatest all-rounder ever or Kanhai the best batsman he had seen, or why Chandra was the match-winner he was. He would go on, his face a mix of excitement and child-like enthusiasm; whenever they were together, Tiger would look at him indulgently. Unlike Jai, Tiger would say something only once, but that was enough to make a massive impact on the listener.

That's not to say that he was not an entertainer. I recall how, one evening, he spoke about Raj Singh Dungarpur, later to become the BCCI president, and his fascination for cricket. How frustrated and theatrical he would get if someone dropped a catch off his bowling. 'Why should this happen only to me all the time?' Tiger mimicked him and pantomimed him walking close to the batsman with outstretched hands reaching towards the sky. 'He'd talk about how he had been deprived of 300 wickets only because of dropped catches.' It was hilarious, the way Tiger enacted the whole scene. He was the master of subtlety, never going overboard but always commanding attention with his pithy observations and wry humour. Evening banters between him and Jai were legendary; Jai would do his utmost to draw Tiger into a discussion, if not a debate, but Tiger would never rise to the bait, choosing to remain his own man.

Like...

> Jai: What a fantastic attitude Sunny has! Just hates getting out. Why do you think so?
> Tiger: Oh simple. He is an opening batsman, what will he do if he gets out early? He'd get bored, so he wants to be out in the middle.

It was all in good humour, and we knew that. They were the inseparables, contrasting personalities but fantastic seniors and great human beings. We were blessed to share grounds and dressing rooms with them.

As the car drove out of the compound and headed to Bangalore, I recalled every moment of the last fortnight. My first interaction with superstardom outside cricket, my first journey that had nothing to do with cricket, my first holiday with special people. The Ooty trip freed me up as a person, it gave me the confidence that I belonged. It boosted my morale and my spirit, almost as much as the 137 in Kanpur had. Tiger had fashioned another roaring success.

13

SIGNATURE STROKE, NOT MY ONLY STROKE

First things first. The square cut was my preferred boundary option, but there always is more to scoring runs at any level than banking on a specific stroke.

I am not unaware that people have been fascinated by the Vishwanath square cut. What I can tell you is that it was a stroke born out of necessity.

My tryst with the cut began with the tennis ball, which invariably got big on you. I was a slight, thin boy with no power to speak of, and while I did play the drive and the flick, seldom would the ball reach the boundary. The cut, by contrast, didn't require me to generate power entirely on my own, I could use the pace of the ball. I am not saying every cut I played fetched me four runs, but it had greater potential to cross the boundary than any other stroke. Over time, because I played it so often, I got quite good at it, though it also brought about my downfall a fair few times. On the so-called risk versus reward charts, however, I was seldom in the red; by a conservative estimate, I reckon more than 4,000 of my 6,080 Test runs came through the cut.

As I graduated through the ranks, from the schools' level to playing against a cricket ball, the square cut and the late cut remained at the top of my boundary options. There was hardly an innings of substance that wasn't dominated by these two strokes, though when I started to play for Mysore and then the country, my reputation had preceded me and teams were trying to deny me my bread-and-butter option.

Therefore, I had to expand my boundary repertoire. The higher you climb up the cricketing ladder, the less advisable it is to rely on one particular shot or on a specific way of getting runs. In any case, I grew stronger and bulked up a little, so the other strokes too started to yield boundaries, but people associated me largely with the square cut. And, as so many have told me so often, the square cut with me, which is both flattering and humbling. The label stuck with me during my career, and has remained so to this day. I am not complaining.

The more Tests I played, the more teams tried to trap me on that stroke, determined to convert my strength into my Achilles' heel. I took it up as a challenge. It wasn't my ego that called the shots. I knew I could play the stroke well, and no matter their plans, if I executed the way I wanted to, it would still be as productive as ever. Some of my teammates, both with Karnataka and India, suggested I stop playing it because it was causing my downfall. I didn't tell them off, but politely pointed out that it was my most prolific scoring stroke, and I welcomed opposition designs of trapping me on the cut. So long as I played the ball on its merit, there were plenty of runs to be had.

I wasn't a blind, compulsive cutter. You can't be if you aspire to be successful. Unless the ball was truly short and just wide enough for me to reach it, I didn't play it in the air when there were no fielders at either deep point or deep third man. Otherwise, it was all about being in control. Of yourself, and of the stroke. You can control your mind through constant reinforcement, but the only way to control the stroke and keep the cut on the ground is to get on top of the ball. Like the hook, this is not an easy stroke to play because of the attendant risks. You need to work really hard to hit the ball on top of its bounce. I put in the work required which is why, I'd like to think, I scored the runs I did.

You must learn from experience, because unless you do so, you will be left behind. When you start off in Test cricket, you tend to be more aggressive if you are a strokemaker because it's that approach which has brought you to this level. Quickly, you understand there is a gulf between domestic and international cricket, that you have to temper your mindset. You have to constantly want to learn. Learn from playing with and against great players, yes, but primarily learn from your mistakes, learn on your own. If you have played 20–30 Tests without gaining any knowledge, it's a waste of time. My philosophy was that you must gain at least one positive from each match, and the best way of doing that was analysing your own batting because at the end of the day, you are your best judge.

We had no coaches, no bloated support staff infrastructure—maybe in a generation or two, there will be a designated coach for each player? All we had was a team manager. When the manager happened to be a Polly Kaka or a Col. Adhikari, who had played substantial Test cricket both at home and overseas, it was a boon because they had so much to offer if you were willing to listen and learn. Teams would fraternize and get together for a drink at the end of a day's play or the end of a Test, and seniors from the opposition too would pass on huge tips. That was good enough for me as a youngster, it was good enough for Sunil, for Ekki. I didn't crave a coach 24/7, 365 days a year. I didn't need one.

Why? Because then, like today, no one could bat for you. You can have all the information, all the inputs, all the knowledge, all the words of encouragement and advice and reinforcement, but it's you who has to play the ball, you who has to score the runs. Not even the non-striker can play for you. My mantra was to absorb everything I had access to, sift through the information and figure out what worked best for me, but eventually figure out my game on my own. Standing at slips, I'd often ask myself why a batsman was able to play a stroke with so much ease. Between balls, I'd replay the stroke, replay the events leading up to the stroke. I'd openly applaud its beauty and effortlessness, but notice his balance, how he managed to get on top of the ball so quickly, whether he had caressed or smacked it. Watching live and breaking it down to its minutest detail was my own personal video analysis tool.

On my first tour of the West Indies, from 65 yards away, I watched Sir Garry Sobers at work during the Bridgetown Test. At the Kensington Oval, the square boundaries aren't too long— they are not exactly short either—and with Pras bowling to the great man, I was stationed at deep square leg for the sweep. Abid was at deep mid wicket, the two of us split by, say, 30 yards. When I fielded in the outfield, I followed the ball rather than the bat, watched it from the time the bowler ran in all the way till it made contact with the willow. From my vantage position at deep square leg, I also had a fantastic straight, uninterrupted view of Sir Garry. He shaped to come forward to start with, saw the trajectory was short and quickly rocked on to the back foot. He didn't play the pull, more a whip with the blade, more vertical than horizontal. Oh, the horror! I wasn't the swiftest runner, I managed three to four yards to my right. Abid, fast as the wind, took eight to nine steps to his left. Neither of us was anywhere near the ball when it crashed into the wall and ricocheted halfway back into the ground. We didn't even have to go fetch the ball and relay it to Pras, Sir Garry had done that too for us. It was a ferocious stroke played all along the ground, the control immaculate. I quickly did my mathematics; he was 34, had played international cricket for 16 years. I couldn't start to imagine what he would have been like at his peak.

My other 'teachers', voluntary or otherwise, included Rohan Kanhai, Sunil and Viv. I have already written about closely watching Kanhai playing spin, and learning from being at the non-striker's end when Sunil was constructing masterpieces. Viv was a masterpiece himself, an uninhibited attacker who intimidated bowlers with his presence. I enjoyed his strokeplay, but I'd watch intently to see how he attacked, when he attacked and why he was so successful despite playing so many strokes. He would nonchalantly take balls from the fourth or fifth stump and deposit them through mid wicket. Why? Because he was moving so quickly. Because he was taking his left foot close to the ball so that when he played the stroke, the whole body was on top of the ball, which was why he was able to keep it down. Viv's early blitzes filled me with amazed wonderment. As I looked closer to find out what made him tick, the answer was obvious: he was on top of the ball, he was in full control.

By the time I was a dozen Tests old, 'control' had become my watchword. When Pakistan toured India in 1979–80, their skipper Asif Iqbal employed funky fields for me. For his fast bowlers, he'd have just one slip but four gullies to neutralize the cut. The first time I saw that field, I turned around and smiled at Asif, gently nodding in appreciation. It was a compliment to me, but it also became a challenge. How do I not go against my natural grain and continue to score in that region, yet not offer a chance to those five men placed strategically?

Short answer, through control. To play the cut, I'd have to be certain the ball was short enough so that I could get on top, but not short enough that I'd have to hit it in the air. It wasn't about seeing a short ball and blindly going after it. If I felt the ball was there to hit, I would hit it, that's how I played my cricket. If I played the cut and it went along the ground, or on the bounce, to the four gullies, fair enough. My endeavour was to not hit it in the air, and I didn't fool myself into thinking that I would deliberately place the ball in the gaps through that tight cordon. No one can say with confidence that they will find the gap off the next ball, and pull that off with regularity. It's something that just happens. You have to play with the conviction that the ball will avoid the fielder, but if you try to guide the ball, especially when it's doing a little bit, it can be costly.

That's why I reiterate: batting is all about self-assessment. It's about judging the pitch, figuring out what the ball is doing in the air and working out how you can assume control. Unless you are driving on top of the ball, you can't keep it down. Even then, what's the proportion of balls that miss a fielder as opposed to finding him? If the ball is swinging and you are trying to guide it through extra cover or cover point, there is a big chance it will fly to slip and gully if you aren't on top of it. That's why it's advisable, especially at the beginning of your innings, when the ball is swinging, to show the full face of the bat and aim to play towards mid off. Worst-case scenario, it will go to covers. If the bat-face is open and you aren't to the pitch, you put the slips in business.

I am not suggesting, however, that all placement is accidental. It can be deliberate once you are in, once you have the measure of the pitch, the conditions, the bowling. I could influence placement through the square cut, so to say. Just as a bowler, the batsman too can utilize the width of the crease. It might take a stroke or two to understand how to get the placement right. If there is a point and a short third man for a spinner and you have cut two balls straight to point, you know that you can get the third one through so long as you allow it to come a couple of inches closer to you, and play it a fraction later than previously. It's the same shot as before, nothing has changed except when you have played the stroke, how you have manoeuvred it into the gap.

I enjoyed the late cut as much as the square cut. To me, it's a more delayed version of the parent stroke, you can either play it on top of the ball or glide it, which comes with risks because it can go into the air towards slips. If you are on top of the ball, you can immediately slice it into the ground, from where the ball generates even more pace. It was a very paying stroke.

I remember with great delight a late cut I played at the Chinnaswamy Stadium in the Ranji Trophy quarter-final against Delhi in March 1974. I was facing Daljit Saxena, the experienced off spinner, and was in my 50s when I went back to cut a short ball against the turn. From the corner of my eye, I noticed the slip fielder move a foot or so to his right, anticipating that the ball would go there. I delayed the stroke, playing the lateglide instead of the square cut, and directing it softly but firmly along the ground through the exact spot where the slip fielder had been standing originally. I enjoyed that shot immensely, but I could only do that because I was aware of what was happening around me. At that level, it's more about your mind than your skills. You have to overcome your mind to play bowling of the highest order, be it spin or pace. And the only way you can control your batting is if you have the basics in order. If your technique is all over the place, you are a goner.

I loved playing the flick, off either foot. If a spinner bowled slightly short, I'd go back and work it off my hips between mid wicket and square leg, milk ones and twos. But no stroke gladdened me more, not even the square cut, than the square drive. If the ball was right up, maybe an attempted yorker or a full ball as the pacer strived for outswing, I would put a little weight on my right foot and hit the ball over cover point. For some reason, it thrilled me no end, with the inside-out cover drive in the air to left-arm spinners not far behind. I didn't hit the ball over the top very often, but whenever I did, I couldn't help pat myself on the back, figuratively.

I didn't play a lot of drives off the front foot down the ground, primarily because I was a back foot exponent. That said, there was immense satisfaction to gain when you got up on your toes and punched the ball off the back foot into the ground and back past the bowler. In itself, it's not an easy shot to play, and we didn't have the kind of bats that provided value for that stroke. You can only play it when you are well set and in total command, but when it comes off like it did against

Keith Boyce during the 97 not out in Madras, the feeling of warm glow it brings is unparalleled.

The common thread binding my batting in stroke-making and defence was my wrists. In my book, a good defensive shot holds the same value as a crunching cut or a cracking drive. There is no greater confidence-booster than meeting the ball with the middle of a dead defensive blade, it shows you are on top of what you are doing. I enjoyed the rush of dropping a rising ball from a fast bowler close to my feet, a forward defensive stroke to a quality spinner on a turning track that ensured the ball didn't even roll off the pitch. That's what you are there to show. Batting is not just a power game. It's about finesse and craft and control. You might say a dead defensive stroke doesn't yield any runs. Can't disagree, but there is more to batting than mere runs.

If there's one stroke I'd have loved to have played with greater frequency, it's the straight drive off the front foot to a high-class fast bowler. To me, that is forever a treat to watch. You show the full face of the bat to the bowler who has thundered in 20 yards and let go. He is helpless; he is in the process of completing his follow through, he can see the ball coming at him, but he can do nothing to stop it. He sometimes glares at you defiantly, but you can't miss the beaten look. Both the batsman and the bowler know, at least for that one ball, who the master is. Priceless.

Perhaps that's why I am a little envious of Sunil. Though we are of similar stature, he used to play that straight drive so well, just so well. It didn't matter to him if it was the first ball of the match, the last ball before stumps or if he was on 99. If the ball was pitched up and he knew he had it covered, he always played that shot. Always so elegantly, always so beautifully. But then again, I did have my square cut, didn't I?

14

SCALING THE RANJI SUMMIT

The Ranji Trophy was, and continues to be, the most prestigious domestic tournament in our country. Yes, the Indian Premier League (IPL) has caught the imagination because of its inherent charm and thrown up the occasional cricketer who has gone to play at the highest level, but it's the consistency in performances in the Ranji Trophy, season after season, that influences a majority of the national team selections.

To me, playing for Mysore/Karnataka meant as much as representing India. My state had given me my first break when I was relatively unknown. It had afforded me the platform from which I could express myself. I am forever grateful for that. I loved playing for the state team, I enjoyed our successes, both individually and collectively. Some of my most cherished memories stem from the long train rides and wonderful times in the company of friends and teammates as driven and committed to making Karnataka successful as I was.

We were always a reasonably strong cricketing unit, but even though Mysore often featured in the knockout stages, we had made only two finals since the inception of the tournament in 1934–35. On both occasions, in 1941–42 and later in 1959–60, we lost to mighty Bombay in the finals, which is no disgrace given Bombay's pedigree but which hurt us because we felt that we too were good enough to go all the way.

Since my first-class debut, we had been there and thereabouts, but apart from making it to the semi-final in 1971–72, we didn't have much to show for our efforts. That semi-final outing at the Brabourne Stadium was an utter disaster from our perspective. As formidable as Bombay were, we surrendered without a fight, shot out for 90 and 111 to be trounced by 372 runs. We weren't a weak side, but we had no answer to the guile of Padmakar Shivalkar, the excellent left-arm spinner who had ridiculous match figures of 13 for 50.

It was a chastening experience, not softened even by Bombay's supreme dominance of Indian cricket. The western powerhouse won 15 titles on the trot from 1958–59 to 1972–73, which speaks volumes of the strength and vitality of their club cricket structure as it existed then, and to the immense pride the players took in maintaining the high standards established by their illustrious predecessors.

A lot of teams were intimidated by the aura around Bombay, and I won't be wrong in saying that several of them lost the game in the mind even before they took to the field. We weren't in that category; we had belief and confidence in our skills, and while we acknowledged the might of Bombay, we weren't in awe of them, ever. That made the Brabourne drubbing even harder to digest.

As luck would have it, we earned another tilt at Bombay two seasons later, again in the semi-final. This time, our state had a new name, the state association had a new home. On 1 November 1973, two days before we kicked off our Ranji Trophy campaign, Mysore had been renamed Karnataka; a few months previously, the M. Chinnaswamy Stadium had taken shape in the heart of the city, and it was here that, under Pras, we found ourselves face to face against Bombay in the four-day semi-final from 15 March 1974.

To us, it was no less than a final. As always, Bombay put out a strong team—Gavaskar, Wadekar, Mankad, Solkar and Shivalkar, among others—but we had a fairly balanced and experienced side as well. Pras had been captain for four seasons and was a brilliant tactician. He and Chandra formed the best spin bowling combine in the country, and we had a solid batting group with Brijesh Patel and myself assuming lead roles.

Bombay was the team to beat, and while everyone wanted to defeat them, not many had the belief that they could do so. But Ajit's side knew that we wouldn't keel over and allow them to walk all over us. They had to beat us, we wouldn't be handing the game over on a platter. That meant the match began on an even keel, and we had a slice of luck at the toss when Ajit called wrong and Pras opted to bat.

We made a horror start, losing opener V.S. Vijay Kumar for a duck with just 10 on the board. I was batting at No. 3 that season and made my way to the middle far earlier than I would have liked, to join Sanjay Desai.

Very early in my innings, I played back to Abdul Ismail, who was on a high after picking up the first wicket, and was rapped on my back pad. There was a huge, concerted and prolonged appeal from the Bombay camp, but after much deliberation, the umpire ruled in my favour. I had feared the worst, to be honest. Ismail was one of the best exponents of swing bowling in the country at the time and had got the ball to come in sharply, though I had perhaps got just outside the off stump when the ball thudded into my right leg. I couldn't really have complained had I been given out.

Drawing a deep breath, I decided I couldn't let this opportunity slide. Sanjay kept me company during a second-wicket stand of 105, but it was when Brijesh came out to bat that I really enjoyed myself. Brijesh was an extremely talented batsman, particularly brilliant against spin, and I marvelled at his footwork and the decisiveness with which he left the crease to attack the spinners. We had a wonderful understanding throughout our overlapping careers, and it is no surprise that we were involved in several substantial partnerships, both for our state and for India.

This partnership was among the most significant of our many associations. We refused to go into our shells, playing our strokes freely and not allowing the Bombay spinners to impose themselves. With the large crowd egging us on, we put on 166, and by the time I was dismissed by leg spinner Rakesh Tandon, I had smashed 24 fours en route to 162. Brijesh weighed in with 106, and even though there was a collapse after our alliance, we posted 385, a challenging total in a knockout semi-final.

It's a score that might have made us complacent against any other team, but we knew what Bombay were capable of. And then, there was Pras, constantly telling us not to relax or take it easy. He chose to lead by example, producing an absolutely magical ball to dismiss Sunil. Standing at slip, I was completely mesmerized by the action that unfolded in front of me, and when I looked at Sunil's face after the ball snaked into his off stump, I could see that he was in a daze too. To this day, he maintains it's one of the best deliveries he has faced.

On the face of it, this seemed no different to the thousands of excellent deliveries that have arced out of Pras's right hand. Watching the ball closely, Sunil did everything right in playing for the turn, covering his off stump and having the pad as his second line of defence. It was the off spinner, not the one which went on with the arm, but while it threatened to turn substantially into the right-hander, it straightened just enough to sneak past Sunil's outside edge and disturb the off-bail. It had taken something special from one genius to outwit the other.

By now, Sunil's appetite for runs was legendary, and to see our captain pack him off for just 30 was a massive shot in the arm. Just to get a batsman of Sunil's calibre out for that score was brilliant, but for the captain to dismiss him with an unbelievable ball lifted our spirits hugely and strengthened our resolve. We knew Bombay would keep coming hard at us, but we were prepared to be patient, we were determined not to panic.

Predictably, Ajit and Ashok held us up with a superb third-wicket stand of 127, negotiating Pras and Chandra with as much comfort as anyone could these two champion spinners. As well as the two senior hands batted, we knew it was a matter of one wicket before we could start to put pressure on Bombay. That breakthrough came on the back of an inspired piece of fielding by Sudhakar Rao, early on the third morning.

Ashok played the ball to point and called Ajit through for what looked like a regulation single, but Sudha swooped down on the ball and scored a direct hit at the batsman's end to catch Ajit short of his ground. Like Pras's dismissal of Sunil, this wonderful piece of fielding galvanized us; to me, that was the turning point of the game.

When Ajit was dismissed, we had nearly 200 runs to play with, and Pras and Chandra got down to work. There were brief pockets of resistance, but the two legends bowled superbly, always asking questions, always probing away, always teasing and tormenting the batsmen. In the end, Pras took five and Chandra finished with four to dismiss Bombay for 307. It was the wicket they didn't get, that of Ajit's, which proved decisive, because after his departure, the defending champions lost seven for 76.

Our lead was 78, more than handy, but there was plenty of time left in the game for Bombay to stage a comeback. They were the kind of side that, if you gave them an inch, they would take a whole mile. We had to be on our toes, we had to bat in the second innings like we had in the first. We had to both bat time and score runs, without revealing any sense of nervousness.

There were few alarms as we pulled away to 279 for eight when Pras applied a token closure. As a team, we wanted to be together in the middle when victory was achieved, never mind if it was on the first-innings lead. The crowd gave us a wonderful ovation when we came out to field late on the final day, and an even bigger one when the teams shook hands and the game ended in a draw.

It was all comfortable in the end, but we had to fight for this victory every bit of the way. It was one of our finest moments; we had broken Bombay's dominance and their chain of victories. And we had done so on the strength of our all-round performance. The result was doubly sweet considering what had happened two years ago at the Brabourne, and we basked in our achievement, bathed in goofy grins.

This was until someone reminded us that we hadn't yet won the title. That we had only reached the final, there was unfinished business ahead of us. That brought us back to earth, though it was impossible for the smiles to be wiped off our faces.

◆

The final was to start on 23 March, five days after our historic win against Bombay. We had to make the trip to Jaipur to face Rajasthan, a domestic powerhouse which had lost seven finals to Bombay between 1961 and 1970. Like us, they were also looking for their maiden title; they were coming off of a thrilling 12-run win in a low-scoring semi-final in Hyderabad and were themselves riding the crest of a confidence wave.

Hyderabad were chasing only 168 for victory on the same day we were keeping Bombay at bay on the final day of our semi-final, but were bowled out for 155 with Gajendra Shaktawat, the off spinner, taking six for 35. That they had prevented a strong Hyderabad batting line-up —Abbas,

Tiger, Abid, Jai and Narasimha Rao—from hunting down a modest target meant Rajasthan fancied their chances against us, particularly with the masterly Hanumant Singh in charge, and Salim Durani, Kailash Gattani and Parthasarathy Sharma as their batting mainstays.

At every available opportunity, Pras would urge us not to take Rajasthan lightly. 'We have beaten Bombay, but that's history,' he would tell us. 'It doesn't guarantee us the title. Rajasthan are a good side, they have some fantastic players. Having come this far, we should not miss out on the title. If they are better than us, so be it. But they must win the final, we shouldn't lose it. We must maintain the same spirit and intensity as we did against Bombay. Never forget that.' To be fair, each one of us was keyed up, though Pras's strong words had their desired sobering effect, too. For everyone in the squad, it was our first taste of a Ranji final. We wanted the sweet taste of success to linger, not be replaced by the bitterness of a heartbreaking defeat.

A huge crowd turned up on all four days of the scheduled five-day match to mainly cheer the home side, but to also appreciate the not inconsiderable skills of the Karnataka team. That was pretty much the norm for the duration of my domestic career—big turnouts everywhere in the country, 25,000–30,000 fans gathering to encourage the players and partake of the entertainment. It's very sad that hardly anyone watches domestic games these days, but then again, that's how it is. Like life itself, cricket has changed. There is a lot more cricket, and because the Indian team is in such demand, the big names are hardly in a position to turn out for their states. Only those who are recovering from injury or eyeing a comeback play in the Ranji Trophy.

That's not necessarily the best development, but what can we do when the top players play non-stop and therefore are either away on international duty during the Ranji Trophy or would rather rest and recharge between national-team assignments? Unless the best players are on view, it's practically impossible for the Ranji Trophy to draw crowds, but spectators have started to stay away even from Test matches in India, which in my opinion is a huge cause for concern.

Back to the final. Pras called right and we batted first for the second game in a row, but our core batting group—Brijesh, Sudha and me—

managed just 33 runs between us. Fortunately, our strength in depth came to our rescue. Vijay Kumar batted beautifully to make 66, and our middle order flourished with all-rounders B. Vijayakrishna and A.V. Jayaprakash chipping in with half-centuries. From 15 for two in the first hour, we had managed respectability at 276. We would have loved at least 100 runs more, but it was a slightly tricky surface, and we had our trump cards Pras and Chandra to fall back on.

I made only 15, caught off Salim bhai's bowling. Salim bhai was playing with an injury and picked up a pair, though he apparently told Hanumant that he would get our main batsmen. True to his word, he picked up Sudha's and Jayaprakash's wickets to go with mine, though we were all relieved and delighted that when it came to his turn with the bat, Pras ensured he failed to trouble the scorers in both innings.

Rajasthan's reply wasn't allowed to gain any momentum by the brilliance of Chandra and Pras. Hanumant was wonderful while dancing to 83, putting on a masterclass in the art of batting against spin of the highest order. But apart from opener Laxman Singh, no one else touched 20, and we took a huge 100-run lead after Vijay cleaned up the tail with the second newball.

We stuttered at the start of our second innings; Gattani's medium-pace claimed Sanjay and myself for ducks, and I vividly remember his unbridled celebrations after I chopped the ball on to my stumps. Jayaprakash and Kiri came to our rescue by putting on 114 for the seventh before Kiri fell to the last ball of the third evening.

By now, our lead was a healthy 297; already, Rajasthan had to score the highest total of the match if they were to win the title, and everyone began to comprehend that that was a very tall order. Even accounting for the glorious uncertainties of our great game, Rajasthan would need a miracle to score 300 in the fourth innings against Chandra and Pras. And while form necessitated that we maintain our composure and poise, all of us mentally already had one hand on the trophy.

After the third day came the mandatory rest day, and the Rajasthan Cricket Association thoughtfully organized a get-together for the teams. There was much back-slapping and camaraderie, though I was pretty much a non-participant. My delight at imminent team success was tempered by my twin batting failures. With the tour of England coming up, I was slightly worried about whether I'd be selected or whether the two failures in the final would be held against me. I was not in a great mental space, all said.

Apart from the usual refreshments, there was *bhang* available too. Having had no previous experience of that drink, I was keen to experiment. Consequently, I have little memory of what happened for the rest of the evening, though everyone present later reassured me that I did nothing to embarrass myself. Apparently, after partaking of the beverage, I went and stood in a corner, facing the wall, sulking about my batting failures for two whole hours, impervious to the goings-on around me despite the constant urgings of players from both teams to join in the entertainment and riotous story-telling. During that entire period, I was informed, Chandra kept laughing. Not at me, no. It was how he reacted to the new liquid in his system.

That didn't prevent him from weaving his magic the next day. By posting 212, we had set Rajasthan an impossible target of 313, and except for a while when Parthasarathy and Hanumant realized 54 for the third wicket, they were never in with a shout. When Chandra castled Hanumant, the wheels fell off and Rajasthan collapsed to 127 all out. Pras returned five for 45, Chandra three for 56. We had won by 185 runs. We had won the Ranji Trophy!

Some officials of our state association had arrived in Jaipur in anticipation of victory and, fearing the worst, slept at the ground to ensure there was no attempt at 'pitch-tampering'. I know it sounds absurd now, but it only goes to show how badly the players and the association wanted this victory. Pras lifting the Ranji Trophy is one of the greatest moments of my cricketing career.

We celebrated long and hard. We had always been a tight bunch and victory drove us even closer. I thoroughly enjoyed playing for the state from my debut till my last game, I have great memories of time spent on and off the field alongside such men as Brijesh, Sudha, Jayaprakash, Raghunath, Vijay Kumar and Vijayakrishna, not to mention the two giants in Chandra and Pras. As more and more youngsters started to come into the squad, we became one big happy family, taking great pride in not just our own individual successes but also rejoicing in the successes of our mates. It's a culture that has been handed down from generation to generation, and I feel that's one of the reasons why Karnataka cricket continues to be in such good health.

Playing for a state like Karnataka was a dream come true for me. And even as we were waiting on the field for the formalities to be completed on the fourth day and for us to take the last wicket that would seal our coronation, the value of being Ranji Trophy champions started to sink in. We needed to portray that we were focussed on the job at hand, but a million thoughts were running through all our minds. All of us didn't just want to play for Karnataka, we wanted to make Karnataka proud. We wanted to win titles, we felt that was our way of expressing our gratitude for everything the state had done for us.

I am sure players of subsequent generations share the same values. I can still see how much it means for players to be a part of the winning team. Every time Karnataka has won the trophy post my playing days, I have been transported back to the events of March 1974. I live the emotions with the current players, I share their delight, I can empathize with their feelings. Winning the Ranji Trophy is the ultimate honour for an Indian cricketer. Not everyone who plays first-class cricket can represent the country; for the vast majority who play only at the first-class level, the Ranji Trophy is the greatest tournament. That's why I am convinced the passion associated with playing for the state and working towards making it a champion side will remain undiminished.

I always made it a point to play for the state whenever I could. Even if landed in Bangalore on the morning of a Ranji game, the thought of taking it easy never occurred to me. I felt it was my duty to represent my state, yet it didn't feel like duty because in any case, I enjoyed doing so, I loved the game. Why would I want to sit idle when I could be out there in the middle? Playing for Karnataka was as fulfilling as representing India.

Playing for my employer, of course, triggered an entirely new gamut of emotions. Through some quirk of fate, I joined SBI. To me, that name symbolized everything I loved and respected: state (Mysore/Karnataka), bank (which paid my salary, put bread and butter on my table) and

India (need I say anything?). I really couldn't have asked for a better institution as an employee.

We received a tremendous welcome when we returned home with the trophy. The next 15 days, till we left for England, are a bit of blur. We were invited to breakfasts, lunches and dinners, and were felicitated by a wide cross-section of cricket-supporters. We knew the magnitude of what we had accomplished, but to see the delight and satisfaction our victory had provided so many people was at once both satisfying and humbling.

One of the highlights was being invited by famous film and theatre/drama exponent Master Hirannaiah to his show in Subhash Nagar in central Bengaluru. His drama troupe was performing at what was then a vast, empty ground where the sprawling bus station has now come up. His father was also a great actor and dramatist who ran the K. Hirannaiah Mitra Mandali, and Master Hirannaiah was continuing that tradition. The entire team enjoyed the play and was touched at his invitation to be special guests that evening. It rekindled the spirit of Karnataka within the boys. We had gone where no team from the state had before. It felt quite special to be the pioneers.

15

SUMMER OF 42

There are certain tours you'd like to forget in a hurry, except that you simply can't. Like our visit to England in 1974, for a three-Test series that promised so much and delivered so little.

We had every reason to be bullish about our chances when we landed in London in the middle of April. Even though our last three series had been spread over 22 months, we had triumphed in each of them, including twice overseas. Just 14 months previously, we had defeated the English in our own turf to complete a rare hat-trick of series wins; we were now facing England for the third time in succession, able to draw inspiration from our last visit to the country.

Pras, Chandra, Brijesh and I were still flying high on our maiden Ranji triumph, and we saw no reason why we couldn't extend our winning run. Or so we thought, until we landed in London. I don't necessarily believe in portents, but I felt a little shiver run down my spine when we stepped out of Heathrow. It was cold, gloomy, damp and windy. Welcome to England, I thought.

Those days, India wasn't considered important enough to merit a full series in England, so both in 1971 and 1974, we shared the summer with Pakistan.[2] But where, three years previously, we had played in the second half, in 1974 we were slotted in to play at the beginning of their summer.

'Summer' is a bit of a misnomer. Admittedly, as the months tick over and you get into July and beyond, the weather is far better. The sun makes more than mere fleeting appearances, and while there are the

---

[2]Usually, unless England are hosting Australia, they play Test matches at home every summer against two teams, mainly in three-match series. The Ashes (England-Australia) is of five Tests.

occasional spells of rain, subcontinental teams who love playing with the sun on their backs find the going a lot easier. However, in April, May and June, the weather is miserable, to even the locals. We weren't used to the bitter cold and the icy winds, which affected not just our psyche but also our cricket.

I realize whatever I say might be construed as an excuse, but I want to make it clear that I am not offering any excuses for our crushing 3-0 defeat. We were comprehensively outplayed by a team that wasn't just familiar with the conditions, but also had the resources and the ability to make the most of the assistance on offer. We should have adapted better. We were an experienced side, several of us had played in England before, we ought to have given a better account of ourselves. But we didn't. Simple fact.

That being out of the way, I would like to highlight a significant change in the playing conditions for the series, a development not even skipper Wadekar was aware of until we reached England. In its collective wisdom, the BCCI agreed to the England board's proposal to restrict the number of fielders on the legside to five. Clearly, the move was to negate the influence of our spinners, who invariably bowled with six men on the onside, including close-in catchers at forward short leg and leg slip for the most part. Our world-class spinners had been the driving forces behind both our previous series wins against England. Perhaps, the result of the 1974 series might have remained unaltered even in the absence of this tweak to the playing conditions, but the change didn't help our cause one bit.

What was equally disappointing was how all of us were kept in the dark until the proverbial last minute about a significant, potentially decisive, change. Had we known of this earlier, the thinktank and the quality spinners could have worked out suitable game plans. All of a sudden, not only was one of their primary weapons seized from them, but they also had no time to prepare and come up with effective alternatives. As it is, the cold made it difficult for them to grip the ball properly, to get the feel of the ball on their magical fingers. Their efficacy was further blunted by the five-on-the-leg restriction. Bishan, the only spinner to play all three Tests, finished with 10 wickets. Chandra, Pras and Venkat, each of whom figured in two matches apiece, collectively picked up five wickets. That pretty much tells the tale, doesn't it? Especially given that we didn't have a pace attack that could make the most of help from the atmosphere and the surfaces.

I am not trying to lay the blame for the whitewash at the feet of the bowlers. As a batting group, we were woefully below par. Only Sunil and I touched 200 runs for the series, Farokh had 195 and Abid ended up with 101. No one else made even 100 runs in six innings combined against an England attack led expertly by Chris Old, far quicker than in India the previous year, and Geoff Arnold, a wonderful swing bowler whose threat quotient was amplified by the conditions.

We did play a dozen first-class games before the first Test in Manchester, but most of them were interrupted by the weather, which, in turn, hampered our preparations. At the same time, we registered convincing wins against Surrey and Derbyshire, respectively, in our last two games before the first Test, so we had managed to wrest a little bit of momentum as we squared off against Mike Denness's men at Old Trafford.

We made a bright enough start by packing off Geoff Boycott and the excellent John Edrich cheaply, but Keith Fletcher held the innings together with a lovely unbeaten century, aided by 50s from Dennis Amiss and Tony Greig. England declared at 328 for nine late on day two; despite the constraints, we hadn't allowed them to run away from us, forcing them to bat 143.3 overs for those runs.

Then began our woes. In the half-hour to close, we lost Ekki and nightwatchman Venkat, and when Ajit perished early the next morning, we were stuttering at 32 for three. Bob Willis, Old and Mike Hendrick were getting it to whoop around corners, but even they couldn't find a way past Sunil's broad willow for five hours.

Before and after his exceptional 101, I have seen several hundreds and doubles cascade off Sunil's bat from close quarters. Each of them has been of the highest quality, but if I had to rate his 34 centuries, this will be right on top of the list. At the very top. It was a stunning exhibition of how an opening batsman, how any batsman in fact, should play swing bowling at pace when the dice is loaded against you. It was poetry in motion, whether he moved forward or back in defence—be it when he showed immaculate awareness of where his off stump was when he chose not to offer a shot or be it when he leaned into drives after getting to the pitch of the ball and cutting out the possibility of late movement that might put the slip cordon in business.

I was an entranced spectator as we added 73 for the fourth wicket. According to me, the best lessons are learnt by watching, not from listening, and Sunil added to my education with this epic. I was already a big Sunil fan, but after this innings, I began to view him in an entirely different light, if that was even possible. In the end, he was dismissed in the only way that looked possible that day; it was a run-out, to end an alliance of 85 for the eighth wicket with Abid.

Bowled out for 246, we conceded a lead 86, and England swelled it to 295 with an unbeaten ton by Edrich studding their second innings. We needed to survive the entire last day to secure a draw—a target of 296 was well out of reach given the conditions—but were bowled out for 182, Sunil and yours truly preventing a total wipeout with patient half-centuries.

Where we struggled to put totals on the board with any consistency, England were extremely competent with the bat. Denness, to date the only Scottish-born cricketer to lead England in Tests, made hundreds in successive games, and found support from Amiss, Fletcher, Edrich, Greig and David Lloyd, who slammed a double-century in the last Test in Birmingham. Their lowest first-innings total was in the first Test, which added to the already huge pressure on us as a batting unit.

Between the first and second Tests, we won both our warm-up games. We were 0-1 down, but not particularly disheartened because we hadn't been overwhelmed. We felt that if we pulled up our socks, we could run the home side close. That wasn't to be, as we suffered one of our heaviest losses, by an innings and 285 runs at Lord's to surrender the series.

A powerhouse batting display with hundreds from Amiss, Denness and Greig catapulted England to 629, from which point we were always playing catch-up. Sunil and Farokh raised an attractive 131 for the opening wicket at a furious tempo, and I weighed in with my second straight half-century, but we were forced to follow on when we were dismissed for 302, very late on day three.

On the rest day, we didn't look too far ahead. We needed to improve our first-innings score simply to make England bat again. There were two days to go, so we had no respite when it came to time either. We decided that the only option available to us was to bat normally, taking everything else out of the picture.

As theories go, that was faultless. However, all our plans lay in tatters on the fourth morning, by a distance my worst day in Test cricket.

We lost Farokh immediately on resuming on two without loss. That sparked an unprecedented, unacceptable and inexplicable procession. As batsmen went and came, you could have knocked the entire team over with a feather. We watched the horror show unfolding in front of us with disbelief, despair and no little shame. In a matter of 17 overs, we were bundled out for 42. The Indian batting line-up had been destroyed for 42, our reputations gone for a six, our humiliation total, our surrender abject.

It was then, and until December 2020, the lowest score in a Test innings by an Indian team. It's the sort of record you desperately want to forget, but it's also the kind of dubious distinction that stays with you for the rest of your life. That 42 all out didn't define our lives, or even our cricketing careers. But for all of us who were a part of that meltdown, it's a painful reminder, an asterisk that will stay with us like our initials do. I can fully understand what the Indian team must have gone through after being bowled out for 36 in Adelaide in 2020, and it's to their great credit that they turned things around in grand fashion to complete a spectacular series triumph.

It's just one of those events that happen, I guess. It was a terribly gloomy morning and the ball was doing a fair bit. Arnold and Old bowled extraordinarily well—the former was swinging the ball a long way and the latter was doing the same at pace. Ekki was the only one to reach double-figures, and Sunil was the sole batsman to play more than 20 balls. Again, it was one of those days when not one ball whizzed past the outside edge. Every time the ball took the edge, it invariably found a fielder's hands. Logic suggested that you write it off as a terrible day in office; after all, we did make more than 300 in the first innings. But when you register the lowest tally in your country's history at the time, all logic goes out the window. With all due respect, England bowled superbly and caught everything that came their way, but our batting was timid and without spark, and that was hard to live down.

Our morale at an all-time low, we were hammered by an innings in the final Test at Edgbaston too, surrendering the series 0-3. The scenes were a far cry from three years back, when we had rewritten history. This time too, history had been created, but not of the kind we would have liked.

During my international career, I played 23 series in all, 12 of them overseas, and figured in two 60-over World Cups. Without a shadow of doubt, this 1974 tour of England has to be my worst tour ever. It wasn't just because of the result, not only because we lost 3-0. Everything that could go wrong went wrong, starting with the twist in the playing conditions and the dismal weather. There were tensions between senior players that started in the dressing room and spilled over to the field, or vice versa. There were off-field incidents that left us disillusioned and a little depressed. Our team manager, Col. Hemu Adhikari, had his hands full though, typically, he soldiered on and tried everything he could to salvage a bad situation.

I felt particularly bad for our captain. This time three years back, Ajit was the man with the Midas touch, celebrated and lauded for leading the team to victories in the Caribbean and England. Now suddenly, he became the most obvious punching bag. We could only imagine what he must have gone through during the entire series. It wasn't his fault alone that we were steamrollered, but that's the way the cookie crumbles in sport, I am afraid.

Once we returned from the ill-fated outing, Ajit announced his retirement from Test cricket. That depressed me even further. I had enjoyed playing alongside and under him, both for India and for All India State Bank of India. He was a great servant of Indian cricket, an excellent batsman, a top-class close-in catcher, a fine captain and a very decent human being. He had done so much for Indian cricket, had brought the country such glory and respect, that he deserved a better farewell. It was an unfortunate exit from top-flight action for one of India's most exemplary cricketing sons.

16

A SHOT AT REDEMPTION

The start of a fresh domestic season always brings with it new hopes and challenges. Within two months of returning from England, our tail between our legs, it was time to get cracking in preparation for the five-Test home series against a very strong West Indies side, to be led by the seasoned Clive Lloyd.

The Duleep Trophy set the ball rolling and was followed by the Irani Cup, where, for the first time in October 1974, I represented Karnataka. There's something about the Irani Cup that brought the best out of me, be it when I played thrice for my state or six times for Rest of India. With all the internationals available, it was the most prestigious one-match tournament in the country, which appealed to the competitor in me.

Having had a quiet time during South Zone's charge to the Duleep Trophy title, I hit my straps in Karnataka's first appearance in the Irani Cup in Ahmedabad. After a first-innings 52, I feasted on an attack that included Bishan on my way to 200 not out. A half-century in Karnataka's first Ranji game of the season, against Andhra, rounded off my preparations as we knuckled down to face the might of Lloyd's men.

West Indies had a formidable pace attack with Andy Roberts as the lynchpin. Andy had played against us on our tour of England for Hampshire in a first-class game, but I sat that match out, so I was looking forward to finding out first-hand why he was rated so highly.

Even though he had only played one Test before this series, Andy had already established himself as among the world's fastest bowlers and picked up the reputation of inflicting physical damage on batsmen in every match he played on the county circuit. I don't know if he enjoyed hitting batsmen, but whenever Roberts played for Hampshire, there were a couple of ambulances parked at the ground as a precautionary measure. The medics were kept busy by the big fella, obviously.

My first taste of Andy would come at the Lal Bahadur Stadium in Hyderabad, where South Zone were playing a three-day game against the tourists. Andy was every bit as quick as he was touted to be, there was no empty hype around him. He spoke little with his lips. He didn't need to because he conveyed whatever he wanted to with his eyes. He was much quicker than anyone I had faced previously, but sheer pace didn't ever bother me, and I was happy with how I approached the task during my first-innings 114.

We had a fair few players who would figure in the first Test a week later, and most of them had a useful outing, as did the West Indians. The game was drifting towards a draw on the final evening when, on a whim, Venkat declared our innings, setting them a token target of 163 in less than an hour and a half.

For the next 18.2 overs, their batsmen tore our bowling apart. They had only one goal, victory. Roy Fredericks got them off to a flyer, Lloyd promoted himself to open the batting and Alvin Kallicharran came in at No. 3, and they picked the bones off our shell-shocked bowlers to rattle to a nine-wicket win. This was in 1974, a good 30 years before the advent of T20 cricket. Against a bowling attack that included three men who would play in the first Test, the West Indians scored 163 runs in 18.2 overs at nearly nine runs per over. It was breathtaking batting. We had been served notice of what to expect over the next two months!

◆

We moved from Hyderabad to Bangalore for the first Test, our heads still reeling from the spectacular assault. My spirit was buoyed by, finally, being able to play a Test match in the state of my birth. Hitherto, only Madras and, occasionally, Hyderabad hosted Tests in the South. Bangalore was to join that list with the M. Chinnaswamy Stadium making its international debut. The prospect of playing in front of family and friends with whom I had grown up was exhilarating. I wasn't nervous, just tingling with anticipation. What an occasion it would be, to walk out to the ground and hear the approbation of the fans crammed into the temporary galleries at a stadium yet to be fully constructed.

The England drubbing had not just scarred us, but also cost us our leader. With Ajit no longer in the fray, the net was cast for the next skipper, and in landed our new 'old' captain—nearly four years after he last led the country, Tiger was back at the helm. It was also his comeback to the Test set-up, after being overlooked for the tour of England. Legend has it that the selectors wanted to appoint him captain for the first couple of Tests, putting him on probation. Tiger would have none of it. 'The entire series, or none at all,' he is said to have told them. Like almost always, he had the last word.

Tiger knew he had his work cut out as we tried to regain the faith of the fans after the debacle in England. That was our motivation. West Indies had their own; they had been bearded in their own den during the last battle between these two sides, and Lloyd had a long memory. He also had a wonderfully talented and skilful side, a great mix of experience and youth, all suffused with typical Caribbean flair.

Apart from the captain himself, there was an array of sparkling batting talent in the Caribbean ranks—Fredericks, Kallicharran and Lawrence Rowe, as well as newcomers Gordon Greenidge and Viv Richards, of whom so much was being talked about even before their Test debut.

Already, Kalli had made a name for himself, as a left-handed mirror image of Rohan Kanhai. He looked a bit like Rohan, and it seems he batted a lot like Rohan too when Rohan was as young as Kalli was now. The two Guyanese had a lot in common, and as the series unravelled, I could see why comparisons were being made. Kalli was a tremendous batsman, technically one of the soundest to come out of the collection of islands in the Caribbean, full of strokes but with a strong defence as his biggest ally.

And then there was the whistling genius, Rowe. What an outstanding batsman he was! A couple of years previously, he had heralded his Test debut by becoming the first batsman to make a double hundred and a century straightaway, and backed it up with a triple century against England. He had this habit of whistling as he settled into his stance and waited for the ball. The longer the wait once the ball left the bowler's hand, the more extended the whistle; the harder he hit the ball, the louder the decibel level. Unfortunately, his career was blighted by injuries, eyesight issues and an allergy to grass—imagine that. Eyesight problems restricted him to just one game, against West Zone, on this tour, which was a shame because he would have undoubtedly entertained the West Indian crowds. In all, he only played 30 Tests in eight years due to his various injuries and ailments. That he didn't play more was a great loss not only to West Indian cricket, but to world cricket as a whole.

We had already heard a lot about Greenidge and Richards, and we were as keen to see what they were made of as how Roberts would go on Indian pitches. As things panned out, all three of them put on supreme exhibitions of skill through the duration of the series, establishing themselves as world-beaters by the time the West Indians flew back home.

These subtexts lent greater excitement to the start of the series, at a first-time venue. Yours truly included, there were four 'local lads' in our XI: Brijesh, Pras and Chandra were as thrilled as I was, and their delight was echoed by an enthusiastic crowd that made us feel larger than life. To be able to start a new season thus was a priceless gift.

◆

Overnight rain delayed the start of the first day, and because the track was somewhat damp, Tiger stuck West Indies in on winning the toss. Greenidge and Kalli continued from where they left in Hyderabad, making light of the challenges offered by a drying pitch. Greenidge immediately announced himself with a brilliant 93 in the first innings and followed it up with 107 in the second, while Kalli was outstanding against the spinners as he danced to 124.

We were without Bishan, left out on 'disciplinary' grounds,[3] but had done well to restrict West Indies to 289. However, we weren't good enough for consistent periods of time and ended up conceding a lead of 29. Roberts was sharp, as was Vanburn Holder, and once the pitch eased up and they batted again, West Indies buried us under a mountain of runs.

---

[3]The BCCI wasn't happy that he had given an interview to the BBC during the fractious tour of England in 1974 without seeking its permission.

Greenidge's maiden 100 was complemented by a blistering 163 from Lloyd, who smashed the ball long and hard. In all, 22 fours and two sixes cascaded off his blade, his runs coming off just 149 balls. By the time he applied the closure, our target was a massive 386.

We were two batsmen down even before starting the chase. Farokh had been hit on his eye while keeping to Pras and had to hand over the gloves to relieved debutant Hemant Kanitkar, who had been given a torrid time deep on the onside by thunderous sweeps from Lloyd. Joining him in the infirmary was Tiger, who had dislocated his ring finger while taking a smart catch to dismiss Keith Boyce. Even with a full set of batsmen, 386 was going to be a tall order; without two of our most experienced and accomplished stars, we stood little chance, especially once Sunil was dismissed without scoring by Boyce.

Throughout the game, Roberts was menacing, three wickets in each innings, just reward for the venom he spewed on a slowish surface. He was quick, hostile and accurate; I had kept him at bay in both innings, but I knew the rest of the series would be interesting. I was looking forward to the battles.

We caved in meekly on the final morning to go down by a huge margin of 267 runs. It was far from the ideal start to the series. We were playing catch-up going into the second Test in Delhi.

A fortnight straddled the two Tests, and it was a fortnight that was to bring us further bad news. Sunil played for Bombay in a Ranji Trophy game against Maharashtra in Nasik, and was struck on his glove by Pandurang Salgaonkar, the fiery pace bowler. The broken finger ruled him out of not just the second Test; his return was to be delayed until the final Test after he received a blow from Karsan Ghavri on the same finger during a practice session before the fourth Test in Madras. Tiger had not yet recovered from his finger injury, so we had two new batsmen and a new captain too, in Venkat.

Like Bangalore, Delhi too was a one-way traffic. Once we were bowled out for 220 on the first day, we were out in the cold. Viv decided to show what he was made of, getting stuck into our spinners with a disdain that was to be his calling card for the next 15 years.

He had fallen cheaply in both innings in Bangalore to Chandra.

Relishing the leggie's absence from the side to make way for Bishan's return, Viv exploded with a series of spectacular strokes. He ran out of partners as he closed in on his double, but his unbeaten 192 had given his side a lead of 273 runs. We scrapped but were well beaten early on day four, by an innings and 17 runs with veteran off spinner Lance Gibbs picking up six wickets.

It was a sickening feeling. We were in a free fall, having lost our fifth consecutive Test. As much as the defeats themselves, it was the lack of fight that hurt us. Our fans deserved better, Indian cricket deserved better, but we were already 0-2 down with three to play. What next, I wondered, with a little shiver.

◆

Calcutta, though, had always energized us as a team. The people there are very emotional, they invest everything in the Indian team, and we were instantly lifted when we hit Eden Gardens for our practice sessions ahead of the traditional New Year's Eve Test. We received a further boost with Tiger back in the fray. And, in keeping with what had happened previously when there was a debutant apiece in Bangalore (Kanitkar) and Delhi (Parthasarathy Sharma), we had two fresh faces in Anshuman Gaekwad and Karsan Ghavri, both of whom would play significant roles in our revival.

We made a customary horror start on batting by choice, losing Sudhir Naik to the first ball of the Test from Roberts. In no time, we were three down for 32, with Roberts on the prowl when Tiger strode out. We had slowly started to rebuild when Tiger deflected a lifter from Roberts on to his chin and then the stumps, blood gushing out of the cut.

It couldn't have been easy for Aunshu, on debut, to walk out to the sight of his captain departing in discomfort, and fresh blood in his line of vision on the pitch. I quickly went down the track to try and help him out, assuring him that there were no demons on the surface and that Tiger's accident was merely that, nothing more. That the track had no role to play in his injury, it was just one of those things that happen on the cricket field.

To his credit, Aunshu fought it out. He showed no outward sign of nerves and made a pleasant 36 while we added 75 crucial runs. It was to be the start of a partnership that is still going strong, I am glad to say.

We finished at a modest 233, but unlike in Delhi, we defended that total with tremendous commitment. Fredericks blazed to a fluent 100, but we kept pegging them back with Madan Lal striking regularly. When Madan dismissed last-man Roberts for his fourth wicket of the innings, West Indies's lead was just seven, and we were still in the game.

Naik and Sharma went cheaply for the second time in the match, but Farokh was already on song when I walked out at 46 for two. We took our lead past 100, but when he fell for 61, we suffered a mini-slump with Tiger, Aunshu and Madan all going cheaply. At 192 for six, our lead was 185, far too few for even our great spinners to trouble the power-packed West Indies line-up.

Karsan had had a quiet debut, but we both knew he was a more than competent bat and this was his chance to showcase his mettle. As the senior and set batsman, it was my responsibility to hold the lower order together; the support I required came from my left-handed partner. For nearly two and a half hours, he hardly put a foot wrong, allowing me to bat freely but carefully.

I enjoyed the challenge of responding to a tight situation, with the team looking to me to bail it out of trouble. Here, I had to occupy the crease and score the bulk of the runs, and I was thrilled to bits to be able to accomplish both those tasks with aplomb. I knew that going into my shell was a recipe for disaster, but also that strokeplay had to be judicious. I struck the perfect balance, batting for more than six hours and hitting 23 fours in making 139, which I consider one of my finest hundreds. I wouldn't have got there without Karsan, whose contribution in our seventh-wicket stand of 91 was a pugnacious 27.

West Indies needed to bat really well to get to 310 and take the series and began brightly with Kalli and Viv building on the good work of Fredericks. Viv was particularly threatening, breezing to a boundary-infested 47 when Madan delivered a peach to pack him off, late on the fourth evening. It was just the shot in the arm we needed as we retired for the day. At 146 for three, the game was in the balance, but I'd rather be in our shoes than theirs.

Chandra's comeback had been anything but spectacular. He had only one wicket to show in the first innings and hadn't been at his best in the second innings either. But Tiger had great faith in his ace leggie and intuitively tossed him the ball at the start of the fifth day.

Most skippers might have taken the leg spinner off after a couple of expensive overs, but Tiger wasn't most captains. He knew his best chance of a breakthrough rested with Chandra, and his perseverance was rewarded when Chandra rediscovered his zip dramatically. He snaked through Lloyd's defences, had Kalli caught by me and trapped Bernard Julien in front in a tremendous burst of great quality. The rest was routine business; Bishan finished with four wickets, West Indies were bowled out for 224 and we were back in the series. It was a much-needed win ahead of the 10-day break before the fourth Test. We were still in with a shout, the series was alive, there was so much to look forward to.

17

WHEN 97 TRUMPED A HUNDRED

In a world where numbers hold such great importance, it's the hundreds and the five-wicket hauls that cricket-lovers tend to remember fondly. I consider it my greatest blessing that the knock that endeared me most to the millions of cricket fans in the country was the 100 which, I can happily say now, got away from me.

I am not sure what would have happened had 97 not out, in our first Test of 1975, been replaced by, say, 101 not out. Would it have invited the same romanticism? The same aura and mystery? The same unfettered expressions of joy and delight I have so gratefully received? I don't know, and I don't want to know.

We spent a week with our families after the Calcutta victory, unwinding, recharging and rebooting. The Calcutta result had come at the most opportune time—imagine being a sourpuss on your brief return home—and when we assembled in Madras for the fourth Test, we felt everything would be all right, that things would work out just fine for us.

Madras was a great place to play cricket in. The crowds were very knowledgeable, and not just statistically. They appreciated a perfect forward defensive stroke just as much as a full-blooded hook. There was a strong cricket culture in the city, propelled by a very competitive corporate structure, and that tradition spilled over to the Pongal Test, one of the highlights of our home international season.

Festivities were the last thing on our mind after we won our fourth straight toss and chose to bat. We had won the first battle, giving ourselves the chance to set the stage for our spinners to come into play in the fourth innings. But winning the toss is of little consequence if you don't put runs on the board.

We didn't, to start with. Julien fired out the openers, after which Roberts produced his most lethal spell of the series. The Chepauk deck was spicy—lots of pace, plenty of bounce. Or, maybe, it looked that way because of how Roberts was bowling. Either way, it wasn't what our batsmen would have liked.

In no time, we were floundering at 76 for six, a rout imminent. I had got a few away, didn't look in any discomfort, but it wasn't until I saw Karsan walk in at No. 8 that I realized the gravity of the situation. How were we six down? What had I missed?

Neither Karsan, nor I panicked. We had added nearly a hundred just two weeks back, so there's no way we couldn't put on a few more in even more daunting circumstances. But I knew that the situation was a lot direr, that I had to take the initiative. There wasn't much batting to come, it was time to take charge.

I am not trying to oversimplify when I say that it was just one of those days when everything I tried came off. I didn't attempt anything fancy, focusing instead on my strengths. The result was spectacular. Even now, when I close my eyes, I can see several of those strokes as clearly as if I am watching a high-definition recording. Such as two or three whips off Roberts, taking the ball from off stump and wristing them wide of mid on. Such as a couple of back foot punches off Boyce that slammed into the pitch and hurtled back past him to the straight boundary.

Those two back foot strokes drove me crazy. I hadn't tried to hit the ball hard, there was no full flourish, but the ball just sped off the bat like a bullet. The effect of my workout with customized 'dumb-bells'—the Tiger-directed buckets of water that had strengthened my wrists—was still evident. As I looked around, I realized that my shock was being reflected in the faces of the fielders. Lloyd, Viv and Kalli were looking at me like *Maan, did you really hit that?* I was as surprised as them, considering I didn't know that I even possessed that kind of punch! I heard claps and 'wows' from the slip cordon. It was uninhibited stroke-making; I completely opened myself up to playing my shots, there was no hesitation. In other situations, you wonder if it is OK to play shots, and what the repercussions would be if you got out doing so. This time, I openly declared to myself that I would play my shots, come what may. I committed myself to it. I wasn't slogging—how could you even contemplate that against an attack of such ferocity?! I played true to my character, an innings to savour.

It's an innings dear to my heart for the emotions it triggered in those who were at Chepauk that day. Even to this day, more than 45 years after that knock, I get letters and phone calls from strangers just to thank me for entertaining them. Every time I go to what's now Chennai, all I hear is about 97 not out. Sometimes, I feel that's the only worthwhile innings I have played! But honestly, I feel humbled when people talk about that magical afternoon. *Wisden 100*, a series from the respected publication, has rated this the thirty-eighth best innings of all time, and the second-best non-century in July 2001. I think it's safe to say that this knock defined my career.

◆

Karsan and I put together a handy 41, gold dust under the circumstances, but we slipped deeper into the quagmire when Pras came and left without troubling the scorers—117 for eight. How much could we eke out?

Fear not, Bishan seemed to say. I had seen him make runs previously in Test cricket, but this was as demanding as it got. Nothing fazes him, though, and he played several fancy shots while keeping me entertaining company for 45 minutes. We put on 52 to stumble towards respectability; I had a smile on my lips when Chandra made his entry. He had more Test wickets than runs, of course.

That afternoon, he made the most important single of his career. In 38 minutes, he only scored one, but he was around long enough for us to add 21. It was a hilarious alliance; between us, we could and should have been run-out at least a dozen times. We always targeted a single off the fifth or the last ball of an over, no matter where the ball went, so that I could be on strike at the start of the next over. West Indies had a great fielding side—Richards, Lloyd, Boyce and Kalli. They were lightning quick and deadly accurate. And yet, from 20 yards or less, they kept missing the stumps. Time after time. Everyone believed Michael Holding was the fastest cricketer when it came to a sprint over 100 metres in his time. The way Chandra ran that day, Usain Bolt would have been hard pressed to keep up.

Chandra blames me for his dismissal which left me stranded three short of his hundred. Maybe he is right.

I was on 96 when I cut the fourth ball of an over from Roberts, one of my best square cuts. I ran casually, confident it would be a boundary. I was so happy I had got to a hundred; luckily for me, I didn't raise my bat, thus saving myself serious embarrassment. I was so bloody sure it would cross the boundary—I thought be it Boyce or his father, there was no chance of anyone stopping it. I had sauntered three-fourths of the way down the track when I saw Boyce pick up the ball. My euphoria vanished, I froze. Chandra had completed the first run and was desperate for the second, but there was no way I could have made my ground in time, so I screamed to him to stay put at the striker's end.

Chandra was now breathing heavily, the excitement getting to him. I calmed him down and told him that he should expect a short ball. 'You will survive, I am sure,' I reiterated in Kannada. He didn't. It was a beautiful ball, a leg cutter that curled away from a length. Chandra had gone right back, and while he didn't hang his bat out to dry like a typical tailender, he didn't play close to his body like a top-order batsman either. The edge was snaffled by Lloyd at first slip. As we walked back, Chandra whirled around and said, 'Because you said he would bowl short, I was expecting a bouncer. It's only because of you that I got out!' He was so miserable I didn't get my hundred. But I told him I was happy with 97 not out. 'You bowl us to victory, I will be delighted,' I told him.

We had scrambled to 190, not humongous but not trifling either. Pras took five wickets to make this a second-innings game and Aunshu made a superb 80 in the second knock. For the second time in two Tests, we were in the middle of an important stand, this time worth 93, and Karsan's industry at the end carried us to 256. A target of 255, the game ours to win with the track now generously helping the spinners.

Pras was once again unplayable, and Bishan and Chandra backed him up beautifully. Between them, they bowled all but four of the 67 overs and picked up all nine wickets to fall to the bowlers. West Indies were rolled over for 154, it was 2-2 with the decider looming.

While I walked away with the accolades, I thought the real heroes were the spinners. In a low-scoring game where 200 was topped only once, they kept their nerve and bowled us to a 100-run win—a monumental effort. Throughout the series, our batting had tottered and teetered. If it was all square going to Bombay, no one was more responsible for that scoreline than our extraordinary spin kings. It was one of those games where magic was floating in the air. For the spinners, as gifted as they were, to keep bowling West Indies out cheaply, you had to be perfect. You had to bowl to the plan, bowl to the field. The captain had to perforce be in command throughout. It's hard to find that perfect combination. But for four glorious days in Madras, we did that. After our first innings, we were in complete command—not from a scoreboard's perspective, but in the execution of our plans. It doesn't happen often, but when it does, there is no greater feeling as a cricketer and as a cricket team.

◆

We were going to finish the series the way we had started it, by playing at another new Test venue. I had played all my competitive cricket in Bombay at the Brabourne Stadium. Now, we would be playing at the brand-new Wankhede Stadium, a kilometre away and constructed in record time.

I had fond memories of Brabourne; the atmosphere was crackling and the facilities were the best in the country. The nature of the playing surface gave bowlers and batsmen an equal chance, the bounce facilitating strokeplay, keeping the faster bowlers interested and bringing the spinners into play. I would have loved for the decider to have been played at Brabourne, but Wankhede it was, on an internationally untested pitch.

Our euphoria at the Madras heroics and at Sunil's return to action dissipated not long after Lloyd called right for the first time in five Tests. In those days, the final Test of a live series was invariably a six-day affair.

West Indies turned in a powerhouse batting display, Fredericks bringing up his second hundred of the series and Kalli making 98 as the two set the base for a large total. It was with mixed feelings that I welcomed taking the catch that deprived Kalli of his hundred. We badly needed to halt the growing second-wicket threat, but Kalli had become a good friend, and had batted so well that he deserved a hundred. Bizarrely, two years later, I again held the catch in Bridgetown when Kalli fell for 93 off Mohinder Amarnath. Some friend!

Our joy at Kalli's dismissal was no more than fleeting. Lloyd, armed with that bazooka of his, destroyed us once more, unleashing such power that we had nowhere to hide. By the time he took pity on us and declared the innings, he had muscled to 242 not out, their score read an intimidating 604 for six. Our best-case scenario was to bat out time, somehow secure a draw and come away from the series with honours intact.

We started well enough despite losing Farokh for another blob. Sunil looked like he had never been away, regaling his home crowd to a sparkling display of batsmanship alongside another hometown hero, Ekki. They had the big crowd eating out of their hands during their partnership of 168; waiting for my turn to bat, I wondered how much our batting would have benefited had Sunil been available for the entire series. We had missed his class and solidity badly.

Gibbs ensured there was no fairy-tale return by getting rid of Sunil for 86, Ekki made his only century, I cashed in on good form with 95 and Aunshu continued his impressive start with 51, but we only narrowly avoided the follow-on, stymied by Gibbs's seven-wicket burst. Armed with a lead of 198, West Indies set about our bowling with ease, scoring at five an over and setting us the near-impossible target of 404. Farokh, Sunil and I were dismissed before stumps on day five; we needed lots of rain and a miracle to get out of jail. I had reached 17 and was feeling good when I received a beauty by Holder, a leg cutter that pitched on leg, jagged away, snuck past my outside edge and hit off. It was a bowler's dream, a batsman's worst nightmare.

Holder shut out all escape routes on the final day with a six-for. We collapsed in a heap for 202, well beaten by 201 runs. But unlike in England, we weren't disgraced. We had shown loads of character in bouncing back from 0-2 down to give ourselves a chance of winning the series, the youngsters had acquitted themselves with credit and personally, I had my best series with the bat.

West Indies were my kind of opposition. They gave it their all on the field, but especially that team was a great advertisement for the sport and ambassadors for their region. The relationship between the two sides was excellent, and I made dear friends for life, chief among them being Kalli. We continue to remain in touch, our bond strengthened by our devotion to Shri Sathya Sai Baba of Puttaparthi and our numerous visits to meet Baba, along with Sunil. Viv and Clive are great mates, as is Holding, who wasn't on this tour but was lying in wait for us for when we would travel to the Caribbean in 1976.

I took tremendous heart from the consistency I had shown throughout the series, and the part I had played in the wins in Calcutta and Madras. I had heard from various quarters that Vijay Merchant, the chairman of selectors, had spoken glowingly of my batting, but it wasn't until after the Bombay Test that I got to meet him.

The chairman told me, 'Well played, young man. And no shame in how you got out here. Any batsman in the world would have got out to that ball, it was a beauty.' Music to my ears. I had earned Mr Merchant's appreciation.

18

THE 'OTHER' CRICKET

I had played only two representative limited-overs games before my, and India's, One-Day International (ODI) debut in England, at Headingley in July 1974. Predictably, we lost both matches of our maiden ODI series to the hosts, whose players had greater exposure to and understanding of the needs of the fledgling format because they played plenty of such games domestically.

Less than 11 months later, we were back in England for the first men's World Cup in 1975. All this while, I had admired people who had dazzled with their skills at the football World Cup. As I had earlier mentioned, I am a big fan of Brazil, I loved their astonishing ball-control and the fluidity of their movement. All of a sudden, here I was at a World Cup myself. I wouldn't say it was the realization of a dream because I had never thought I'd be a World Cupper, but it was special to be a part of the tournament that would, for the first time, bring multiple cricketing nations on a single platform.

Unlike now when the stakes have become high and the attendant preparations have mushroomed beyond imagination, the World Cup was a relaxed affair, played over 60 overs an innings. When we landed in London, I was transported to a world of feel good and affection. Three or four teams were housed in the same hotel, allowing us to interact with each other, share stories, renew old relationships and build new bonds. I imagined that was how, but on a much grander scale, the Olympic Games might be.

We were pooled with England, East Africa and New Zealand; no one expected much from us and, truth to tell, we too expected very little of ourselves. None of us had a worthwhile taste of the overs-limited version. My experience was restricted to the two ODIs in England, and five matches in the inter-zonal Deodhar Trophy, instituted in November 1973. We were ripe for the picking, if you like.

Our inaugural World Cup face-off was against England, the hosts and one of the favourites in the eight-team draw, along with West Indies and Australia. Predictably, England feasted on our inexperience, as one would expect of a professional, well-rounded outfit well versed in the nuances of 60-over cricket.

Dennis Amiss hammered a century, Keith Fletcher made a measured 68 and then Mike Denness and Chris Old shocked us with a breezy fifth-wicket stand, at the end of which England's tally read an unbelievable 334 for three. Most teams struggled to post those many runs in an entire day's action in Test cricket; England had done so in half the time! We knew at the break that victory was out of the question. We had little idea of how to approach a chase of this magnitude, comical as it might sound now.

The general consensus at the end of our reply was that it had been a bizarre run-chase—if you could call it that—and I can't say I disagree. We comfortably batted out the 60 overs, finishing on 132 for three. I top-scored with 37, off 59 deliveries. Sunil remained unbeaten on 36, from 174 deliveries, with one four.

It's Sunil's story to tell, and he has done so many times. All I can say is that it was one of those days when nothing worked for him. Even when he tried to get out, he couldn't manage that successfully. Then again, when you have played all your life trying to protect your wicket, it's not easy to be dismissed by design. By the batsman's design, that is.

We did unto East Africa in the next match what England had done to us. We had at least played some limited-overs cricket, the Africans were a motley bunch and we brushed them aside by 10 wickets. Bishan bowled with such immaculate control that he conceded just six runs from his 12 overs. And Sunil made an unbeaten 65 as he and Farokh knocked off the 121 runs needed for victory.

It was all to play for in the last game against New Zealand, and even though we had our limitations, we scrapped all the way. In the end, it took an unbeaten century from Glenn Turner for the Kiwis to overhaul our 230 with seven deliveries to spare. Our campaign had gone just the way we had envisaged, no surprises. Fair to say we would have surprised ourselves had we somehow put it past Turner's men and made it to the knockouts.

Luckily, because the tournament only lasted two weeks, even the teams that didn't progress beyond the first stage were invited to stay back till the final. We were thus witness to some brilliant cricket in the knockout games, not least in the final. What a feast that was, being able to watch the title match, with the two strongest teams in the fray—West Indies and Australia—going toe to toe. It was such a fabulous contest, one team nosing ahead and the other fighting back to regain lost ground, until Lloyd's men trooped home winners by 17 runs.

The skipper himself dominated the final with a spectacular 102, full of muscular strokes that only he could conjure. Watching him take the fight to Australia's Dennis Lillee and Jeff Thomson (Thommo) was electrifying, as was witnessing Viv's brilliance in the field. Lillee and Thommo threatened to ruin the West Indian party by adding 41 for the last wicket, but they ran out of steam against a relentless, pace-heavy attack.

As an advertisement for the limited-overs format, the final was just what the doctor had ordered. The World Cup was a huge success, even though we had only played a bit part. Personally, I was delighted to have been a slice of history.

◆

Four years later, in 1979, with still no more than a handful of games under our belt, we landed in England for the second edition of the World Cup. This was an unmitigated disaster as we ended up losing to New Zealand, West Indies and even Sri Lanka, not a Test-playing nation then. It was a chastening experience, but there was no great disappointment because, for some reason, many of us felt one-day cricket wasn't a part of the mainstream.

Paradoxically, it was during our darkest hour that I fashioned my best limited-overs innings. Unsurprisingly, it was against West Indies in Birmingham, on a typically cold, overcast, gloomy English morning. The pace attack was populated by Andy Roberts, Michael Holding, Joel Garner, Colin Croft and Collis King. If you looked for relief, it lay only at the non-striker's end, or in the dressing room.

We were in trouble right from the off, with Holding doing most of the early damage. For perhaps the only time in my limited-overs career—25 ODIs out of a total of 59 List-A games —I felt the same intensity as in a Test match. That was entirely due to the quality of the attack; there wasn't a moment's respite, the examination was long, thorough and searching. You had to be on top of your game to come out unscathed, and I enjoyed every one of the 134 deliveries I faced while making 75, my highest ODI score.

By today's standards, it was a laborious innings, strikerate 55.97, but in an innings where the next highest contribution came from extras (16), I cherished keeping the celebrated attack at bay for more than two and a half hours. Mohinder Amarnath keeps referring to it as the best knock he has seen, and I consider it high praise, given how masterful he was against quality pace, especially on the twin tours of Pakistan and the West Indies in 1982-83.

To be brutally honest, I didn't enjoy playing one-day cricket. I suppose much of that stemmed from the fact that we had been brought up on days cricket, and even when we were introduced to over restrictions, we didn't play this format with any regularity. I never felt the seriousness of the format, so I almost went through the motions. It didn't touch an emotional chord in me like Test cricket did, and because I always felt something was missing, I couldn't concentrate or give my 100 per cent to every game. Don't get me wrong, I didn't go out to fail or to try fancy strokes. I didn't fool around with my batting. But maybe subconsciously, I didn't believe it was the *real* deal, so it was difficult for me to gear myself up for battle like I did at a Test match.

That doesn't mean I am not a fan of 50-over cricket, though. How would I have adapted if I were an active player now? Quite reasonably, I would like to think, because I would have had no choice. Today, 50-over and T20 cricket are as much a part of the sport's landscape as the traditional version is, so if you aspire to play across formats, you can't afford to be blasé like I was 40 years ago. That's a no-brainer.

We had at least one win to take back home four years previously, but this time around, we didn't even have the crumbs. Despite our slightly enhanced exposure to this version, we were woefully inadequate at the global level. We weren't too despondent, however. In our minds, one-day cricket was a distraction, nothing more.

We stayed back in England at the end of the World Cup for a Test series, and it was then that I met Richie Benaud for the first time. Having retired after a long and illustrious playing career, the former Australian captain had established himself as a wonderful commentator and analyst, much loved and respected. I had been hoping to meet him in Australia during the 1977–78 tour, but our paths didn't cross, though whenever possible, I listened with rapt attention as he shared his wisdom on television.

The first Test was in Birmingham, a match we lost by an innings; I made half-centuries in both knocks. Some of us would gather around the television in the evening to watch the highlights. To my great annoyance, I heard Benaud constantly refer to me as 'Vishnawath'. Each time he pronounced my name wrongly, my irritation grew, but what could I do?

One evening, as we left the dressing room to board our coach for the hotel, we ran into Benaud. Sunil knew him and introduced me, saying, 'This is Vishy'. Benaud smiled sweetly and I returned the compliment, adding, 'Nice to meet you, Mr Bednau'.

'My name is not Bednau, it's Benaud,' he said, with feeling.

'And I am Vishwanath, not Vishnawath,' I countered, in kind.

I boarded the coach and sat in my seat when, within seconds, Benaud walked in and started scanning the faces. When he spotted me, he strode forward with a big smile and said, 'Beauty, that was brilliant, I like you!'

◆

It's amazing how the same tournament that had embarrassed us was to take Indian cricket to glorious heights four years later. I'd have loved to be a part of the 1983 World Cup as well, but I had been dropped from the Indian team after the tour of Pakistan. Consequently, I missed the tournament that galvanized the Indian limited-overs revolution, under the stewardship of the extraordinary Kapil Dev.

Just like our series wins in the Caribbean and England in 1971 had given Test cricket the fillip it needed in our country, the unexpected triumph at the World Cup in 1983 was the turning point in India's evolution as a limited-overs force. For the first time, the knockout games of the tournament were being telecast live in India, and as the millions of fans breathlessly watched their heroes go all the way, it sparked an interest that is alive and kicking in every corner of the country to this date.

India mounted a remarkable campaign after entering the tournament as 66-1 outsiders.[4] Even though they had beaten West Indies for the first time a few months previously in Berbice, I am not sure many members of the 14-man squad believed they could make an impact at the World Cup. Luckily, there was one man who believed; who believed that no peak was insurmountable; who believed that impossible was a word that only existed in the dictionary; who believed in himself, and his band of warriors. Kapil's belief triumphed in the end, the mercurial captain at the forefront of a fairy-tale run with a dream ending.

While I wasn't a part of the squad, I was in England, nevertheless. At the end of India's run, whenever that was, a bunch of us including many in the World Cup side were to travel to the United States (US) to play a series of matches. Since England was the midway point, I decided I would fly out to watch all of India's matches instead of joining the team at the last minute. It turned out to be one of the best decisions of my life.

India served notice in their very first game by defeating the two-time defending champions, West Indies, reiterating that their recent win in the Caribbean was no flash in the pan. The match that ignited their collective fire, however, came against Zimbabwe, in unfashionable Tunbridge Wells. It was a match that they had to win to keep their prospects alive.

Within 45 minutes, I watched in horror as there was a beeline for the pavilion. India slumped to nine for four, then 17 for five. I was hoping I was in the middle of a bad dream and that I would wake up to see the ball flowing sweetly off the broad blades of our batsmen.

Zimbabwe had scythed through the top-order but hadn't bargained for the brilliance of the captain. There were no television cameras around due to prioritization protocols at the British Broadcasting Corporation

---

[4]The bookmakers had given India the unflattering odds of 66 to 1 to win the title. No one realistically thought India would be genuine contenders for the title.

(BBC), so there is no footage of that knock, but I can play that innings over and over again in my head whenever I feel like. It has to be one of the two greatest knocks in one-day history, on par with Viv's unbeaten 189 against England in May 1984. Then again, Viv was a pure batsman—he did bowl off spin, agreed—whereas Kapil was a genuine all-rounder. And he made 175 not out of the finest in the most trying circumstances, with elimination looming large and the team in a deep hole.

I was transfixed as Kapil rebuilt the innings in Roger Binny's company. Kapil was careful, but not tentative. He focussed on occupation of the crease, blunting the bowling and gently ticking the board over. But when he decided to hit the ball, he did so with utmost confidence. It was clean, beautiful ball striking; there was no hesitation when he lifted the ball over the infield or deposited it into the stands. Zimbabwe hoped Kapil would make a mistake sooner than later, India prayed the entertainment would last the duration of the innings. As it were, India's prayers were answered. Kapil switched gears effortlessly towards the end, smiting 16 fours and six sixes in his 138-ball epic. With support from Roger, Madan and Kiri, he lifted India to 266 for eight. That was enough to secure a 31-run win and energize the team. Kapil's belief was beginning to rub off on his men.

◆

Whether by design or by accident, India had the perfect bowling attack for the conditions. Kapil was the only quick bowler, but Roger, Madan, Balwinder Sandhu and Mohinder were accomplished swing bowlers who capitalized superbly on the assistance offered by the atmosphere. The batting was a good mix of experience and dashing youth, with the dynamic Kris Srikkanth, the dour Yashpal Sharma and the debonair Sandeep Patil holding fort.

India's reward for making it to the semi-final for the first time was a showdown against England. Contrary to expectations, India trooped out commanding winners, with the bowlers leading the way again. England was rolled over for 213, and Sandeep Patil fired the team home with a bruising half-century. Should the country dare to dream now? Even with the mighty West Indies up against them, in the 25 June final at Lord's?

I was fortunate enough to watch the final from the dressing room, thanks to the generosity and thoughtfulness of Kapil and P. R. Man Singh, the team manager. I had come to the ground, along with the rest of the team in the same coach, and I could see how much it meant to India's passionate fans to see their team in the final. Victory would drive them to delirium; that's when it struck me that if this run could impact the Indian diaspora overseas so much, it would catalyse a seismic change back home in the way the one-day game was viewed. As I looked around me, I sensed that my former colleagues who were gearing up for the biggest day of their lives shared a similar sentiment.

There are dreamers, and then there are doers. The 11 men in the final belonged to the latter category; if at the halfway stage, the 10 others didn't feel they were in with a shout of pulling off a victory, they were converts by the time Kapil finished with his pep talk.

India's 183 wasn't going to seriously challenge West Indies. That was the majority opinion, and I must confess I too was in that vast majority. Never have I felt more proud or happier to have been proved wrong.

During the break, Kapil pointed out to his players that India had put the runs on the board, it was up to West Indies to go and get them now. 'We will fight till the end,' he proclaimed. India's hopes ratcheted up when Sandhu cleaned up Gordon Greenidge with a beauty, until Viv took the wind out of their sails like only he can. By then, he was an acknowledged world-beater, and threatened to single-handedly dismantle India's best-laid plans. He was batting beautifully, the ball making a sweet—or sickening—sound as it screamed off his bat. It seemed as if Viv was intent on getting the job done in 35 overs.

Heads were dropping and shoulders were drooping on the park, but the fire shone through in one pair of eyes. And when Viv offered a quarter of a chance with that pull off Madan, those eyes remained steadfast on the ball as Kapil embarked on a run from mid wicket that only ended when he gobbled up the ball in his giant hands, not far from the boundary. To me, it was the fielding equivalent of his 175 not out, magnified by the occasion and the batsman he had accounted for. It's a run I can summon any time I want to. Lithe, fast, focussed and iconic.

There was still work to be done, but the balance of power seemed to transfer perceptibly from that point. Lloyd, Larry Gomes and Faoud Bacchus came and went in a jiffy, and even though Jeff Dujon and Malcolm Marshall offered staunch resistance, they couldn't deny India their tryst with destiny. My joy knew no bounds. I could only imagine what Kapil and his boys must be experiencing at that moment.

It was a super team effort all the way through, and Kapil handled the team beautifully from the word go, even though he wasn't a very experienced captain at the time. He was the kind of cricketer who relished leading from the front, and who knew not what it was to give up. That manifested itself in the way he approached the game.

For the record, the cricket tour of the US that had taken me early to England in the first place was cancelled because Mrs Indira Gandhi, the then Indian prime minister, wanted to felicitate the World Cup-winning team in its entirety. It was a great gesture that reiterated the significance of the occasion; as for me, cricket or no cricket, I went ahead with my plans, enjoying myself in the US.

◆

Kapil is one of the most naturally gifted cricketers I have seen in my association with the sport. He descended on Indian cricket like a breath of fresh air with God-given athleticism, searing pace and a beautiful outswinger that tested the most accomplished of right-hand batsmen.

Everyone felt he should have been on the flight to Australia in 1977–78 under Bishan. I am convinced it would have been the perfect start to his international career, bowling on pitches with pace and bounce against an inexperienced Australian batting line-up. By then, I had played against him a couple of times, and he was by a distance the fastest Indian I had encountered. I dare say the result of that series (India went down 2-3) would have been radically different had he been with us.

You can't keep a player of his calibre down for too long, and it came as no surprise when he was picked for the tour of Pakistan in late 1978; even on placid surfaces, he harried and hustled Pakistan's high-class batting line-up with his pace and movement. His speed through the air alone meant he brooked careful watching. That he could swing the ball late at that pace made him a potent threat. He had a lovely, rhythmic run-up and got classically side-on at the time of delivery, turning even the coaching manuals green with envy.

Even at that early stage, we all knew he would go on to achieve great things, but none of us had bargained for the peaks he would scale. That Pakistan tour offered the first, early glimpse of a great cricketer in the making, testified by the fact that his bowling skills didn't overshadow his batting. A wonderful striker of the cricket ball, he never forsook his aggression, yet finished with upwards of 5,000 Test runs.

There had been all-rounders of various skill levels in my time—Abid, Ekki and Madan, to name a few—but Kapil was good enough to hold his place in the team either as a bowler alone or a batsman alone. He was cavalier, dashing and high-risk, but also exhilarating, entertaining and effective. And he stayed that way till he played the last of his 131 Tests, aged 35. I am not being anything but sincere when I say I feel really privileged to have played alongside two of the greatest cricketers of all time—a batsman as accomplished as Sunil, and easily the most versatile all-rounder of my time, Kapil.

◆

Apart from his batting and bowling, Kapil was also one of the finest fielders of his generation. In that regard, he was way ahead of his times. Now, of course, with the white-ball formats here to stay and necessitating cricketers to leave no stone unturned, fielding standards have improved beyond recognition. Especially since the advent of T20 cricket a decade and a half back, cricket has moved from sheer skills to a high level of creativity and inventiveness. I enjoy the ebbs and flows of T20 cricket, the rapidity with which matches change course, but occasionally, I do feel that I am not actually watching cricket.

Call me old-fashioned, because that's what I am, but give me a lovely cover drive or a cracking punch down the ground off the back foot ahead of going down on one knee and scooping the ball over the wicketkeeper's head. I admire the courage of batsmen who attempt such strokes, but when I see a classicist not compromising on aesthetics in a 20-over game, it stirs wonderful emotions in me. I revel in the knowledge that there still are players who maintain the technicality of the game, and yet are able to adapt to the demands of this unforgiving format.

The exponential growth of the 20-over game has triggered an unqualified improvement in running between the wickets, and especially in fielding. Over the last several years, efforts by boundary riders involving tossing the ball up in the air, stepping out of the field of play and then coming back in to nonchalantly pouch the offering have become the norm rather than the exception. Relay fielding or catching is a wonderful concept that symbolizes teamwork and unity of purpose.

Diving stops have become commonplace now, which for some reason takes me back to our days when diving was restricted to the swimming pool. With the nature of the outfields being what they were, we could ill afford to dive; any such attempt was likely to be the last slice of action on a cricket ground, with the guarantee of injuries ranging from flaky skin to broken bones.

I'd like to think we didn't need to dive, of course. That we had the anticipation and the alacrity to get to the ball without having to throw ourselves around! Having been brought up on gravelly outfields in India, there was no switch which would encourage us to slide and dive when we played on more forgiving outfields.

When I say we couldn't afford to dive those days, I do mean it literally, too. On our first few tours of England, our daily allowance was two pound sterling, and that included what we spent on laundry as well. A dive translated to a green patch on our trousers, and a spell in the washing machine. That also meant going without one, sometimes two meals.

I shared a cricket field with some truly outstanding all-round fielders, among them Ekki, Ramnath Parkar and Brijesh. I haven't seen anyone cover angles and anticipate in the covers and extra cover better than Ramnath. As importantly, he was excellent at throwing down stumps; on an average, he scored direct hits seven times out of 10 attempts, a more than acceptable strikerate. Brijesh chased down balls like a hare, among the quickest I have seen across the turf. And Wadekar and Venkat were brilliant close-in catchers.

But there was no one to match Kapil, and Tiger before him. I have seen Tiger appear disinterested while fielding at cover or mid off, allowing batsmen to coast to easy singles after playing the ball in his direction.

He would do it a couple of times, lulling the batsman into a false sense of security and comfort, before pouncing on the ball and flattening the stumps in one quick motion. His power-packed throws from 40–50 yards away sent wicketkeepers into panic mode even though they were wearing protective gloves. And I believe in domestic cricket—two or three fielders generally backed up his throw, just to be on the safe side.

I had seen the best of Tiger in the infield, but Ted Dexter stunned me by waxing eloquent about his prowess as a close-in catcher. Dexter had come to Bengaluru for an India-England Test, and as we rolled back the clock at the M. Chinnaswamy Stadium's Diamond Box, the conversation veered to fielding, and inevitably to Tiger, who Dexter had captained at Sussex. I spoke enthusiastically about Tiger in the covers when Dexter perked up and said, 'Covers? Close-in, he is the most brilliant fielder I have come across.'

That was news to me. Dexter wasn't to be taken lightly, though I had never seen Tiger in a catching position. 'Naturally, after his accident, he didn't field in the inner cordon,' Dexter explained, correctly interpreting my perplexity. 'But in his early days, he held amazing catches at slip and leg slip.'

I should have known. Like Kapil, Tiger was a born sportsperson, an excellent polo player and a crack cueist with a penchant for snooker. For all his brilliance. I never saw him work more than cursorily on his fielding. Then again, when you are Tiger, you don't need to, do you?

19

AT HOME IN RECORD CHASE

We went straight off the drawn three-Test series in New Zealand to the Caribbean for a four-match showdown in March–April 1976, with happy memories of our historic last outing.

West Indies had just been pummelled 5-1 in Australia, and even though they boasted Roberts and Holding, we believed we had what it took to extend their recent poor run. How wrong we were proved in the very first Test.

The two quicks took nine wickets between them, and Viv and Lloyd made hundreds. We were crushed inside three days by an innings at the Kensington Oval in Bridgetown, the worst possible start to our campaign, our confidence hitting rock-bottom.

If there was any consolation, it was that we couldn't do worse. And, that the next Test would be at the Queen's Park Oval, in Port of Spain.

The Trinidad and Tobago capital was a home away from home for us. There has always been a significant Indian presence there, and we had struck up strong friendships from five years previously. Indian families would turn up in large numbers to the biggest ground in the Caribbean at the time, both in dimension and capacity. As importantly as their support, they brought home-cooked lunch on match days, going out of their way to make us feel comfortable. Our epochal win on the last tour had come at this venue on Sunil's memorable debut, so we were determined to dig into pleasant memories and shed the disappointment of Bridgetown.

It helped too that of all the surfaces in the Caribbean, this was the one that assisted our spinners the most. Chandra and Bishan capitalized on the conditions to pack West Indies off for 241 in the first innings and, after we declared at 402 for five with centuries from Sunil and Brijesh, reduced them to 215 for eight when the game was called off. The score card showed a draw, but we had had the better of the exchanges and were in a far better frame of mind as we emplaned for Georgetown, the Guyanese capital, for the next leg—a first-class match to be graced by Lance Gibbs, who had ruled himself out of the Test series, followed by the third Test.

As fate would have it, it bucketed down in Georgetown, and the Bourda Oval looked more like a lake than a cricket ground in the lead-up to the practice game. With more rain forecast, it was clear that any play in the Test would, at best, be minimal. After hasty deliberations, it was decided to move the third Test out of Georgetown, back to Port of Spain.

◆

As we boarded the aircraft, I could sense the joy and excitement at the unexpected bonus of playing a second successive Test at the Queen's Park Oval. The backing of the Indian population in Port of Spain, and our record at the ground, convinced us that we could pull off something special. The conviction wavered for four days. Then came deliverance.

The Port of Spain pitch started off as a batting beauty, then gradually changed character and became a spinner's ally, so it was imperative to win the toss. Bishan called wrong, so West Indies had the best batting conditions of the game to work with. Our bowlers did brilliantly to restrict them to 359, despite a third successive century by Viv.

Like the rest of his mates, Viv had had a torrid time in Australia against Lillee and Thommo, but back at home, he feasted on our bowling. In this innings, he was unstoppable, fusing aggression with consistency and dictating terms to our wonderful spinners. His footwork was a delight to watch and his strokeplay spectacularly destructive. We didn't seem to have any answers until, when he reached 177, he took mercy and holed out.

We didn't have a great time with the bat. Several of us got off to starts but only Madan and I reached the 40s. Holding grabbed six and we ended up conceding a significant lead of 131. With the pitch gradually wearing and three spinners in their midst, we were up against it.

Lloydy wanted to seal the series then and there, so he declared at 271 for six immediately after Kalli got to three-figures, midway through day four. West Indies had over four sessions to bowl us out, we had to survive more than eight hours to keep the series alive going to Jamaica.

Our target was 403, pretty much out of reach. In 774 Tests—interestingly, the number of runs Sunil made in his maiden series—till that point, only once had a team chased down 400-plus successfully, and that was Don Bradman's 'The Invincibles' against England in Leeds in 1948. Few gave us a chance to draw abreast of the Aussies; truth to tell, even we didn't think about victory when Sunil and Aunshu walked out to begin our fourth innings.

Our first objective was to secure the Test, ensure we batted time and didn't fall 0-2 behind. West Indies had the advantage of a mountain of runs in the bank, and three spinners to exploit the pitch—left-armer Raphick Jumadeen, offie Albert Padmore and the leggie, Imtiaz Ali. But to get to them, we first had to negotiate Holding and Bernard Julien. Roberts had sought time off after the second Test to rest body and mind, so we had at least one less threat to worry about.

The message from the captain was clear to our two openers: play your natural game, hang in there, try to save the game. Sunil and Aunshu took Bishan's words to heart and kept Holding and Julien at bay while adding 69, when Jumadeen effected the breakthrough. Even though we lost Aunshu, we took heart from the solid start. There was a lot of work ahead of us, but we had taken one little step in our quest for safety.

Mohinder was Sunil's ally during an excellent second-wicket stand that yielded more than 100. By then, it was accepted by everyone—the Indian and West Indian teams, the fans at the ground, the cricket world—that if Sunil played in Port of Spain, he would get a hundred. True to type, he breezed to 102, a superb four-hour knock with Mohinder largely an admiring but passive ally during their lovely association.

Uncharacteristically, Sunil was dismissed reasonably early on the final morning soon after getting his hundred, caught behind off Jumadeen. Two down for 177, more than five hours left, eight wickets in hand. Dry land didn't seem that far away, though we couldn't afford any slip-ups.

Jimmy and I made sure we avoided all banana skins (in other

words, potential slip-ups) for the next three hours. The ball was turning, sure, but it was true turn, the bounce was predictable. It wasn't as if one ball was shooting through and the other taking off alarmingly. I don't mean to disparage their fine spinners, but we had faced far more threatening members of their ilk on worse surfaces in domestic cricket. Our game was tailored to tackle these conditions, the bowlers' steadiness notwithstanding. They were consistent in their disciplines but didn't trouble us too much, and Jimmy and I carried on unflustered, every over survived a nail in West Indian aspirations of victory.

The rate of scoring, though, was not very high. The ball became softer and softer, and while we had dissipated some of the pressure by occupying the crease, we hadn't transferred any on to the opposition because the boundaries would simply not come. Lloydy was frustrated at the lack of wickets, and by three successive meaningful partnerships. Even though he still had a fair few runs to play with, he chose not to go for the kill, refraining from unleashing Holding and Julien with the second new ball because this fraying, old ball was making it impossible for us to get a move on.

Ultimately, the umpires had to step in and get the ball changed. By now, it was coming apart at the seams, and there was no chance of a replacement ball, so Lloydy had no option but to accept a shiny new cherry. This was to be a key influencer.

The new ball can lead to one of two things: a rush of wickets or a torrent of runs. We were 223 for two when Holding and Julien returned to the bowling crease. Jimmy had been batting for a very long time, I had spent more than two hours, so we were well set and easily negotiated what could have been a tricky passage. I got a few fours off Holding, Jimmy began to play a few more strokes and within eight overs, we made 37 runs and had wrested the initiative out of nowhere.

A cover drive after tea took me to my first overseas hundred, as good a feeling as any. By now, the balance had clearly shifted. Victory was no longer in the realms of the impossible, we needed less than 100 runs in 100-odd minutes and had eight wickets in hand. Jimmy and I had strung together 159, and I could see West Indian shoulders drooping, Lloydy's frustration slowly giving way to something close to panic.

I threw them a lifeline by getting myself run-out. If memory serves me right, I played to short mid wicket and set off for a single. Jimmy sent me back, but I didn't make it in time to beat the direct hit from one of Greenidge or Kalli. I was enraged at myself; I should have stayed on and got the job done. Sure, 112 was all nice and good, but I was now exposing a new batsman. We required 67 more for the unlikeliest of victories, in a little over an hour. So much could happen...

What happened, was a brilliant batting display by Brijesh. His confidence was at an all-time high after his 115 not out in the previous Test, and he batted as if he was resuming from that score, not starting a new innings from zero. He kept peppering the boundary while Jimmy opened up as well, knowing that 65 in the last hour with seven wickets standing wasn't too daunting even in 1976. A fourth straight handy partnership got us to within 11 runs of victory when, like me, Jimmy too was run-out. That was the only way West Indies could have ended his 440-minute vigil. There was no hundred for him, much as he deserved it, but as he smiled all the way back to the pavilion, he knew that we were nearly there.

Brijesh sent us into delirium by pulling Jumadeen to the boundary to power us over the line. As he sank into Madan's arms, we were beside ourselves. We had reached 406 for four, then the highest successful chase in Test history. We were in the same rarified space hitherto occupied only by Bradman's Class of 48. Wow! Squaring the series seemed almost incidental, such was the scale of our monumental accomplishment.

I didn't, but I am sure some of my friends might have thought back to Lord's, and 42 all out, and viewed this as redemption. We had made Indian history then. Now, we had rewritten world history in cricket, this was sweet history. To win so convincingly after needing to do so much for so long was a terrific pointer to our skills, character and temperament. One of my finest Test wins, a result I will cherish forever, like all those who were a part of that match will.

Champagne and spirits of other variety flowed in the dressing room, followed by a visit to the Indian High Commission straight off the ground for more festivities and celebrations. Several of the prominent members of the Indian community who had helped us out with food and who had created a homely atmosphere were in attendance, and the joy on their faces humbled us. We were happy to have given them a reason to smile, this one was as much their victory as it was ours. After all it is they, the fans, who make us.

Little did we know at the time that we had sowed the seeds of a revolution in West Indian cricket. We had no idea our successful chase would reshape Test history.

◆

Lloydy was feeling the heat. His captaincy was already under a cloud after the rout in Australia. The stunning defeat after failing to defend 400 in the final innings of a home Test heaped more pressure. He had given his spinners a dressing down after the game. He also decided that he wouldn't rely on spin again. His mode of attack would revolve around a battery of four pace bowlers for all conditions, against all opposition. No more teasing and tormenting batsmen, just terrorizing and blasting them out. And just like that, out of the ruins of the Queen's Park Oval humiliation, surfaced the legacy of West Indian cricket, a legacy that saw the climb to prominence of such luminaries as Holding and Roberts, Croft and Garner, Marshall and Bishop, Walsh and Ambrose.

We expected a backlash at Sabina Park in the final Test, on the hardest, paciest, bounciest strip in all Caribbean. But not even in our wildest, most terrorizing nightmares, did we envisage what lay ahead.

Out went Padmore and Ali, in came Wayne Daniel on debut and Vanburn Holder. The first West Indies pace quartet had taken shape, and we were the sacrificial lambs as Lloydy's quest for revenge and vindication reached unprecedented levels. To make matters worse, there was a 'ridge' on the pitch just short of a good length, the preferred area of operation for the West Indian pacers.

We seemed to have weathered the storm on being put in, with Sunil and Aunshu kicking on from the previous Test. Despite repeated intimidation, they refused to cow down. And I don't use the word 'intimidation' lightly.

Within a matter of minutes, they were subjected to a barrage of bouncers and beamers from Holding and Daniel. Admittedly, there were no restrictions on bouncers at the time, but to have four or five balls an over directed at your throat and head was definitely not the norm. Protection was basic, we had no helmets. All Sunil and Aunshu took with them was courage and guts, and no little skill.

Those traits served them wonderfully during their stand of 136. At one point, after the bouncer-bouncer-bouncer-bouncer-beamer routine, Sunil put his bat down and raised his arms in silent protest, but umpires Douglas Sang Hue and Ralph Gosein were unmoved. In the dressing room, there was a growing sense of apprehension and anger; apprehension at the imminent danger our openers were in, anger at the apathy of the gentlemen tasked with running the game. This free-for-all was unacceptable, lives were on the line.

Uncomplainingly, though, Aunshu and Jimmy batted on after Sunil's dismissal for 66, steering us to 175 for one on a first day prematurely halted by bad light. The top three had been outstanding in the face of extreme provocation, showing character and bravery beyond the call of duty. Aunshu sported numerous bruises on his body proudly, like a badge of honour, seeking to make light of pain with his inimitable humour.

If day one had been a searching examination, day two descended into absolute chaos and disarray. Armed with the second new ball, Holding produced a snorter that homed in on Jimmy's throat. He put his hands in front of his face in self-defence, the ball lobbed off the blade and backward short leg pouched the skier.

Aunshu was playing as well as possible under the circumstances, not once flinching, always getting behind the line of the ball, riding the blows, ticking off the runs slowly. He greeted me with a wry smile and a 'good luck'. I needed that luck straightaway.

I have little memory of sighting the first ball I received from Holding. I saw the round little orb leave his right hand, but by the time it hit the ridge just short of good length, it had become a blur. It took off and came straight for my head. Like a rabbit transfixed by headlights, I stood frozen. At the last instant, I closed my eyes and lifted my hands. The ball thudded into my gloves, and when I turned back, I first heard and then saw it smack into the sightscreen after having flown over Deryck Murray's head.

The sightscreen wasn't made of cloth, it was a brick wall painted white. The ball made a fearful 'thwack' as it hammered into the wall, and flew almost all the way back to Murray. The wicketkeeper nonchalantly picked it up and tossed it to a fielder, while my heart beat furiously against my chest, my throat parched, my lips dry.

Nearly five years later, I received a similar delivery from Len Pascoe in the MCG Test of 1981. The ball was even shorter, kept following me and brushed my gloves as it sailed over Marsh. That was the quickest ball I have faced, but I saw it all the way. I saw the red sphere then, not a blur. But this, this was the nastiest, most dangerous delivery of my career.

At the end of the over, I asked Aunshu, 'Did you see that ball? Did you notice how it took off? I didn't even see it.'

Aunshu dead-panned, 'Vishy, you have faced only one ball this innings. What do you think I have been doing since yesterday?'

There was an eeriness to the atmosphere, as if something untoward was about to happen. It did. And again. And again.

I got another unplayable ball from Holding, again smacked flush on my right glove. This time, it nestled in the hands of leg slip, and I made the long walk back, out for eight. Halfway through, I felt unbearable pain, like someone was crushing my fingers. I stopped dead in my tracks and managed to take off my right glove. Oh horror, where was my middle finger now?

With mounting trepidation, I searched for the missing digit inside the glove. Had it detached itself from my hand and found a new home? No, it hadn't. So where was it?

I scrutinized the empty space more carefully, and discovered to my absolute terror that the finger had retreated inside my hand. I mean, it had been forced back, into my palm. I have never felt more alone, more helpless, the mind-numbing pain making me dizzy and light-headed. I somehow dragged myself off towards the dressing room, thinking, what if it had been my leg? What if it had been my head?

I slumped into a chair, still in a daze, when P. Krishnamurthy, our twelfth man, sidled up. I raised my right hand in his direction, and he said, 'Don't worry, Vishy, I know what to do.' He reached in and pulled my finger out, after which the pain reduced considerably. But clearly, the finger was shattered.

As I was being taken to the hospital, Aunshu was struck on his left ear by Holding and went down in a heap. He was unconscious for a long time, and we prayed hard for him. Even today, he says that from time to time, he can't hear in his left ear. God forbid, had the ball struck him a couple of inches higher, somewhere near his temple...

Aunshu and I were soon joined in the infirmary by Brijesh, who had been struck on his mouth by a short ball from Holder and needed three stitches on his upper lip. Between them, Holding and Holder had sent three of us to hospital, ripped the heart out of our batting. We should have been in the same dressing room, on the same ground. Yet, here we were, practically lying in the same hospital bed. Brijesh and I attempted some dark humour, but soon gave up.

Bishan declared at 306 for six in our first innings when Venkat was dismissed, determined that neither Chandra, nor he would bat. West Indies replied with 391—Viv made 'only' 64— and even though we were just 85 behind, that didn't mean anything with three of us ruled out. Jimmy batted bravely to smash a counter-attacking 60, but for the second time in the match, Venkat's was the last Indian wicket to fall. We were 97 for five, ahead by 12, with Bishan and Chandra nursing finger injuries and not in a position to bat either. But with five people unable to bat, we were also 97 all out.

West Indies knocked off the runs easily to win the match and the series, but we felt there was a hollow ring to it. We did question the West Indian tactics, but more than that, we were angered by the umpires allowing them to do what they wanted. They were supposed to ensure fair play and ensure that the game was played in the right spirit. I am afraid they did neither in this instance.

Saying that, the relationship between the teams didn't change a huge deal, there was no animosity between players even when this was transpiring. Whatever happened on the field was left behind when we ran into each other in the evenings. We bore them no grudge, and they didn't feel they had come too hard at us, though I did believe they went overboard.

It was a terrible way to end an otherwise enjoyable tour. We had gone from the high of a world record chase to finishing the series with only six fit men in a fortnight. Fortunately, our next Test was seven months away, I'd be fit to resume battle. The war, the Bloodbath at Sabina Park, was behind me.

20

ROMANCE REKINDLED

In the eight years since my Test debut, we had played England home and away more than once each. We had travelled to the Caribbean and New Zealand and hosted them too. But for some reason, we didn't run into Australia post 1969. All that was to change towards the end of 1977.

To say I was excited when it was announced that we would be travelling to Australia for a five-Test series would be a gross understatement. From my formative years, I had enjoyed listening to the exploits of their legends, I admired the way they played the game, I liked their history. Sir Don Bradman, the greatest batsman of all time, was from Australia. So was my hero, Neil Harvey.

We knew this would be a challenge like no other. None of the batsmen in our side had played in Australia previously, but our spinners had been there earlier and enlightened us on the extra bounce which characterized surfaces Down Under. In England and New Zealand, you had to watch out for swing; in Australia, it was more seam and bounce, aspects of the game I hadn't encountered too often in the past.

That several of Australia's top players were unavailable did little to dampen my enthusiasm. Agreed, without the Chappell brothers, Doug Walters, Dennis Lillee and Rod Marsh, they were a depleted side short on experience, but there has never been a dearth of talent in Australia despite a relatively small talent pool to choose from. We knew no matter which 11 men took the field sporting the Baggy Green, we would have a fight on our hands.

One of the big points of interest was who would lead them. Australia had a great record at home and the establishment, at loggerheads with Kerry Packer's World Series Cricket which had weaned away the superstars, was determined to ensure that didn't change. They turned to old warhorse Bob Simpson; to no one's surprise, the 41-year-old readily agreed to return to international cricket, even though he hadn't played at that level for nearly a decade.

Ahead of the tour, we had our first full-fledged fitness camp under Major Tandon in Chennai, as I have alluded to previously. Already confident of our skills, we were further buoyed by physical conditioning and genuinely believed that we could become the first Indian team to win a Test series in Australia.

Our conviction stemmed not merely from Australia's inexperience. We were a settled and established side, and even though the batting group hadn't played in Australia yet, we boasted a wealth of experience in the shape of Sunil, Mohinder, Ashok Mankad, Brijesh and myself, with the gifted Dilip Vengsarkar lending additional class. We might not have had crack fast bowlers, but Pras had shown 10 years back that spinners could feed off the extra bounce by finishing as the highest wicket-taker across both teams.

I had started my own little preparations once the tour was formalized. These revolved largely around getting used to the extra bounce. Pras and Chandra reassured me that the bounce would be consistent, which brought a twinkle to my eyes because as a stroke-maker, I wanted the ball to come on to the bat at a good height. Depending on the lengths and therefore the positions one got into, you could play forcefully off both the back and the front foot. Even though the outfields were massive, there was value for strokes; in any case, working with Major Tandon had boosted our endurance and speed, and we knew we could run threes and fours on a regular basis if need be.

To adjust to the additional bounce, I faced up to tennis balls soaked in water, and hurled at me at a short of length from 15–17 yards. The idea was to get in line and either play it off the back foot or let the ball sail by. My routine was three-fold: sway out of the way, drop the ball down at my feet with soft hands, or play horizontal-bat shots square on the off or legside, depending on the line. For obvious reasons, I didn't have to practise ducking under the ball a great deal!

For about a month prior to our departure for Australia, I played more than 100 such balls a day without fail. As it is, my back foot play had been honed by the circumstances as they existed. All our league fixtures were on matting surfaces, as were all Ranji Trophy games in Karnataka outside of Bangalore. From the very beginning, that facilitated my back foot play. The wet tennis-ball workout augmented that experience, and when we emplaned for Australia, I felt I was as well prepared as could be expected.

I am of the opinion that generally, back foot players are a little more attacking than those with a penchant for committing to the front foot. When you go back, you have that extra fraction of a second to adjust; by the same token, when you play forward, you are trying to get as close to the pitch of the ball as you can, allowing you to play aggressively or defensively secure in the knowledge that you have covered for potential swing. In the end, it all depends on how quickly your feet are moving and how close you get to the ball. It's up to each individual to make that adjustment, first in your mind and then with your hands and feet.

I also didn't change my style depending on where I played. Of course, you must make minor modifications to your technique if you aspire to succeed, but even in England, for instance, I didn't play forward blindly to counter the swing. Playing off the back foot was equally productive, particularly because the ball often swung late and when you stayed back, you could address it after it had done its thing. Again, it's an individual thing. Unlike now, we didn't have video analysis or batting coaches to help us out; you had to figure out on your own what worked best for you, and in my book, that's the best kind of learning. That's where experience and instinct comes into play. All the adjustments I made, be it in India or in other parts of the world, happened intuitively.

Throughout my career, I never tinkered with my backlift either. That wasn't out of ego or stubbornness. I knew what worked for me and what didn't. I wasn't interested in where my bat was coming from, only where the ball went after it made contact with my bat. Experts asserted that because my bat came down in an arc from around point and not straight down from first slip or the wicketkeeper, I was susceptible to the yorker. Sure, I did get out to yorkers occasionally, but who doesn't? When you have a long career, there are bound to be multiple modes of dismissals. But I don't think I was especially vulnerable to the full ball.

Like the backlift, I didn't change the weight of my bat one gram. I played with a very light bat largely because I played square of the wicket on both sides—from cover point to deep third man on the off, and from mid wicket to fine leg on the on. I preferred the light bat because the bat would come down faster and assist in my aggressive intent. It suited my game, my character and my style.

The one change I did make was eschew the hook from my repertoire; unlike now, the hook was more fashionable at that time than the pull. Early doors in my Test career, I wouldn't think twice about taking the ball off my face and hooking it behind square. I did so in the West Indies in 1971; against Chris Old in England in 1974 when he was pretty quick, I distinctly remember hooking him out of the ground. But after 20-odd Tests, I decided not to play the conventional hook. It was a fairly high-risk stroke, and because you are hitting in the air, you can't always be sure of being in control. I started to come inside the line, take the ball outside my left shoulder and tap it on its head at the top of its bounce, playing it fine and keeping it down. It's not an easy stroke, especially when you are vertically challenged, but it was safer than the hook, especially against express pace of the kind I encountered quite often in my career.

◆

The series in Australia didn't go as well as we had hoped. We lost the first two Tests, in Brisbane and Perth, by narrow margins. The batting let us down in Brisbane, while in Perth, we didn't have the resources to hurt Australia with the new ball despite posting 400-plus in the first innings. Nightwatchman Tony Mann got a hundred and Australia scaled down a target of 339 with two wickets remaining, which was very deflating.

The batting group felt it had let the team down in the first Test because Australia were without Lillee. But there was Jeff Thomson, fiery and slippery due to his unique action. Thommo had built up a huge reputation, he and Lillee masterminding a 5-1 rout of West Indies in 1975–76. He was still one of the quickest in the world when we went there two years later, and was brilliant throughout the series, with Wayne Clark for company.

Fortunately for us, this was an extended series, our first five-Test showdown overseas since the West Indies tour in 1971, so we had a chance to work our way back. We hadn't been that far off the mark in the first two games, so even though we were disappointed at the scoreline, we backed ourselves to turn things around.

We were in control from the time Bishan won the toss at the MCG. We didn't post a huge first-innings total, though I did make my first half-century in Australia. But we had 256 on the board and an inspired Chandra itching to run rings around Australia.

When Chandra gets on a roll, he is impossible to counter. He never allows you to feel you are 'in', the ball an obedient slave to the masterly right wrist that sent it snaking this way and that, hustling through at pace or climbing from a length. His six for 52 gave us a handy lead which we translated into an overall advantage of nearly 400, thanks to another customary second-innings century from Sunil, his third in as many games. Unlike in the two earlier matches, this brought glad tidings.

Like in the first innings, Chandra was all over the Australians. He reprised his earlier heroics by returning identical figures, giving him a match haul of 12 for 104. Consequently, India achieved their first Test win in Australia, by 222 runs. We felt this was a truer indication of where the two teams stood.

That the fourth Test was in Sydney gave us greater encouragement. For one thing, our confidence was sky-high. For another, we knew there would be more help for our bowling legends at the traditionally spin-friendly Sydney Cricket Ground (SCG), and I could picture Chandra, Pras and Bishan licking their lips in anticipation.

Predictably enough, we shot Australia out for a very small total on the first afternoon, then set about trying to build a platform from which we could eke out a series-levelling win. With consistent contributions throughout the order, including a gritty 64 by No. 8 Karsan, we reached 396 for eight and a big lead of 267.

I top-scored with 79, my third half-ton in a row. It was a particularly satisfying knock against one of the fastest spells I have had to tackle in Test cricket. Evidently, no one had told Thommo about the nature of the SCG deck, or he wanted to show that the character of the surface would have no impact on his bowling. Whatever the reason, he bowled frightfully quickly. For 27 relentless overs, he put us through a serious examination.

Later, I came to know that this wasn't even Thommo at his quickest. He had dislocated his right shoulder after a collision with Alan Turner in a Test against Pakistan in 1976, which apparently took some sting off, but you wouldn't have known; he bowled like the wind. By then, we had faced the West Indian greats with the exception of Malcolm Marshall, we had played Bob Willis and Chris Old, but this was something else. It was quite an experience to keep Thommo at bay, though he was rewarded for his fire with four for 83 on a reasonably benign pitch.

That evening, I ran into Simpson in the elevator. The moment he saw me, his face contorted into a look of disbelief and admiration. 'How did you manage that?' he asked me. 'It was just unbelievable. I had kept a fielder there (short leg) and there (silly point). Thommo got all the Pommies (slang for Englishmen) there last year, 28 of his 40 victims were caught there. But you, you just kept dropping the ball down at your feet. Beautiful, what control!'

I didn't show it, but I was bursting with pride. Simpson was one of the giants of the game, a brilliant opening batsman who had formed a great alliance with Bill Lawry. He was a top-class leggie and one of the shrewdest brains in the business, and that showed in how he marshalled his greenhorns in this series. Despite advancing years and time away from the game, he batted beautifully, tackling our spinners with a felicity that only comes to a few. It wasn't coincidental, perhaps, that Australia lost the two Tests in which he didn't make a half-century.

Back to the game. We had lots of runs and time to play with, and even though Australia put up a better fight, Pras's guile was too much for them and we ran out victors by an innings. After two bitter losses, we had pulled off two commanding wins of immense significance. We departed for Adelaide with momentum on our side, and with high hopes of completing a dramatic series triumph.

That wasn't to be, however. Once Simpson won the toss on a flat pitch, we had our work cut out. Graham Yallop and the skipper slammed centuries and Australia piled up more than 500. Our reply was timid and we ended up conceding a huge lead. Australia batted on and set us a target of 493, out of reach 99 times out of 100 even for us, who owned the record for the highest successful run-chase in Test history. We did come close but when Chandra fell to Simpson, our brave chase fell 47 short. We were proud of how we had approached such a steep target, but bitterly disappointed that for all our experience and skills, we hadn't been able to seal the series.

I added to my list of half-centuries with 89 and 73 in Adelaide, giving me five scores of more than 50 on the trot. Personally, I converted a steady start into a very successful outing, finishing with 473 runs even though I didn't make a hundred. The Australian tour had been a great challenge, every bit as entertaining and demanding as I had expected it to be. I had enjoyed my battles with Thommo and Clark, and watched excellent batting from Simpson and Peter Toohey. Only the fact that there was no trophy to show for our efforts acted as a dampener. It would have been great had we become the first Indian team to win a series in Australia too, like we had in the West Indies and England.

While we hurt at not being able to translate our superiority to consistent results, we couldn't help but admire Australia's resolve and resilience. They had a competent batting group with Toohey and Yallop among the youngsters catching the eye, and their pace attack was of the highest order even without Lillee. John Gannon, the left-arm quick, played excellent foil to Thommo and Clark even though he didn't figure in all five Tests.

My admiration for Simpson went up several notches as the tour progressed. His knowledge and expertise were phenomenal, and his footwork even in his 40s against our spinners was a treat to watch. He was a wonderful mentor and guide for a team woefully short on experience, justifying the faith reposed in him by the authorities who brought him out of decade-long retirement. I left Australia with mixed feelings; delight at a great time overall and no little individual success, but despair at collectively looking a gift horse in the mouth. I couldn't wait to return there.

◆

History suggested a long gap between tours, but fortunately, we were back Down Under three years later for a three-Test series against a full Australian side. All issues between the Australian board and Packer had been resolved, which facilitated Greg Chappell's return as captain. Doug Walters was back, as were Lillee and Marsh. Allan Border and Kim Hughes added class to the batting line-up, while Len Pascoe and Rodney Hogg were as menacing as Lillee. This was a formidable outfit, and we knew we had to be at our best to keep pace.

However, we could fall back on the experience gained from having recently played there. A majority of the batsmen had toured in 1977, though there was a new look to our bowling attack. The spin kings were all missing, Dilip Doshi and Shivlal Yadav entrusted with carrying the legacy forward. Most importantly, we now had a proper pace attack to speak of, Kapil having made the world sit up and take notice.

We started very poorly, comprehensively beaten in Sydney by the same margin by which we had won on the last tour—an innings and four runs. As expected, their pacers were a handful, while Chappell made a gorgeous 204 and contributed more than half of his team's total. The start was far from ideal; 0-1 down overseas with two matches remaining all but ruled out a series win.

A triangular series also involving New Zealand overlapped with the Test series, so there was a three-week gap to the second Test in Adelaide. One man who used that time to excellent effect was Sandeep Patil, our hard-hitting middle order batsman.

Sandeep had batted brilliantly in the first innings in Sydney, taking the fight to Australia before he was struck on his head by Pascoe. In the extended break between the first and second Tests, he acclimatized to batting with a helmet, and produced one of the great innings in Adelaide.

Australia had amassed more than 500 and we were struggling at 130 for four when Sandeep walked out to an expectedly hostile welcome from Lillee, Hogg and Pascoe. As it is, they were very quick. The sight of Sandeep walking out was like a red rag to a bull because they thought he would be rattled and shaken up by the events of Sydney. Instead, in the space of a few minutes, they went from the hunters to the hunted, Sandeep turning it on in style.

No part of The Oval went untouched as he smashed 174 of the very best runs. Punctuated by bruising strokes, he earned grudging admiration and respect from the Australians, who lauded his courage and character as much as we did. For five hours, he kept blasting away, taking us to within 109 of the Australian total. It was as courageous a display as I have seen, the perfect illustration of fighting fire with fire.

We were to finish off the Test series in Melbourne. The series was still alive, but I wasn't in a great personal space. Coming off scores of 26, 24, 3 and 16, I was worried about the lack of runs, though I didn't feel out of form. In fact, had it not been for a conversation with Sir Don Bradman during the Adelaide Test, I would have been in far worse shape.

Sir Don and his wife Jessie had invited Sunil, his wife Pammi, Kavita and myself to dinner. For two hours, I was entranced by his simplicity, his knowledge and wisdom, his humility and his passion for cricket. Understandably, much of our conversation was dominated by the sport we all love so much. Sunil was curious about Sir Don's playing days, his preparation, his approach to batting, things like that. I was generally quiet, until Sir Don turned to me with a questioning look on his face.

'What's bothering you, young Vishy?' he asked me.

Grateful for the opening, I spoke to him about not getting runs. He listened to me patiently, then said, 'When you have a long career, these things happen.' *Not to you, they didn't*, I thought to myself. 'There is one more Test left in the series,' he continued. 'Don't think about what's happened. Just concentrate on what's ahead, and you should be able to get out of this little rut. Good luck to you.'

As we left after one of the most fulfilling evenings of my cricketing career, I was wearing a smile for the first time in days. Dinner with the greatest batsman of all time was itself a huge honour, but to hear his words of reassurance meant the world to me.

◆

However, as we closed in on the start of the final Test, on 7 February 1981, my anxiety started to mount again. Sir Don's words were ringing in my ears, but I still had my apprehensions. Seeking to put me at ease, Dilip Doshi sought me out on the morning of the first day and asked me if I would like to have a word with Sir Garfield Sobers. Dilip had played alongside Sir Garry for Nottinghamshire in the English county circuit and shared a great rapport. I was touched by his offer and readily took him up on it.

Sir Garry lived in Australia at the time, so Dilip rang him and passed the phone to me a little before we left the hotel for the MCG. I told him pretty much what I had told Sir Don less than a fortnight back—the lightness of runs was driving me crazy.

'I have seen you bat in the past, and I have watched you on this tour too,' Sir Garry sing-songed. 'I don't think you are doing too much wrong. You may not have scored a lot of runs, but you have been hitting the ball well. If I were you, however, I wouldn't play square of the wicket at the beginning of my innings. Take your time, assess the pitch and the conditions, see what the ball is doing. Try and play in the "V" as much as possible at the start, and then take it from there. Like I said, you should be all right, there are no major issues with your batting.'

Immediately, my mind went back to what Tiger had told me when I was waiting to bat in the second innings of my debut Test, after my duck in the first. The impact of Sir Garry's words was the same as Tiger's had been 11 years ago. In the space of 15 days, I had received endorsements from the greatest batsman the game has seen and the greatest all-rounder to grace cricket. It was impossible not to be optimistic and positive.

As Sir Garry had predicted, Chappell put us in because of the up-and-down nature of the surface. The square at the MCG hadn't been relaid for a while, and it was clear that the bowlers would have the edge. Our top three were dismissed cheaply and we were 43 for three with half an hour to lunch, Sandeep and I needing to put our heads down and get us out of trouble. I felt nice and light, my self-doubts having dissipated even though Lillee and Pascoe were making the ball talk. Sir Garry's advice about playing in front of the wicket kept coming back to me, and I made a conscious effort for the first 20-odd runs to refrain from playing the cut.

Sandeep was looking good when Lillee had him caught in the slips, after which Yashpal and Kapil perished without contributing much. We did have depth, so I managed handy stands with Kiri and Shivlal. By the time I was ninth man out, I had shed my lean trot with an immensely satisfying 114, fashioned in four and a half hours. Not for the first time, I had delivered with the team in trouble; the quality of the attack, the nature of the pitch and my own form coming into this game added to the satisfaction, though I knew that against Australia's in-form batting unit, 237 was anything but a competitive total.

With Border leading the way, Australia topped 400 in the first innings for the third time in the series. In a patient display, the hosts found runs throughout the order and by the time they were bowled out midway through the third day, their lead was a healthy 182. The series was down now to the last two and a half days. For us to make a match of it, we had to score big, but also give ourselves enough overs to bowl them out a second time. The only positive was that because we had been shot out on the first day itself, time wouldn't be a factor.

Thus it was that Sunil and Chetan kicked off India's fightback. By the end of that evening, they had constructed their first meaningful partnership of the tour, lopping 108 off Australia's lead without being separated. We knew we were still well behind the eight-ball, but the start had been promising and we weren't out of the game by any means.

The next day, the openers continued their good work and had put on 165 when calamity struck. Sunil had rediscovered his touch with 70 when he was adjudged leg before to Lillee by umpire Rex Whitehead. Sunil was adamant he had hit the ball, but the decision had been made, and he had no choice but to leave the field. In the meanwhile, Lillee ran down the track and pointed to the exact spot where the ball had thudded into the pad. After a long pause, Sunil was just beginning to leave his ground when one of the Australian players made one comment too many which upset our captain. He returned to the crease and started to drag Chetan along with him towards the boundary line, more in protest at what the player had said than at the umpire's decision.

Seated in the viewing area, we watched this unfold in front of us, bemused and perplexed. The dressing room at the MCG was literally a changing room, its location preventing us from catching any action and forcing the entire team to retire to the players' box unless it was time to pad up. We weren't quite sure what to make of it but fortunately, our manager had his wits about him. Wing Commander Shahid Durrani quickly made his way to the ground, urging No. 3 Dilip Vengsarkar to follow him.

The manager stopped Chetan from crossing the boundary rope and asked Dilip to accompany the opener back to the middle, thus preventing anything more untoward. I didn't know at the time but had Wing Commander Durrani not forced Chetan to stay inside the rope, it would have meant India forfeiting the match and surrendering the series 2-0. Full credit to our manager for his quick thinking and decisive action.

We kicked on to wipe out the deficit and were on course for a big lead at 243 for two when I was bowled by Lillee. Wickets tumbled in a rush thereafter and we bowled out for 324, an hour before close on the fourth evening. Australia needed only 143 to complete a 2-0 triumph, but even though Kapil, Dilip and Shivlal were all nursing injuries, we felt we stood an outside chance if we picked up early wickets, because the up-and-down character of the pitch would make life difficult for the batting side on the final day.

By stumps that evening, we had gone from quietly optimistic to hugely confident, thanks to Karsan's new-ball heroics. After getting rid of John Dyson, he cleaned up Chappell first ball. In his eagerness to dominate from the beginning, the Australian captain had walked across his stumps, exposing middle and leg in trying to flick. Karsan defeated his designs and bowled him behind his pads. It was a huge moment in the game, and though we still had plenty of work ahead of us, 142 suddenly loomed as a mountain.

Kapil, who had an injured ankle, was convinced to take the field on the last day and destroyed Australia with a sensational burst. His five-wicket haul precipitated Australia's collapse, while Dilip kept wheeling away, unmindful of his discomfort. Australia were shot out for 83, and we had completed an incredible, commanding 59-run win to come away with a share of the series honours.

We were due to leave for New Zealand the following day—my thirty-second birthday—and my cup of joy was full to the brim. We had become the first Indian team to leave Australia with a drawn series to our credit, and I had been named Player of the Match at the MCG. As the teams got together post-match to reflect on the series, Lillee told me, 'Little giant man, I like you a lot even when you make runs against me, you are made of steel.'

21
CAPTAIN'S LOG

To lead a cricket team, any cricket team, is a massive honour. You aren't just the captain or the skipper, but a leader of men, making spot decisions under pressure and looking out for all the members, not just yourself. I didn't covet that status, but when it was conferred upon me in the natural order of things, I was thrilled to accept it. I tried my best to do justice as a captain; whether I was good or otherwise is not for me to say.

I have heard some people referred to as 'born leaders'. With due respect, that is balderdash. You might have certain qualities integral to leadership, but just as you aren't a born batsman or a born bowler, you can't be a born captain. Experience counts; without hard work and dipping into lessons learnt, you can't succeed in any endeavour. So many players have excelled at the junior level but faded away on graduating to the next stage, or not even made the subsequent grade. People say, 'If he had played Test cricket, he would have definitely succeeded.' But there must have been a reason why they didn't make the step up. Captaincy isn't too dissimilar.

It's also a massive myth that batsmen alone make good captains. There are numerous examples of successful bowler-captains even without delving deep into history. In my generation alone, we had Kapil and Imran, all-rounders for sure but primarily bowlers, both of whom led their countries to World Cup glory. Like Richie Benaud much before him, Bob Willis too was a very good skipper, as was Bishan. And then there is Jason Holder, until recently the West Indian Test captain who led by example and has a towering presence, no pun intended.

Having said that, I do admit that batsmen-captains have the edge in that when you are on the field, you don't have to worry about your own bowling, you don't carry that extra load of focusing on what you should do as a bowler while also working out field placements, bowling changes, strategies and tactics. A bowler-captain can end up over-bowling or under-bowling himself, which isn't a judgement, just an observation.

Not for once did I believe I was earmarked for captaincy. When I made my first-class debut, Mysore state had several stalwarts. I debuted in 1967–68 under Y.B. Patel, who was only in charge because V. Subramanya was away with the national team in Australia. Mysore had a host of glittering cricketing and intellectual talent, and it was no surprise that when we won our first Ranji title—as Karnataka—it was under the stewardship of the astute Prasanna.

State Bank of India had several pedigreed stars when I joined them. Mr Shivshankar, a new-ball bowler, was the captain during my early days. Later, established names like S. Mahendra, M.S. Hanumesh (Anmesh), Kiri and Raghu were in charge, and I was happy to be a foot soldier.

It was in 1977–78, following the retirement from the bank, or from cricket, of several leading lights, that I was appointed the captain. It was my first experience of leadership in cricket, I had never been captain at Spartans. I immediately relished the responsibility that came with the position. We had Kiri, Roger and Raghuram Bhat, all first-class cricketers, but we also had to rebuild the team because we had lost our core. It was a great challenge, and I enjoyed being involved in the recruitment of talent and in ensuring that SBI's stellar reputation as a cricketing entity was maintained. League cricket in Bangalore was extremely competitive, and I looked forward to pitting my tactical skills against more experienced captains, looking at each outing as a learning experience.

◆

I was elevated as captain of Karnataka in December 1978, for our South Zone Ranji Trophy league clash against Tamil Nadu in Madras. That was the non-batting highpoint of my cricketing career till then; the privilege of leading your state isn't commonplace. It was a strange feeling to take over the reins from Pras, who retired after this Madras clash. He had been my skipper for the last half a decade or so, and I was glad to have his counsel if required. To lead a team that included Chandra, Roger, Brijesh, Raghu and Sudhakar, friends as much as colleagues, was a fantastic feeling.

Even if I say so myself, I wasn't a dictatorial captain. I didn't lay down the ground rules, I didn't expect players to toe the line. I don't think that's how a captain should operate. You don't have any special powers because you have '(Capt.)' against your name. You are not the boss that barks orders and demands discipline and loyalty. Such a style is guaranteed to fail. More significantly, that was against my character.

I would like to think of myself as an inclusive captain, eliciting suggestions, someone who is open to ideas from grizzly veterans as well as hopeful newcomers. But I was mindful of the fact that the buck stopped with me. That, while success was a result of collective effort, I was the one responsible for failure. So even though I invited opinions, I knew I had to take the final call and live with the consequences. Because I didn't lead by consensus, I was more than happy to accept criticism, warranted or otherwise. For me, the team had come first when I was just another member. Why should anything change because I was now the captain?

Captaincy provides insights into players you might not have had access to as a colleague. For instance, I knew Pras liked to set his own fields when he bowled, so while we would have brief chats, we both knew he had the freedom and luxury to position fielders depending on what lines he intended bowling. Chandra was the exact opposite. He mandatorily needed fielders in three positions (slip, short leg and leg slip) and perhaps a fourth to the left of the square leg umpire. The rest, he left to his captain. His contention was that when he bowled well, these four positions would suffice. When he didn't, it didn't matter how many were on the field, or where they were stationed!

I was happy for bowlers to take responsibility so long as they stuck to their plans. We all know how much pacers and spinners alike invest physically and mentally in their craft. They want to deliver more than you want them to, so there is no point constantly being in their ear, talking to them every ball or every over. At the beginning of the day, or a spell, I would check with a bowler about his plans, and if I was convinced, all I wanted was that they stick to those plans, whether that meant instant success or not. When they consistently deviated from their own plans, I'd quietly point it out. It helped that, by nature, I am not an angry or agitated person. The last thing the players want to see is their captain losing his cool. Even if you have your backs to the wall, you must project an air of calmness and composure, not allow your inner disappointment to surface.

You can't expect that every time a bowler sends down a delivery, they will get a wicket. I know, as a batsman, that they have to work for wickets. You are trying to get the batsman out bowling line and length, bringing your variations into play, playing the wait-and-watch game. Of course, you want wickets but as captain, I never placed expectations in terms of the number of wickets we needed in a session. The idea was to control the session, whether through penetration or economy. But when there was help for bowlers, I encouraged them to go for the kill, to look for wickets. If, in that process, they don't succeed, fair enough. But working out game situations, fields and making plans on the fly, my enjoyment lay in that.

Captaincy can impact individuals differently, there is no set pattern or one-size-fits-all strategy. Some are weighed down by the prospect of devoting time to so many different aspects to the detriment of your own game, others are buoyed by the responsibility and reinvent themselves. Captaincy didn't affect my mindset or my batting. I didn't change anything about my cricket, except perhaps become determined to do more for the team. That doesn't mean I didn't want to perform when I was not leading. But as captain, sitting in the dressing room after being dismissed, waiting for the batsmen to come in during an interval to discuss ideas, isn't a pleasant experience. Instead of watching from the inside, it's better to be one of the two batsmen out in the middle, build a partnership, infuse confidence in your colleague and inspire the team with your deeds. To me, captaincy was the ultimate affirmation of your abilities as a cricketer and a human being. I'd do everything in my control to justify that show of faith.

◆

To be perfectly honest, I didn't expect the India captaincy to come my way. I had played under numerous captains—Tiger, Ajit, Bishan, Venkat and Sunil—and even though I was vice-captain to Sunil towards the end of the 1970s, Sunil wasn't going anywhere, was he? Therefore, when I did become the captain, even if only briefly, it came as a pleasant surprise.

From an era when we had to wait two years between series, we played 26 Tests against Pakistan, West Indies, England and Australia in a 15-month spell between October 1978 and February 1980. We were scheduled to travel to the Caribbean a little over a month after our final home game of the 1979–80 season, the Golden Jubilee Test against England at the Wankhede Stadium.

Sunil had played all these Tests and had been captain for most of them. He was mentally exhausted, more than anything else, and expressed his inability to go to the Caribbean in that state for what was bound to be another arduous assignment. This was towards the end of the home series against Pakistan in January 1980, when we had already taken a winning 2-0 lead in the six-Test showdown with one to play. Kapil cited similar reasons and said he too was pulling out of the West Indian tour. Sunil suggested that, with the series already won, it would be better for whoever would captain in the West Indies to ease into the job by leading in the dead rubber against Pakistan, as well as the Jubilee Test. Since I was his deputy, that honour was bestowed on me.

The intensity of emotions when I was informed of this development left me speechless. To lead your country is the ultimate honour, a moment of great pride and a vindication of your efforts all these years. I knew I was warming the seat for Sunil, that once he was available he would return as captain, but that didn't matter. I had a job to do, I couldn't afford any distractions. It did take some effort, however, to wrap my head around the fact that I was now G.R. Vishwanath, the Indian Test captain.

As luck would have it, my captaincy debut was at the hallowed Eden Gardens, the ground with the greatest energy and the most infectious atmosphere in the country. Playing in Calcutta lifted your spirits, it galvanized you, and I felt the hair on the back of my neck standing up when, sporting the India blazer, I walked out for the toss on 29 January 1980, alongside my Pakistani counterpart Asif Iqbal.

Nearly 90,000 fans were packed into the Eden, one of the best Test centres in the world for its sheer size and vibrancy. I was swept away by the emotions, but I also desperately wanted to win the toss. The pitch looked good for batting, which added to my desperation even though I had no say in the matter. All I could do as the home captain was flip the coin, and hope Asif called wrong.

With only a couple of press photographers clicking away—this was long before match referees, even longer before the television commentator interviewed captains at the toss—I flicked the coin and Asif called. It landed in the middle of the hard pitch and started to roll away from us before coming to a halt. Asif got to the coin before I did, picked it up, turned to me, put his hand out and said, 'You have won the toss, Vishy.' I hadn't seen which way the coin had landed, but what reason did I have to doubt Asif? I was thrilled I had won the toss, that we would be batting first.

The match didn't produce a result. Asif declared with Pakistan 59 behind our 331, and Imran finished with nine for the match as we were bowled out for 205. With a little more time, we could have forced a result—chasing 265, Pakistan had slumped to 179 for six. I would have loved a winning start as captain, but this wasn't too bad. Ominously though, I was dismissed for 13 in each innings.

We lost my second and last Test in charge, to Ian Botham's all-round genius at the Wankhede. Like the toss in Calcutta, this game is remembered for our decision to recall Bob Taylor to the batting crease, and his subsequent association with Botham which put England in a winning position. My stint as India captain might have been short-lived, but it was anything but uneventful.

As it turned out, the proposed tour to the Caribbean was called off. For better or worse, the trip didn't come through. There's two ways of looking at it: if the tour had gone on, I would have captained for a few more Tests. If the tour hadn't been pencilled in in the first place, it's more than likely I would never have led the national side. When we played our next series, in Australia in early 1981, Sunil was back in command and I knew I wouldn't captain India again. I was fine with that, no disappointments, no regrets. Would I have liked to have captained in more Tests? I'd not have said no. But did I secretly eye that honour? Certainly not.

◆

I have been fortunate to play under a string of fabulous readers and analysts of the game at various levels. All things considered, my best captain is Subramanya. In so many ways, he was my role model, the one I wanted to emulate when I became captain. His situational awareness was exceptional, the way he dissected the game was at once simple and marvellous, the way he talked to his players was inspirational. I didn't play much under him, just a season or two, but that was enough to make a lasting impression. Had he played a little earlier for India, and scored more consistently, he could have gone on to lead the country, he was that good.

Jai was another terrific skipper. He was obsessed with the game and could talk endlessly about it, dismantling every play minutely and staying one step ahead of where everyone else was. We spent a lot of time together, especially when we travelled to Hyderabad. He'd call us over to his Marredpally residence, where the evening would be about cricket, more cricket and only cricket. His ability to not just analyse but also explain was unparalleled; he talked to a 15-year-old on an equal wavelength as he did a 40-Test veteran, and was a master at summing up batsmen and working out plans in a jiffy. Tiger spotted all of this. That's why even when he was the India captain, Tiger was more than happy to play under Jai for both Hyderabad and South Zone. Jai was as good as the best international captains, and certainly far superior intellectually to many others.

Tiger, of course, was Tiger, my Skip. I have reflected on his man-management skills elsewhere, all I have to add is that he was the best attacking captain of my time.

Sunil was very firm in his decision-making, and whenever he sensed a shot at victory, he invariably went for it immediately, not waiting for things to unravel on their own. However, for a majority of his stint, he had to work with serious limitations. Our batting wasn't the most formidable, and the spin quartet had run their course, so he had the responsibility of batting long as well as making sure we weren't unrealistic about our prospects. The arrival of Kapil lent him a weapon that captains before him didn't possess, and he handled Kapil superbly. But as awesome as Kapil was, he often had to plug away single-handedly as a pace force. Sunil was more studious than instinctive, and while he wasn't defensive, circumstances and resources necessitated him to put safety above bravado. Given all this, his record is not bad at all. When he finished with his captaincy stint in 1985, he was the first Indian captain to have more Test wins than losses.

The obvious overseas options whose captaincy I admired are Ray Illingworth and Mike Brearley. Illingworth led superbly in our series in 1971, and especially at The Oval when we were chasing 170-plus for victory. He didn't give up until the last over of our chase when, in an inspired move, he brought on Brian Luckhurst and was rewarded with my wicket! But seriously speaking, he also led England to a famous Ashes win in Australia just before that series, and was a masterful strategist.

Brearley carries the reputation of having a degree in people. He possessed the wonderful ability to bring the best out of Botham, exemplified by Botham's Ashes of 1981. Brought in to turn England's fortunes around after captaincy seemed to weigh the great all-rounder down, Brearley extracted one searing performance after another from his ace to fashion a remarkable 3-1 victory. England owed that result in equal part to Botham's incandescence and Brearley's motivational and analytical instincts.

◆

Increasingly, there is a tendency to coach the captain from the sidelines, which I am not sure is a great look. Agreed, at the junior level, the skipper might require guidance and advice from outside, but with time, he must be allowed to develop his skills, to rely on his instinct and intellect, to make his own decisions and to learn to live with their consequences. You might have 40 people around you: the coaching staff, the support staff, the data analyst. But just like no one can bat or bowl for you, the coach can't lead in your stead either. In any case, how does one lead from 100 yards out on a consistent basis? When you are the captain, you have to carry the baby. Do the job in the middle. Take ownership of your responsibility. There is a reason you have been made the captain, therefore you are the best judge and the buck stops with you. You might as well sink or swim on the basis of your convictions.

At the end of the day, a captain is only as good as his team. If you don't have the resources, you can't win. The first pre-requisite, therefore, is balance. In some ways, it's like batting. If you don't have balance as a batsman, it's unlikely you will have a long career. Likewise, in the absence of a balanced side, the captain will struggle to deliver. The odd extraordinary talent is a welcome addition, but it's the balance of the composition that is pivotal.

It's essential for a captain to contribute in his primary discipline; it's a must to have the respect of your colleagues. You need to make tough calls if the situation so demands, secure in the knowledge that you are not there to please an individual but to do what is best for the unit. To possess that courage to make the difficult decisions is a unique trait.

No matter what, you need a little bit of luck. Gary Player, the great South African golfer, once famously said, 'The harder I practise, the luckier I get.' True as that might be, sometimes you need the benevolent hand of good fortune on your head, for catches to go to hand when you set meticulous fields, for balls not to fly aerially through the very spot from which you have just moved a fielder.

Just as a captain shouldn't rely on consensus, he can't take unilateral decisions. For instance, you can't tell a bowler that these are my fields, you have to bowl according to them. That will make him a different, less effective bowler. That's not to say that the captain should give in to every demand of the bowler, but this is a game of give and take and, as a leader, you must know when to push and when to hold back. How do you know that? Through experience.

Most importantly, you must learn to control your emotions. I don't believe in elaborate gestures and showboating. Walking up to the stumps at the bowler's end, asking gully to move three millimetres to his right or short leg half a centimetre to his left? Really? Or maybe, it's just me.

22

PLAYING CRICKET, MY WAY

I have had plenty of time since retirement, more than three decades back, to reflect on my playing days. I count my blessings that I lasted 20 seasons in first-class cricket, that I was good enough to represent the country for more than 13 years.

Do I have any regrets? Would I do anything differently if I had the chance? No, and another emphatic no.

I played cricket because I enjoyed doing so. I had great fun pursuing my passion, and I was fortunate my passion became my profession. From my first day to the last, I played cricket *my* way. My approach didn't change one bit, nor did I make significant modifications to my batting. I had a certain notion of how cricket should be played, and I derive immense satisfaction in having stuck to my guns, my conviction.

Like you must if you have to be successful at the highest level, I made minor modifications depending on where I played and in what conditions, and which bowlers I faced. That's imperative, that comes from experience. You can't follow the same template everywhere, otherwise you will get left behind. But I never felt the need for a complete technical overhaul. I knew my game, I understood what worked and what didn't. As a cricketer and batsman, I was the best judge of my game. I had to be brutally honest with myself, not hide behind excuses.

I was ruled by my instinct, a constant companion through my roller-coaster journey. My instinct dictated that if the ball was there to hit, hit it. Don't overthink, don't stress over consequences, but don't manufacture strokes, don't go looking for the ball when it isn't there. If you want to try out a new stroke, don't do so in a match unless you have practised extensively in the nets. Don't let your heart rule your head.

My instinct warned me to be mindful of situations and conditions. Like, can you afford to play expansive shots right now, or wait for your turn, see off five overs or half an hour, and then dictate terms? It compelled me to analyse my game, analyse situations. Again, that's something you can only do from experience.

If you apply your mind, you will be amazed at how much you are able to accomplish. If you don't put your mind to the task, if you stumble from one Test to another, you will end up making the same mistakes over and over again. What's the point of playing cricket then? What's the point of playing anything, if you are not better today than you were yesterday? There is no shame for a batsman in getting out, but you must know how and why you got out, and work on it so that tomorrow, you avoid committing the same errors.

There were plenty of well-wishers who would offer advice and suggestions when you sought them out, or at times of their own accord. The way I looked at it was that all advice was good, but I couldn't take it to the middle willy-nilly. I had to try it out in the nets, see if it worked for me. Ultimately, it's about you, you are the boss in the middle. People can point out chinks and offer solutions, but they can't bat for you, they can't score runs for you.

You have to think for yourself. You are the one facing the bowling, you know perfectly well how the contact between the bowler and you, between the ball leaving his hand and the bat in yours, has been. When you get out, you know why and how, that impact will be with you. It has to be. You then put that in perspective, work it out by yourself, then work on it. That's called experience; your strength lies in how fast you learn. We didn't have slow-motion replays, video analysis, any of those tools. Don't get me wrong, I welcome the modern developments which help break down and minutely analyse every second of the action. We didn't have these luxuries, so, essentially, the onus was on you. You were your best friend, but if you didn't apply yourself, you were also your worst enemy. That was my way of thinking, of playing.

I operated under the assumption that everyone who had an opinion on your technique, everyone who offered a suggestion with regard to your batting, did so with good intention. That they wanted you to succeed, to do well. But even if someone didn't have your best interests at heart, don't ignore those tips. Who knows, if you think deeply and work hard, you might still be able to unearth something that might benefit you. Don't ignore advice, no matter which quarter it comes from. Don't be swayed by a third party suggesting that someone was misguiding you. You are the one listening to the advice, you should know if it's good for you or not, forget about the third party's interference. But don't feel obligated to implement every tip, every suggestion. Try it out, and then try it out again in net sessions. Then decide whether to embrace it or dump it.

The one thing which satisfies me greatly is that I played according to the situation, I didn't throw my bat around. I didn't play for show, I played to contribute to my team's needs and to entertain the fans, in that order. I took all the runs that came my way, but I enjoyed a boundary if the cover drive went where it was intended to go, not if it skewed off the edge behind point or to third man. It wasn't that I was a perfectionist; I was more an aesthete, if you like.

I finished with 14 hundreds and 35 half-centuries from 91 Tests. Clearly, my conversion rate wasn't the best, I might have missed several hundreds, but that never meant anything to me when I played. Now when I think about it, I would have loved to have scored more centuries, it is such a milestone. But that's only now, all these years later, though I won't say it is a regret. I am not really a man of regrets, you see.

When I was an active player, I never counted my hundreds. What purpose would it have served? Weren't you in the team in the first place to make runs, to score centuries if you could?

◆

Before I talk about it in some detail, I'd like to make it clear that 'walking' is an individual choice, the batsman's prerogative. One isn't a saint if he walks, nor a sinner if he chooses to wait for the umpire's decision.

I have no recollection of when I first 'walked' on the cricket ground. I gave it no thought, it was something that happened. I knew I had edged the ball, I knew I was out, so off you go to the pavilion. It wasn't a conscious decision, I didn't tell myself it was the right thing or the moral thing to do. I just did it.

All of that changed in my second Test, at the Kotla against the Aussies. Ashley Mallett, the tall off spinner, had troubled me in Kanpur, and he was the one who dismissed me in the second innings. I don't know what it was about him, but I had my fair share of problems as we approached tea on the second day, replying to Australia's 296.

Off the last ball before the interval, there was a huge appeal for a bat-pad catch. I didn't think I hit the ball, so I stood there, and then the umpire removed the bails and called tea. I walked towards Ashok Mankad and we started to head for the dressing room when I felt someone kick my bat from behind. I whirled around but couldn't identify which of the five–six fielders walking behind us had done so. I hated that moment; for me, for any batsman, the bat is our most revered possession. It is the most important tool of our trade, a spiritual companion, to be treated with love, care and respect. It angers me when I see batsmen hurl their bat after being dismissed. What's the bat's fault?

Anyway, I was both enraged and hurt at the kick to my bat when I heard someone call out 'You cheat'. I didn't react, but I felt terrible. I was not a cheat, I had no intent to cheat. But those two words kept ringing in my ears as I went inside the dressing room and plonked myself in a chair.

Tiger sauntered in and sat next to me. 'Vish, did you nick it?' he asked, more out of curiosity. I am sure he wouldn't have lectured me on the virtues of walking even, had I told him I knew I had edged the ball.

'I don't think so, but I am not sure,' I replied.

'Okay, don't worry about it. Just carry on.'

But I did worry about it. As the day wore on, those few seconds kept playing themselves over and over in my head. I could feel the bat move as someone kicked it, I could hear 'You cheat' as loudly as if someone was screaming in my ear. For the first time, I started to doubt myself. I am no cheat, I thought, but I was now not convinced that I hadn't got bat to ball. I didn't like being called a cheat, no one does.

That night, I made a commitment to myself. I would never give anyone the chance again to call me a cheat. If I knew I had nicked the ball and the catch had been taken cleanly, I wouldn't even look at the umpire. I didn't feel I was doing anyone a favour by choosing to walk. It was my decision, I was committed to walking, whatever the situation of the game, whatever my score might be. My record subsequently was spotless. Almost.

Only once thereafter in more than 250 first-class games did I not 'walk', and even then, it wasn't by design. It was at a Ranji Trophy game against Tamil Nadu at Chepauk towards the end of 1974. I stepped out to on drive Venkat. I knew I edged the ball on to my pad, after which it ballooned to short leg and was easily gobbled up by P. Mukund, who had previously played for Mysore too in the Ranji Trophy.

The pavilion was behind me, so I had to turn around to walk back. I thought that's what I was doing when I heard a loud 'No' from the umpire in response to the fielders' appeals. I stopped right there. I wanted to walk, I was desperate to drag myself from the middle, but I don't know what came over me. I froze, I became a statue for the next 15 seconds. My body just would not respond to my mind's urgings.

By the time I regained control of my body, it was too late. It would have been embarrassing to walk after 15 seconds—embarrassing to me, and to the umpire who had adjudged in my favour. I put my misgivings behind me and batted on, as a completely perplexed Mukund asked me with concern, 'Are you alright, Vishy? What happened there?'

'I don't know,' I shook my head. 'I knew I was out, I wanted to walk, but I couldn't. I couldn't move my feet at all.'

A little while later, I edged the same bowler to the same fielder at the same position. This time, I whirled around and trudged off.

Even today, Mukund ribs me about that incident. We ran into each other at a function in Madras a couple of years back, and as we slipped into nostalgia, I was the one who brought up that incident. With a twinkle, Mukund said, 'You, Vishy? Even now, I can't believe what happened!'

Oh well, it did happen. Not my proudest moment on a cricket field.

I didn't then, and I don't expect now, that everyone who knows he is out must walk. That, as I have said before, is up to each individual. Some say these things balance out, that sometimes they are wrongly given out, so why try and make things easier on the umpire. I don't judge them, I have no issues with that line of thinking.

However, whether you are a walker or not, you must not make a song and dance of it when you are ruled out even though you know you aren't. That's just not on, it's unacceptable. The umpire's word is final, and right or not, you have to respect that. I have had my fair share of disappointments in this regard in Test cricket, ironically, mainly in England. The one that stands out is when I jabbed a full ball from off spinner Peter Willey into the pitch, from where it flew to Mike Brearley at cover. It gathered pace after hitting the ground and was caught shoulder-high by the England captain. My jaw clattered to the ground in astonishment when I saw the umpire's finger shoot skyward. It was The Oval, September 1979, and we had reached 410 for four, thanks to Sunil's memorable 221, chasing 438 for victory. My 'dismissal' triggered a collapse of four for 13, and we eventually had to hold on to secure a draw. I looked at the umpire for a second, wide-eyed in disbelief. Then, it was time to get on the bike and head to the pavilion.

♦

Sledging isn't a new concept, though the form it has taken is both novel and unsavoury. While I never engaged in it, I enjoyed a good banter between my colleagues and some of the opposition. I am not sure what we are seeing, sometimes hearing, these days is anywhere near the 'banter' category.

I can't remember more than one or two instances, if that, when someone said something to me on the cricket ground, other than the the 'You cheat' episode obviously. Then again, for the most part, not many felt the need to use the lip, and certainly not the West Indian fast bowlers. They didn't have to sledge, they didn't have to swear or open their mouth. They'd send down a thunderbolt, bless you with a chilling stare and go back to the top of their bowling mark. If you had done something even unintentionally to upset them, the parfum ball[5] would be their sledge.

My philosophy was very simple: if you hit a fast bowler, any fast bowler, for a four, don't look in his direction. Just admire the stroke, watch the ball speed to the fence. Do not make the mistake of looking

---

[5]The short ball that would whiz past the batsman's nose. 'Parfum' is a Caribbean variant of perfume.

at the bowler. Ignore him. Any fast bowler, but especially if it was a West Indian paceman. Otherwise, if the ball you had hit for four had been delivered at 85 mph, the next one would zero in on your head at 95 mph. Not the stumps, mind you, not the stumps.

Of course, these days, more and more batsmen are staring at bowlers after hitting fours and sixes, some of them even make crude gestures and say angry words. They are not afraid of getting hurt anymore because they have all the protection in the world, covered as they are in high-quality gear from head to toe. Protection has made a huge difference to the way cricket is being played these days, which is great, though at the end of the day, safety gear alone can't transform a mouse into a lion.

◆

Back then, and to this day, I appreciate excellence. I love watching a beautiful stroke, a peach of a delivery, a sublime piece of fielding. When I was active, I enjoyed such spectacles, whether they came from your teammates or your colleagues.

I didn't always believe in expressing my appreciation visibly or vocally. Can you imagine what would have happened had Viv smashed three-four boundaries in an over and I was clapping from the slip cordon? What the bowler, my colleague, would have thought of me, how he would have reacted? Often, appreciation was conveyed through eye contact, or a whispered word in the ear as you crossed sides at the end of the over. You restrict yourself to clapping for every tenth good stroke, and Viv pretty much guaranteed you that every innings.

I vividly remember my first encounter with Sunil in competitive cricket, at the Buchi Babu tournament in Madras when All-India State Bank of India took on Nirlons. The Bombay team batted first on a green pitch, the ball was seaming and skidding through. Rajinder Goel was bowling beautifully when Sunil got on the front foot and creamed him through the covers. Just creamed him. It wasn't a half volley, but he smashed him on the up and it raced to the fence, I got goosebumps. It's a stroke I will never forget, just as I won't forget the ball with which Pras got Sunil in our Ranji Trophy semi-final when we won our first title. There's nothing wrong in showing your appreciation, even if you are at the receiving end. Bishan, for instance, openly applauded batsmen when they hit him for six, but he was already plotting their dismissal. In a way, that sums up the essence of my cricket.

I waved the bat at fans when I reached a milestone, because you have to acknowledge those who are watching and appreciating your craft. That gentleness, I wanted it in me, and as far as I am concerned, I got it. My nature was like that and so I probably got it back, too. I played several hostile bowlers. Sometimes, they appreciated my shots; they gave me a very gentle appreciative look, and I accepted it with the same gentleness. I liked that, I enjoyed those exchanges. That smile on the bowler's face when I play a very good shot, he knows it is a very good shot. He accepts through his eyes without showing it to anyone else. Likewise, if I got a beautiful ball, completely beaten, the smile I gave the bowler—I really enjoyed that moment, that contest.

◆

It might appear old-fashioned, but my idea of aggression is not necessarily what is visible. Aggression for a batsman is not trying to hit every ball out of the park. It is taking charge of the situation, it is about playing your strokes with authority. It is trying to get the measure of the bowler's line and length so you let him know that you are in complete command through authoritative stroke-making, not with wild shots. Patchy strokeplay is not aggressiveness. Yes, sometimes you might try to hit your way out of trouble, but that's a different kind of aggression. Total and complete aggression is being in supreme command of everything you do throughout your innings, and it doesn't come to many, or very often.

Aggression isn't also only about hitting fours and sixes. People talk about aggressive running between the wickets, about tapping the ball and running without any risk being involved. It's about subtly transferring the pressure on to the bowler, by annoying him through rotation of strike, by throwing him off his rhythm and getting into his mind. Ask any bowler, and he would tell you he'd rather be hit for three fours than concede six singles. If the strike keeps turning over, he has a different batsman to bowl to each time, which means he must change his length accordingly.

If one of them is a left-hander and the other a right-hander, it means he has to be vary of his line too. Now, that's aggression from two intelligent, aware batsmen. It's not merely raving and ranting, puffing up your chest, making gestures and using words. To me, aggression is more internal than external.

Aggression on the field is concentrating every second of every hour of every day. Sometimes, there is no help for the bowlers, and the quicker ones are running in from 15 to 18 yards, giving their 100 per cent, toiling away without result, running in with rhythm, delivering with purpose, working their backsides off. In that situation, if you drop a catch, what a waste of energy and effort that is.

A fielder's aggression lies in constantly figuring out ways to help the bowler, whether it is by trying to convert half chances, or looking for every opportunity to effect a run-out. Chandra and I were talking during the 2020–21 Australia-India series about how many catches were being put down. We then lapsed into a comfortable silence when he suddenly said, 'In that regard, Ekki was amazing. When he was at short leg, we were confident everything that went in the air would be taken. That confidence reflected in the way we approached our bowling.'

Even if you are not the greatest fielder or catcher, it doesn't mean you are out of the game so long as you give it your all, every ball. Catches will be dropped, that's a given, but the objective must be to minimize them to the extent possible. As it is, you spend a maximum of six hours on the field, with breaks for lunch and tea thrown in. There are several moments of respite between balls, and also between overs. If, with all these perks, you are lazy and indifferent, that is inexcusable. You have to keep working on the possibility that every ball will present the chance of a run-out. When you are at slip, you must believe the next ball will be a catch to you. Once you get into that mindset, it becomes a lot easier to concentrate.

I always tried to concentrate harder towards the last 45 minutes of a long, unfruitful day. It's tempting to let the mind wander when for five hours, not an edge has flown in your direction. So when an edge *does* come in the last hour, it invariably goes down. You have to be there mentally, all the time. That's aggression, not the bowler advancing menacingly towards the batsman, shooting his mouth off, or fielders whizzing throws just past the batsman's head and into the keeper's gloves.

◆

The Bob Taylor recall in the Golden Jubilee Test of 1980 has been discussed in as much detail as my unbeaten 97 at Chepauk. I didn't think at the time that I had done anything extraordinary, I don't think that now either. Perhaps we would have won the Test had I not withdrawn the appeal, but what's the value of such a victory?

It was my second and final Test as India's captain, a one-off match to commemorate a special occasion. We had been dismissed for 242 at the Wankhede Stadium, but England themselves were struggling at 85 for five when Kapil got past the outside edge of Taylor's bat and Kiri caught the ball behind the stumps. As is instinctive, we all went up in appeal, and umpire S.N. Hanumantha Rao, also from Bangalore, upheld our appeal. Immediately, though, I knew Taylor had not nicked the ball.

I was at first slip, and when I looked at Kiri to my left, he mouthed 'No' to indicate there was no edge. Sunil was to my right at second slip, and he shrugged his shoulders.

The three of us got together, joined by some of our mates, to discuss what we should do. Sunil told me, 'You are the captain, it is up to you whether you want to call him back, but we are all with you, no matter what you decide.'

Taylor hadn't uttered a word in protest, though he knew from the activities that something was brewing. He walked very slowly towards the boundary, his eyes on us, when I went up to Mr Rao and told him, 'Sir, I'd like to withdraw my appeal.'

'No, no, no,' he replied, 'I have already given him out.'

I slowly started to trudge back to my position at slip, clearly I couldn't overrule him. Out of the blue, he called me back. 'Vishy, what did you just say, that you are withdrawing the appeal? If you are sure, go ahead and call him back then, I have no issues.'

Ian Botham at the non-striker's end had been a keen but silent observer, and as soon as the last word escaped Mr Rao's mouth, he alerted Taylor to stop walking. I told him to come back and resume batting, and both he and Botham told me, 'Well done, Vish, good show.'

After that, it was they who put on a good show! With Botham cutting loose, they added 171 for the sixth wicket. Botham was quite the star, batting beautifully to make 114, then taking seven wickets in the second innings to go with six wickets in the first. It was Botham's match all the way—13 wickets, a century and the central figure in England's 10-wicket win.

I had absolutely no regrets. We had been beaten fair and square. I couldn't have said the same, or lived with it, had we not tried to recall Taylor and then gone on to win the Test. That's not cricket, is it?

Just for the record, my recalling Taylor had nothing to do with walking, there was no relationship between those two whatsoever.

From memory, I have lost my cool only once during a game of cricket, in the Christchurch Test against New Zealand in early 1976. I was fielding in the slips when Glenn Turner played the ball through point and set off. I ran towards square leg to back the throw up, and watched from dead square, right next to the square leg umpire, when Turner was run-out by at least two metres but was ruled not out.

I couldn't believe it, it was not even close. As I walked back to the slips and passed Glenn, I said loudly, hands wide apart, to no one in particular, 'No wonder he gets hundreds in New Zealand all the time. He was run-out by this much. Unbelievable!'

Next to me in the slips, Sunil was more amused than annoyed. 'What's happened to you, Vishy? Relax, take it easy,' he said with a smile, clearly enjoying this rare flash of anger from an unexpected source.

I am not ashamed of what I had said. It was the only time I lost it a little on the field, but no, I don't regret it. I am not soft. After all, I am a Bhadravati man—all iron and steel!

∞

23

MY PRIDE AND JOY

As a batsman, you are expected to score runs, just like as a bowler, it's your job to take wickets. By fulfilling your core responsibilities, you aren't doing the team a favour. That's the mantra around which my approach to cricket revolved.

There are some efforts, however, that bring you great satisfaction for the circumstances under which they have been fashioned. They have little meaning if they don't help the team's cause, needless to say. There is no joy to be derived from making a fabulous hundred if it comes in a loss. From a batsman's point of view, while the conditions, the quality of the opposition and the situation of the game are exemplary factors in determining the value of runs, eventually the biggest determiner is what those runs have translated into. Sometimes, they could set up victories. At others, they might steer the side to safety from a precarious position. No matter what anyone says, these are the knocks that remain dear to your heart.

I was blessed enough to never have been on the losing side when I made a Test hundred. Don't get me wrong, I am not saying we won or drew because I reached three-figures. It's just one of those coincidences you are grateful for.

Some of my favourite innings have been dissected in previous chapters. The common thread to these is challenging conditions and the final outcome. The other constant is while I made adjustments to my approach, I never changed the basics—my stance and my movements.

All the way through, I took leg and middle guard, right and left legs equidistantly positioned either side of the popping crease. The gap between the two was perhaps two feet. I crouched a little, but not excessively so. The first time I went into this stance, I immediately felt comfortable. It was a stance I stuck to for the duration of my career, against both pace and spin.

I was a big fan of an initial trigger movement. Against fast bowlers and medium-pacers, both on quicker tracks overseas and more benign ones at home, my initial movement was to go back with my right foot. Whenever I encountered spinners or slower bowlers, the trigger was to come forward. But those movements were only in the mind. They were not physical. In reality, I didn't move even a centimetre before the ball was delivered.

Essentially, my brain was telling my body what my style of batting necessitated it to do. The feet were primed for these movements, but not in a pre-determined fashion. I'd be completely still till the ball left the bowler's hand—still feet, still head. Only when I judged the length as it travelled through the air did I commit to movement of any kind. I am not saying that's the only way to go, just what worked for me.

I have had well-wishers come up to me and lament the lack of 'cheap runs' in my resume. If that was meant as a compliment, I beg to disagree. There is no such thing as cheap runs in any grade of the sport, let alone at the international level. Playing on a flat surface doesn't guarantee you a hundred. You still need to retain focus and concentration, and play perfect strokes. Because it's overcast, the atmosphere is heavy and the ball is swinging around, you can't take bowling success for granted. Bob Massie's 16-wicket haul on debut is often attributed to the generous assistance he got from the conditions. I am not disputing that, but he himself has gone on record about how the big challenge was to control the swing enough to catch the edge of the bat. It looks great when the ball travels a mile in the air and beats the outside edge. But hey, what about wickets? The art of bowling, even for high-quality spinners, on a raging turner is as demanding as batting on flat decks is. Think again before you talk cheap runs and cheap wickets.

That being said, it is true that at the start of my career, I hardly made a big score if I went in after a long partnership. That bugged me, and I sought out Polly Umrigar's advice on how to shed that unwanted habit.

Polly Kaka wanted to know my routine as I waited for my turn to bat. I told him how I'd be glued to my seat hours on end, watching every ball, concentrating hard, trying to figure what the bowler was doing and what was happening off the pitch.

'There you have it,' Polly Kaka told me. 'You are already mentally very tired *before* going out to bat. I am not saying you shouldn't watch, but you must learn to switch off. You must rest your eyes, your brain, to retain the freshness. Every 20 minutes or so, leave the viewing area, go to the dressing room and do 30–40 skips. Move your eyeballs. Get the circulation going in your body and your mind.'

It seems the most obvious thing. It probably is too, but it was one of the several career-changing tips I was fortunate to receive at various stages of my cricketing journey. I could see where Polly Kaka was coming from. From that point, I followed his advice, and the results were immediate.

◆

I loved the thrill of pitting my skills against the wares of the bowlers in their backyard, and especially when there was assistance for them; it strengthened my resolve. It wasn't an ego battle, not the 'I'll-show-you-who-I-am' thinking. I wanted to know if I had the wherewithal to counter them, if I had the ability to tackle something that didn't happen every day.

From among the knocks not discussed elsewhere in the book, here are my top picks, in no particular order other than chronological:

83 AND 79 VS NEW ZEALAND (CHRISTCHURCH, II TEST, FEBRUARY 1976)

The previous week in Auckland, we had scored our maiden Test win in New Zealand, Pras and Chandra sharing 19 wickets. We suspected the South Island city of Christchurch wouldn't be as kind to our spinners, and one look at the surface confirmed our belief. A carpet of green, indistinguishable from the lush outfield, dictated that the team winning the toss bowl first. On the morning of the match, some water had seeped through the covers and there was a damp, fresh, live feel to the grass. We were naturally delighted when we learnt that Bishan had won the toss.

Bishan had pulled a leg muscle in the first-class game against Northern Districts, which kept him out of the Auckland game. In his first Test as skipper, Sunil scored 116 and steered our modest second-innings chase with an unbeaten 35, and was readying for a stint in the slips when Bishan walked in and told us we were batting. That he had chosen to bat. There was stunned silence before we accepted that we had no choice. We'd just have to tell ourselves that Glenn Turner had won the toss and put us in. It was a strange call by Bishan, though am not blaming him. I am not sure these two innings would have transpired if we had bowled first, come to think of it.

New Zealand had what you might call a gun attack—Richard Collinge, Dayle Hadlee, Richard Hadlee and Bevan Congdon, with Hedley Howarth, the older brother of future captain Geoff, as the lone specialist spinner. For the time being, we could forget about Howarth, he'd be lucky to get a bowl in the first innings. If New Zealand were forced to bring him on, it meant we had done a good job as a batting group.

Collinge was a tall, powerful man, very fast and a very senior left-armer. Dayle, Richard's older brother, was also very quick although injuries prevented him from playing as long as he should have, while Richard himself was fairly ferocious those days. In three years, he had played only a handful of Tests, but you could see why he was rated so highly. We had our work cut out.

We lost Sunil and Dilip Vengsarkar early on, only 41 to the good when I took guard. That soon became 52 for three when Collinge claimed Surinder Amarnath as his third victim. The ball was seaming around like it had a mind of its own, jagging in or away very late at great pace. You had to be watchful, but you couldn't afford to go into your shell either, because you never know when you will get a ball with your name on it.

I took pride in the confidence my mates had in me. 'If India is in trouble, Vishy will bail us out,' they'd say. There is no greater feeling than enjoying the respect of your teammates. In difficult situations, as focussed as I was on the task at hand, I was also mindful that I carried their hopes and aspirations.

As a batsman, you can't complain that the dice is loaded against you. You do have a bat, don't you? So, use it. And judiciously.

I managed to do so, adding 98 with Mohinder to make sure we had a respectable total on the board. We scored too quickly for our liking though, 270 in 60.6 overs (they were eight-ball overs then in that part of the world), but with our limited pace resources—to their credit, Madan and Mohinder accounted for nine wickets—we were able to keep them on the field for a day and a half even though they made 400-plus.

Rain at various stages during the match helped cut down the number of overs we had to survive to preserve our series lead, but we still had to bat out the entire final day. Even though the conditions had eased a little, the ball was still doing a fair bit. We had consistent contributions throughout the order, and unlike in the first innings, I put my head down and focussed on occupation of the crease more than scoring runs. We wiped out the deficit and a draw was inevitable when I fell for 79, caught behind off Andy Roberts. Ha, got you! New Zealand, too, had an Andy Roberts at the time, a batsman who bowled a bit of medium-pace.

You might say two hundreds missed, but to me, these were two vitally important knocks. Much-needed, timely, in challenging conditions against a superb attack, resulting in the team securing a draw. I will take these over even one 100. Any day.

79 NOT OUT VS ENGLAND (BANGALORE, IV TEST, FEBRUARY 1977)

They called him 'Deadly' for a reason. On uncovered pitches in England where the bounce was unpredictable, Derek Underwood was lethal. He was an exceptional left-arm spinner even when there was no help, but at the first sign of encouragement, he grew fangs. It wasn't uncommon for him to run through formidable batting line-ups, even at home, in the third and fourth innings of matches.

Underwood was elated at what greeted him at the M. Chinnaswamy

Stadium in early 1977. England had already taken a winning 3-0 lead in the five-Test series, and were hopeful of making it 4-0 in my city, on a track expected to deteriorate increasingly.

After a low-scoring first-innings face-off, we had grabbed a crucial 58-run lead but given how the series had panned out and the form England's batsmen had shown, we felt we had to give our spinners at least 300 runs in the fourth innings. As skilful as you might be, the twin pressures of containing and taking wickets can be daunting to the very best; if we hoped to pull one back, we had to allow our spinners to attack, not bowl containing lines and wait for mistakes.

Underwood was in his elements in the second innings, the lynchpin around whom Bob Willis, John Lever and Chris Old operated. Our designs of a big lead crumbled as he got on a roll, dismissing Sunil and Brijesh to leave us gasping at 124 for five.

That was when I came out to bat. At No. 7, I had not fielded for much of the England first innings after sustaining a blow to my right thumb. The pain was immense, and the digit swelled up profusely, but fortunately, there was no fracture. I was plied with painkillers—injection and tablets—as the doctors worked hard to get me to a position from where I could go out and bat. Because I had spent so much time in the dressing room, I could only come out at the fall of the fifth wicket. Underwood had his tail up, our lead had not even touched 200. Yajurvindra Singh, on debut, was defiant for two and a half hours before perishing to Deadly's guile, leaving me with only the lower order for support.

The ball was spinning like a top, and England were high on confidence. As feisty as Kiri and Karsan were, I knew I held the key—I say this with absolute humility. Despite the painkillers, I felt discomfort every time the ball hit the bat in the first few minutes. The way my bottom hand gripped the handle too was impacted, but soon, I put all that out of my mind. There was a job to do. I could look for excuses in case I failed, maybe I even had good reason, but that's not how I played the game.

It was one of only two instances when I carried an injury or illness into a Test innings. The other was to come four years later in the famous Melbourne victory of 1981, though by the time the match actually started,

I was almost pain-free. I had severe toothache in the days leading up to the MCG Test. Destiny took me to dinner at an Indian family's house, two days before the match. The man of the house was a dentist, and he made it a mission to set me right in time for the game. Thank you, Doc, for playing your part in us squaring that series.

Underwood brooked careful watching with the ball hissing and spitting and turning viciously. I had to play with soft hands and perhaps in some ways, the injury to the bottom hand proved beneficial in defence, actually. Kiri, Karsan and Bishan each helped me add 30-plus for the seventh, eighth and ninth wickets, respectively. Kiri and Bishan were typically creative, while Karsan was more obdurate and stubborn. By the time Bishan waved us in with an hour and a half left on day four, we had reached 259 for nine, I was 79 not out, our lead was 317. Almost home.

Bishan and Chandra did the rest, spinning us to a massive 140-run victory. It was to be the only time I was part of a Test win in Bangalore. When I was batting, I was so in the zone that it never occurred to me that I was doing so in front of old friends and family members. But once the final wicket fell, I was delighted to have played my small part in an Indian victory in the city of my cricketing birth. Like Christchurch, this wasn't a three-figure knock. But we won, so to me, that unbeaten 79 with a badly injured right thumb is right up there.

124 VS WEST INDIES (MADRAS, IV TEST, JANUARY 1979)

West Indies were without several key men in this six-Test series. The cream had been lopped off by Kerry Packer's World Series Cricket, so Kalli had a fairly young and inexperienced team under his command in one of the most difficult places to travel to in world cricket.

There is, however, nothing called a weak Caribbean pace attack. For decades, they have had an assembly line of wonderful fast bowlers, not unlike us and our spin riches. This time around, their quicks were Sylvester Clarke, Norbert Phillip, the seasoned Vanburn Holder and a young tyro answering to the name of Malcolm Marshall. For some reason, West Indies left out Marshall for this fourth Test, on easily the quickest, bounciest track I have come across in India. There might have been a different tale to tell otherwise.

At the risk of sounding immodest, I consider this one of my greatest knocks, perhaps even better than my 97 not out at the same venue against the same opposition five years previously. Even then, it was a reasonably bouncy track, but one man made the difference—Andy Roberts. The impact he made on that game was far more pronounced than the others, even if his partners in crime were all very capable and experienced. That is more a testimony to Andy's brilliance than a censure of his colleagues.

For obvious reasons, this attack didn't possess the same class or inspire the same awe. However, seeing them go about their business at Chepauk, you would never have guessed. The ball was flying through at great pace and considerable height, making each of the bowlers appear far more potent than they actually were. Just as well that Marshall didn't figure in their attack.

This was the fourth Test of what had been a fairly back-breaking tour for the visitors, who had toiled hard on unresponsive decks in Bombay, Bangalore and Calcutta before arriving in the Tamil Nadu capital. At the first sign of pace and bounce, they couldn't help themselves. Like kids in a candy shop, they were all over the place, bowling far too short as they got carried away. All they had to do was concentrate on line and length, and allow the pitch to do the rest. But because they were hell-bent on testing out the bounce and resorting liberally to the bumper, they played right into my hands. We would have been in greater trouble, I suspect, had they had even one thinking paceman in their XI.

Kapil had shown them the way by taking four wickets and keeping them down to 228, but Clarke, Phillip and Holder didn't seem to have watched him closely. Having said that, they were still quite a handful. Clarke was most deceptive, operating off a short run-up but generating tremendous pace on the back of a heavy right shoulder. Phillip and Holder were more than brisk and we had to be on our toes. The pacers felt their plans were working because they made early inroads with the short stuff, but I wasn't complaining.

The bounce and the width allowed me to play the cut freely; I was pleasantly surprised that Kalli didn't employ a third man till I got into the 60s. We kept losing wickets, but that didn't stop me from playing my strokes, mainly off the back foot and mostly through the off side.

Kiri's 33 was the next highest score as we were bowled out for 255. I was last man out, with 17 fours in my 124. Our lead wasn't massive, but in the most un-Indian of conditions, I had given us a fighting chance. Players from both sides were surprised at how the pitch behaved. Madras had the reputation of having more pace and bounce than any other centre in India, but previously, the bounce would gradually drop and the surface would slow down after the first day. This one was different, the track as lively on day four when we completed a nervy three-wicket win as it had been on the first morning.

We went 1-0 up—the only match to end decisively, as it turned out—ironically on a pitch that seemed more out of Sabina Park than Chepauk. I weighed in with a useful 31 when we were chasing 125 and slumped to 17 for three. But that 124, ah, how much I enjoyed it!

222 VS ENGLAND (MADRAS, V TEST, JANUARY 1982)

I have three hundreds at Green Park, including the one on debut, and average in excess of 85. It is with Madras, though, that people identify me. I have two centuries in 10 Tests at Chepauk, my average is a little under 50. But several of my most impactful performances have come in Madras, which has undoubtedly contributed to the legend.

From the time I joined the SBI, I had been very comfortable playing in Madras. SBI didn't have a Bangalore circle those days, we came under the Madras circle. All inter-circle matches in the South were staged in Madras, so I travelled there often and played numerous matches. It became a second home of sorts, and the people of Madras took a liking to me as well, cementing a bond that has only grown stronger over time.

I found the Madras crowd extremely knowledgeable and situationally aware. They enjoyed good cricket, whether it came from the home side or the visitors. They would come to Test matches armed with the statistics of members from both squads, and would welcome individual as well as team accomplishments. I liked the manner in which they expressed their appreciation, I loved their involvement in the game and I enjoyed putting on a show for them.

That's not to say that I had any less fondness for the Bangalore crowd, or the fans in Delhi, Bombay or Calcutta, for that matter. I am grateful for their love and support, and I have tried my best to reciprocate by entertaining them and being respectful of their contributions to my success. But for reasons beyond our comprehension, Madras has been the stage of multiple dramatic performances.

This particular innings makes the list for slightly selfish reasons, you might say, though it didn't harm the team one bit. It was my first—and as it turned out—only double-hundred, the magical number of 222. In so many ways, it was a personal victory.

The bounce was not as pronounced as three years back against West Indies, but England had a pace attack out of the top drawer—Bob Willis, Ian Botham, Graham Dilley and Paul Allott. Underwood was still around, and we were in a spot on day one when we lost Sunil and Pranab Roy with 51 on the board.

Willis was fast and furious, thundering in off a long run-up, arms by his side, exploding into a frenzy of pace, bounce and movement. He bowled as quickly in that first innings as I have ever seen him, reminding everyone that he was not just one of England's greatest fast bowlers but one of the best of all time, worldwide. I had to be on full alert to keep him at bay, and with Dilip playing his strokes with freedom, we took the score to 150 when calamity struck.

Dilip was caught in no-man's land as a short ball from Willis uncharacteristically didn't bounce as much as expected. Down on his haunches, Dilip turned his back on the ball, which thudded into the back of his unhelmeted head. He was carried off the field, and Yashpal Sharma walked in, not unlike Aunshu on debut, to the sight of blood on the pitch.

When, as a non-striker, you see your partner struck on the face or head, your heart starts pounding. As it is, it's just the two of you against the 11 of them, and then this. Your first instinct is to rush down the track to make sure the blow is not serious. To be fair, the concern is universal. As much as a few bowlers might claim so, no one enjoys injuring and maiming batsmen. As an ally, your concern is perhaps greater, if at all there can be varying degrees of concern in such instances.

By this time, I had played more than a decade of Test cricket, I was a veteran. It was my responsibility to settle Yashpal's nerves, if any. I had to tell him that it was an accident, that there was no spite in the pitch, that he should back himself and play his natural game. To give him that kind of confidence, you first need to have that courage yourself. You can't tell him one thing when your voice and your body language are screaming out something totally different.

You have to try and put the incident out of your head as quickly as possible, because if you allow it to grab hold of you, it's impossible to apply yourself. You must find ways of breathing normally, of getting back into the zone. I realized that I had to lead the way in how I carried myself, not just for the sake of the next batsman, Yash in this case, but for the rest of the guys sitting in the dressing room.

England's overrate was quite poor, even accounting for the Madras heat and humidity. Yash showed great character in fighting through the day, which we finished on 178 for two. Not massive, but not bad at all after losing the openers with not many on the board and another batsman to injury.

Day two was historic. Yash and I knew we had to bat deep, not overthink and just build our partnership. As the day wore on, our alliance grew stronger and stronger. I went past my 100, then 150, and a little before close, Yash brought up a richly deserved century of his own. When stumps were drawn, I was in a tizzy.

Not even when I started playing at the highest level did I imagine batting out an entire day in a Test match. And here I was, 181 not out at the end of a day when I had started on 64. What made it sweeter was that my partner too had achieved the same feat. It's not often that you go a whole day without losing a wicket. I was particularly proud of that.

One of the criticisms in my initial days in Test cricket was that I was prone to lapses in concentration, as I have mentioned earlier in the book. I thought if this knock didn't explode that myth, nothing else would. By the time I was bowled by Willis a little before lunch on day three, I had batted for 643 minutes and faced 374 deliveries. Maybe, I could concentrate a little, after all? Just a little.

The Test ended in a draw once we stacked up 481, after which Graham Gooch treated us to a special hundred with a bat that seemed to have only the broadest middle and no edges whatsoever. That evening, some of us caught up with Underwood at the bar, and he whispered in my ear, 'When you are tired, Vishy, give me your wicket. No rush, whenever you are tired.' Apologies, Derek, I didn't tire easily.

24

CROSS-BORDER BLUES

Into my tenth year in international cricket, I had played home and away against all other nations, but still hadn't pitted my skills against the country closest to us geographically. India and Pakistan hadn't played each other since 1960-61, when all five Tests on Indian soil ended without a result. The last time India had travelled across the border was in 1954-55, another indecisive five-Test face-off.

Our excitement, therefore, was understandably palpable when India's first tour of Pakistan in 24 years was announced. We'd play three Tests and as many ODIs from October 1978, a tour where the results were important as always, but where diplomacy was paramount. We weren't going there as only cricket players; we were ambassadors of India, and winning hearts was the greater priority.

I'd met several Pakistani players in England on our 1974 tour. A plethora of them played county cricket—Majid Khan, Asif Iqbal, Zaheer Abbas, Mushtaq and Sadiq Mohammad, Imran Khan and Sarfraz Nawaz—and we struck a good rapport during brief encounters. I was looking forward to renewing old relationships and building new ones; exciting times lay ahead of us on and off the field.

The first few days in Pakistan sped by. Beyond practice, we met with people of reasonably high societal standing, very polished and suave, very polite and hospitable. The air was of goodwill and camaraderie, and we enjoyed our interactions even though secretly, some of us were envious of our manager who attracted plenty of attraction.

Mr Fatehsinghrao Gaekwad was then the titular Maharaja of Baroda, a regal and aristocratic presence who wowed you with his charm and intellect and had an unmistakable aura around him. He was a wonderful human being, cheerful and unpretentious. If you felt you were in the presence of royalty, which you were, it was despite his best efforts to put you at ease. He was the cynosure at all social gatherings, treated like the celebrity he was, and his popularity soared as the tour progressed. I am certain he received more garlands, and affection, than all of us players put together!

As pleasant as the evening crowds were, those that came for the cricket were decidedly partisan and hostile, which is no more than what we had expected. Anybody who says an India–Pakistan contest is just another match is talking through his hat. There is an added edge. We had no issues with the fans supporting the Pakistani team; after all, it came with home territory.

The first Test was on a batting beauty in Faisalabad. Our hopes of Bishan winning the toss dashed, we watched Pakistan flex their batting muscle through Zaheer and Javed Miandad. Zaheer was an accomplished destroyer of bowling. He had made his debut a month before me and loved the English attack so much that he once let them off the hook after making only 274. Javed was relatively new but had served notice of his smarts and his combative batting. Both made 150-plus scores and put on 255 for the fourth wicket, the bedrock around which Mushtaq declared at 503 for eight.

Our best result would now be a draw. We were straightaway on the back foot, having conceded 500 in the first innings of the series, and even though the track was lovely to bat on, we were under pressure. In a great show of character, we responded in kind. Sunil and Chetan set us on the way with a stand of 97, and when the former uncharacteristically fell for 89 with a century for the taking, Dilip and I assumed control.

I was coming off half-centuries in my last five Test innings—59, 54, 79, 89 and 73—in Australia earlier that year. As far as consistency went, that was excellent, but I was beginning to get annoyed at not converting even one of them into a three-figure knock. My last hundred, an unbeaten 103 against New Zealand in Kanpur, had come two years back. It was time to end the drought.

Pakistan had a high-quality attack. Imran was pacy, Sarfraz and Sikander Bakht were more than just support acts, left-arm spinner

Iqbal Qasim was a handful and skipper Mushtaq ripped his legbreaks considerably. Against that versatile attack, Dilip and I bedded in, batting untroubled while putting on 166. By the time I was bowled round my legs by Mushtaq, I had scored 145. Mushtaq sparked a mini-collapse thereafter, but once we had closed to within 41 of Pakistan's tally, there wasn't enough time left for them to force the issue.

It was a good start to the series for batsmen from both sides, and we left Faisalabad buoyant. To come to Pakistan, stare 500 in the face and secure an honourable draw was an excellent result. As a bonus, the players got along famously. There was plenty of laughter and leg-pulling off the field, but on it, the cricket was tough, with no quarters asked and none given. It was easy to make friends in that era, but Indian and Pakistani players naturally gravitated towards each other faster. I became very good friends with Wasim Raja, a true gentleman. He spent a lot of time in our dressing room and we renewed our association after our playing days when we both became ICC match referees. His demise (in 2006) came as a shock and left me in grief for a long time.

◆

Our euphoria at the first-Test performance dissipated within minutes of the start of the second, in Lahore, on a greenish pitch where the ball did a fair bit. Bishan called wrong again, and Imran and Sarfraz worked through the order, only Dilip offering any resistance with 76. When you are bowled out for 199 on the opening day of a Test, it's practically impossible to bounce back unless you have the bowling to exploit the conditions. We didn't. As well as Kapil bowled on his first Test tour, he didn't have support at the other end, and Zaheer once again feasted on our spinners. Perhaps disappointed that he had eased up at 176 in the first Test, he plundered us to remain unbeaten on 235. Pakistan's lead was well in excess of 300, and we mounted a strong response with Sunil, Chetan, Surinder and myself, the top four, all making at least 50. We kept Pakistan on the field for 170.3 overs in making 465, and thought we had earned ourselves another merited draw, but they hunted down the target of 126 in a mere 20.4 overs. Surprisingly summoned to the bowling crease, I conceded the runs that took them to an eight-wicket victory, and a 1-0 edge.

By now, it was apparent that, in unhelpful conditions, our legendary spinners were making no impression on batsmen accomplished against the turning ball. Led by Zaheer, Pakistan played them superbly; in our heart of hearts, we knew the remarkable era of our glorious quartet was drawing to a close. No one spoke out loudly, but everyone felt the same, a feeling that was reinforced when we lost in Karachi too.

Not for the first time, Sunil showcased his wondrous skills as he waged a solitary battle in the final Test. In both innings, the rest of the top order caved in and the only support came from Karsan and Kapil at No. 8 and No. 9, respectively. Sunil had been the recipient of one of several dubious umpiring calls in the second innings in Lahore when on 97, and responded with 111 and 137 in Karachi, the second time he scored twin hundreds in the same Test. By batting deep into the final day and opening up a lead of 163, we thought we were safe, but in an encore of Lahore, Pakistan blasted to victory.

Asif opened the batting, and he and Javed ran us ragged with their alacrity between the stumps. Imran then arrived in a blaze of sixes off Bishan, and incredibly, Pakistan clattered to 164 in just the twenty-fifth over. I admired the spark in the Pakistani chase—they had scored at 6.69 an over more than 40 years back in the fourth innings of a Test—but knew that heads would roll, careers would end. Unsurprisingly, Bishan lost the captaincy after the 2-0 defeat, while the Lahore Test would be Pras's last. Bishan and Chandra didn't play beyond the series in England in the summer of 1979 as the seeds sown in Pakistan germinated viciously.

Where one era was on the verge of ending, another was unmistakably in its infancy. Overlooked for Australia, where he would have thrived on helpful surfaces, Kapil made an immediate mark in Pakistan, hustling the batsmen with the pace that was his ally for his first couple of years at the international level. He had a smooth, lovely action, his outswingers curled away late, and while he didn't have a bucketful of wickets against his name, there were enough glimpses to suggest he would touch great heights. He played a couple of free-flowing knocks lower down the order and fielded brilliantly, thanks to his natural athleticism. Indian cricket had unearthed an uncut diamond that would serve it with distinction for the next decade and a half.

Apart from watching the disintegration of the spin quartet, my other disappointment, strangely, stemmed from not seeing too many runs flow off Majid Khan's bat. I had heard so much about him, how lovely he was to watch, what a great batsman he was. My desire to watch beautiful batsmanship didn't bear fruit, but I kept my feelings to myself. I am not sure our bowlers would have taken kindly to me.

Until the final ODI, this had been a dream tour for those using cricket diplomacy to regularize relations between the two nations. We had managed to endear ourselves to the crowds even though they continued to support the home side vocally, and despite the loss of the Test series, our overall quality of play had been more than decent. The ODI series was beautifully poised at 1-1 when the teams reached Sahiwal, 200 km from Lahore, for the decider.

The umpiring hadn't been of the highest order, though we hadn't made a song and dance of it, not even when Mohinder was given a final official warning for running on the pitch in just the second over of the first Test! We found the call too hilarious to get worked up. Imagine, Mohinder Amarnath, ambling to the crease, receiving a final warning in the second over of a Test that yielded 1,272 runs and saw a mere 21 wickets fall in five days. I am still trying to figure that one out.

Anyway, in Sahiwal, we restricted Pakistan to 205 for seven in 40 overs and were well on course, with Aunshu and Surinder leading the charge. The finish line was in sight, we were looking to round off the tour with the ODI series win when Sarfraz launched into a bouncer barrage that the umpires did little to prevent. There were four, sometimes five, bouncers in an over, sailing over our heads. In protest, Bishan called Aunshu and myself in when we had reached 183 for two in 37.4 overs.

The Maharaja tried to persuade Bishan to resume the game, but that didn't happen and Pakistan were deemed to have won because India 'conceded' the match. It was an unsavoury end to an otherwise lovely couple of months, and my teammates flared up when an official associated with the Pakistan team said, 'Why couldn't your captain have sent a taller batsman, why send Vishwanath, who is so short?' As much as it was an admission that they had bowled too many bouncers, I was stunned by this question. Sir, hello, who do you think you are?

◆

Our next tour to Pakistan, from December 1982, would be my last tryst with international cricket, though none of us knew that at the time.

We were to play six Tests and four ODIs—I wasn't in the limited-overs squad—against a formidable outfit that had several players from our earlier tour and two exciting new names, Salim Malik and Abdul Qadir. Even though I had contributed 249 runs in 1978–79, we had lost the series. I was determined to make my runs count three years on, little aware of what lay in store.

Long story short, we were swept aside 3-0 in the Tests, 3-1 in the ODIs. Pakistan overwhelmed us, overran us, didn't so much as give a chance. Three of their batsmen topped 500 runs—Mudassar Nazar led the way with 761, Zaheer had 650 and Javed 594. We had only two who touched 250. Imran finished with 40 wickets, only nine fewer than our entire team managed. It was carnage, any way you looked at it.

Sunil was customarily stoic, making nearly 450 runs, while Mohinder was outstanding. While the rest of us floundered, Mohinder showed exemplary courage and excellent determination, stacking up 584 runs. It was batting of the highest order, made even more impressive because largely, he didn't have much support. Ravi Shastri celebrated his elevation as opener with a steely century and Sandeep Patil threatened a couple of times, but our batting was primarily about Mohinder.

Even in Australia on the previous tour, he had batted brilliantly. In Perth, when Thommo was bowling really quickly, Mohinder received a sickening blow to his hand. I rushed from the non-striker's end, fearing the worst, and when Mohinder managed to extricate his hand from the glove, we saw blood gushing out of the deep cut to his middle finger. The calmest man on the field, Mohinder signalled to the dressing room for water, cleaned up the blood and proceeded to bat like nothing had happened against the express pace of Thommo and Wayne Clark, eventually finishing with 90.

In Pakistan, he was totally in control, tackling Imran with rare assurance. Imran was making the ball talk—later, we came to know how Pakistan had 'maintained' the ball, scuffing up one side and keeping the other smooth, shiny and heavy to facilitate reverse swing—and looking like getting a wicket every time he ran in with the old ball. Strangely enough, the new ball hardly swung for him or his colleagues, but after the drinks break, it would start to go alarmingly. I am sure it was because the drinks break energized their wrists unspeakably. Mohinder alone seemed to pick the late swing, earning the grudging admiration of the opposition and our immeasurable respect.

I had a couple of reasonable starts, made one half-century and got into the 30s once, but didn't kick on to anything substantial. Throughout my career, I'd done well in say four or five innings in a series. This time, I felt I was on to a good thing in the second Test when I got to 24, and in a couple of other knocks, when I believed I was wrongly given out. This is not an excuse, I am only expressing what I experienced at the time. Had I gone on to one or two good scores early on, it would have done wonders for my confidence and I am sure I would have played a little longer for India. But that wasn't to be. Like I said, no excuses, maybe I was only destined to play 91 Tests.

Imran was outstanding all through the series, no two ways about that. On our previous tour, he was predominantly an in-swing bowler but now, with greater experience, he was able to get the ball to straighten or tail away just that shade. You could see that this version was a marked improvement from the previous one.

I was fortunate to play in the era of four stunning all-rounders. I rated Ian Botham and Kapil above Imran and Richard Hadlee because apart from their huge bag of wickets, both of them made more than 5,000 Test runs, and were naturally gifted fielders. Botham had great hands and took special catches in the slips, while Kapil was an effortless all-round fieldsman, gliding across the turf and possessing one of the finest arms of his time.

In my book, Hadlee was the best bowler among them—I am not including Kapil because, obviously, I couldn't bat against him in Tests. When we went to New Zealand in 1976, Hadlee was quick but erratic, but over time, he mastered accuracy. He played a lot of cricket in England for

Nottinghamshire, imbibed the virtues of accuracy and constantly asked questions of you. He seldom strayed from the corridor on and outside off stump, making it impossible to leave balls because you couldn't say with confidence which one would nip back and which would nibble away. I probably got out to Imran more often, but I'd place Hadlee above him and Botham, and among the greatest, most difficult bowlers I have faced.

As the tour progressed and my runs dried up, I could see the writing on the wall. I also sensed that, like Bishan in 1979, Sunil would lose the captaincy at the end of the series. That was unique to Indian cricket, how captains went from very good to very bad, based on the result of one series. We had had one bizarre experience on our way back from England in 1979, when the pilot of our aircraft congratulated Sunil on being appointed the skipper. It was news to both Sunil and to poor Venkat, who had just led us at the World Cup and during the Test tour. A captain congratulating another captain, while the BCCI didn't deem it necessary to thank Venkat for his services as the captain of the national side and inform him of their decision to replace him as the skipper.

We were due to tour the West Indies immediately after the Pakistan series, and my suspicions that I would be left out were confirmed by Kapil, the only choice to succeed Sunil. One evening in Pakistan, he walked up to me and said, 'Vishy, this is probably your last tour. I don't think you will be there in the team to tour West Indies.' What could I say—'No, please take me to the Caribbean'?

Like the previous outing, this visit to Pakistan too ended sadly. We had surrendered the Tests 0-3, our captain faced the axe and I was being dropped. I was sure I still had what it took to play for India, so I competed at the first-class level for a few more years and scored plenty of runs, too. But there was no Test comeback for G.R. Vishwanath.

West Indies visited India towards the end of 1983 for a six-Test series, and midway through the campaign, there was talk that I'd be recalled. I received a call asking me to report to Ahmedabad for the third Test—not from a board official but from an 'insider'—and to carry my kit with me. I travelled to Ahmedabad for the first Test at the new ground in Motera, but I had more sense than to take my gear. I watched Sunil make an excellent 90 and Kapil take nine wickets in an innings, but not as a teammate. The comeback didn't happen, just as I had suspected. Had I been drafted in, I'd have had to do a Tiger, borrowing a bat from someone, pads from someone else, gloves from a third colleague.

In separate conversations during that series, each of the five selectors told Kavita that they tried their best to push for my inclusion, only for the others to shoot it down. So, the five men who decide the composition of the team all wanted me, still I was out. Kavita and I shared a hearty laugh about it. What else could we do? It hurt to be dropped after the Pakistan tour, but you can't carry that agony forever. For the record, I am still wondering how all the selectors wanted me to play against West Indies, and yet how I didn't even figure in the squad. If you work that out, please give me a shout.

25

GOLF, AND OTHER BALL GAMES

Sometime in the mid-1970s, during a Ranji Trophy game, Pras started shadow-practising golf swings in the slip cordon. From first slip, I glanced at Kiri to my left, and we could barely conceal a guffaw. We were both thinking the same thing. 'Golf is an old man's sport, what is he up to? Is he planning his retirement?'

Obviously, we couldn't say that to Pras. Instead, we asked him, 'What are you doing?'

'Golf is great fun. Why don't you guys start playing it too?'

Kiri and I exchanged another meaningful glance which said, 'Hey, we are still young. We are a long way away from golf.'

Oh, I wish! How I desperately wish I had taken up golf then. Of my various addictions in life, none has been more all-pervading. Anyone who has played the sport will understand where I am coming from. The lockdown and the subsequent stay-at-home in the wake of the pandemic opened my eyes to exactly what the sport means to me. Then again, maybe it was a good thing that I waited a decade after my last Test to try my hand at golf. Who knows, my obsession might have weaned me away from my original sport, the one I love and breathe.

◆

I played five seasons of first-class cricket after my last Test in Karachi, in February 1983. My final Ranji Trophy game was the pre-quarterfinal against Bombay in February 1988, a game we conceded on the first-innings lead. In my only hit, I managed 13 before falling to the left-arm spin of Padmakar Shivalkar. I had played three matches in the South Zone league phase, with a highest of 41 in five knocks. I wasn't enjoying playing anymore.

At the start of the season, I knew I had slowed down a little, as was inevitable. Going into the Bombay game, I decided that this would be my last outing, win or lose. The time had come to walk away. I didn't have the will to carry on, which means it should be the end of your playing career. Even 30-over matches in The Hindu Trophy had become too long, I felt lost after fielding for 10 overs. I wasn't in the game, I'd ask myself what I was doing on the field. Standing in my stance, I'd mentally query the bowler, 'Why are you running in from so far to get my wicket?'

In the days immediately after being dropped—much as I dislike that word, in reality, I was dropped, wasn't I?—from the Test squad, I was seized with the thought of staging a grand comeback to the national team. I made runs for Karnataka, a fair few of them, I knocked off centuries, but there was no recall. I was having fun on the field though, and I was energized by the rush of youngsters breaking into the side. I was still getting runs, I wasn't a burden on the team and I felt being with the youngsters, playing alongside them, would be to their benefit.

Young batsmen such as Carlton Saldanha, Sadanand Viswanath, Srinivas Prasad, Arjun Raja, Kartik Jeshwant and P.V. Shashikanth had broken into the senior state side, and I thought I could be of help by sharing my experience, sharing the dressing room and sharing partnerships.

After the Bombay game, I was reasonably sure I was done with cricket in any capacity. Naturally, I missed playing the sport that had dominated my childhood and adult life. I missed the camaraderie of the dressing room, the long train journeys and the exchange of stories, the leg-pulling and the laughter and banter. I did what I thought was the next-best thing—watch matches on television, no matter who was playing whom in which part of the globe. I subconsciously started to analyse Indian batsmen in particular. If someone got out, for instance, I'd wonder how I would have played that ball. If India won, I'd reflect on our victories, on the good times we had following those wins. I was swimming in nostalgia, occasionally maybe even wallowing in self-pity.

I told myself to snap out of it and just like that, all those thoughts were flushed out of my system. I began to enjoy others' batting, no longer wondering how I would have tackled a particular bowler or played a specific shot. Gradually, I stopped missing playing cricket.

Within months of retiring, I was unexpectedly reunited with cricket as manager of the national team during New Zealand's tour of India, under John Wright, from November 1988. I had watched several Tests since my last game in 1983, but none from the dressing room. To be able to enter the dressing room by right, not as a guest or an invitee, was a moment to cherish, and the start of a long non-playing association with cricket in various capacities.

◆

In 1992, I was made the chairman of the senior national selection committee. It was a great honour; my team was tasked with carrying Indian cricket forward, and I was fortunate to have a fabulous bunch—Kishan Rungta from Rajasthan, Sambaran Banerjee from Bengal, Ravinder Chadha from Haryana and my old mate Aunshu.

We were a very close-knit unit, all pulling in the same direction. It's not as if we agreed on everything, but our discussions were meaningful and nuanced, and we put all biases behind us when we congregated to pick teams. I was mindful of my stature both as a cricketer and the chairman of the committee, and of the fact that I should not be seen as misusing that. I'd encourage all the other members to speak their mind first at selection meetings, digest their observations and only then express my views. I didn't want to put them in a position where, if I spoke first, they might feel the pressure to agree with everything I said. My word was not final in that I didn't impose myself; we'd talk about our vision for the Indian team, and what parts would fit the missing pieces of the jigsaw. In any case, when you sit down, you are not selecting 15 or 16 players, essentially mulling over two or three places at the most.

I encouraged, indeed demanded, that my colleagues and I watch as many domestic games as we could, and preferably not only those involving our respective states of domicile. That way, we would get to see a cross-section of players, so that Aunshu wouldn't have to bring up the names of performers from Baroda or I didn't have to espouse the virtues of the Karnataka boys.

I trusted my colleagues implicitly. I knew they wouldn't talk someone up for the sake of it, they wouldn't sing praises of players they hadn't seen. We'd have several hours of conversations about specific players—not just how many runs they scored or how many wickets they took, but about their temperament, their comfort level at first-class cricket and the potential that might not yet have been realized. Ours was a process of give and take, at the end of which I would lead the discussions that would take us to a balanced combination.

It so happened that a half-dozen Karnataka players were in the national side during my tenure as chairman, but clearly, that was a mere coincidence. Our predecessors had already given us a strong batting line-up to work with, but I'd like to think we laid the base for the golden generation of Indian batting, as it's called. Sachin Tendulkar was already well established, Rahul Dravid and Sourav Ganguly broke in during the England tour in the summer of 1996 and V.V.S. Laxman made his Test debut that same year. In time to come, this would, alongside Virender Sehwag, become the best batting line-up in the world for a long period.

I loved being a selector—I never thought of myself as the chairman—and thoroughly enjoyed the process of identifying talent. To be able to see budding talent in its formative stages gladdened my heart, and my fellow selectors added to my delight with their balance, equanimity and sense of fair play.

I had imagined the job to be very stressful and tough, but within days, I realized that it was as smooth as batting. Like I did before every Test, I felt the jitters ahead of each selection meeting, which I construed as a good sign. I was excited about the challenge, I wanted to do a good job. The butterflies were an indication of caring, not fear. They didn't subside one bit during the four years, but as I said, the road became smooth in no time, the selection process started to resemble my batting more and more.

♦

The International Cricket Council (ICC) had, by now, felt the need for match referees to oversee proceedings during international games and ensure things didn't get out of hand in the heat of the battle. Given my long association with the sport as player and selector, I got into the

ICC's international panel of referees in 1999, though I had reservations about what the job would entail. My biggest fear was that it would be a tiring job, watching every ball, making notes, looking on eagle-eyed like a policeman. I need not have worried. This was a wonderful experience that brought back international travel to watch cricket, especially Test cricket. I was able to go to South Africa, a country out of bounds during my playing days due to their apartheid policy. I made a couple of visits to the land of the Protea, including during the 2003 World Cup which was a cracking affair driven primarily by the vision and energy of Ali Bacher.

It was not long into my match referee days that the match-fixing scandal exploded in early 2000. It came as a massive shock to the system, I found it hard to believe it was true. This should not happen in sport, in any sport. It shouldn't be allowed to happen. My faith and belief took a hit, I felt really bad for a very long time, and took my job even more seriously, if that was possible. I knew the match referee's position came with great responsibility, but this episode made me more determined to be extra vigilant, alongside the anti-corruption machinery in place.

I had some memorable experiences as referee, including one involving Shoaib Akhtar in Sri Lanka. Pakistan, New Zealand and Sri Lanka were battling in a triangular one-day competition; this match in question was being played in Dambulla between the two visiting sides, on 20 May 2003. From my position in the referee's box, I felt that something was amiss on the field, and watched what was going on with great attention. To my dismay, I found Akhtar gouging the ball with his thumbnail during New Zealand's chase of 204.

Under the rules as they existed, I was helpless. The match referee could only react to a report from any of the four umpires: the two on the field, the television umpire and the fourth umpire. I couldn't tell the third umpire, Gamini Silva, what was going on. So I merely nudged him in that direction, suggesting that he watch the ball closely in case something untoward were to transpire.

It didn't take Gamini long to figure out what was going on, and he in turn alerted his colleagues on the park, Daryl Harper and Peter Manuel. At the end of the game, they reported the incident to me, and the umpiring team and I sought footage from the television director of the relevant instances assiduously noted down by Gamini. Our PCT (the Playing Control Team comprising the referee and the umpires) sifted through the footage and easily gathered that Akhtar was clearly tampering with the ball, so I summoned Akhtar for a hearing along with Rashid Latif, the captain, manager Haroon Rashid and coach Javed Miandad, my old friend.

Seemingly taken aback at the charge of ball-tampering, Akhtar asked me, 'Sir, how can I do that with 22 cameras around?'

After a minute's silence as the quartet waited for my reply, I told him, 'Exactly. You tell me how you can do this, with 22 cameras around?'

When he saw the footage, he again protested his innocence, saying he was only cleaning the ball, but I suppose that was a token and natural defence. By then, it was late in the night, so I informed them that I'd deliver my verdict the following day.

As they got up to depart, Javed told me with a twinkle in his eye, '*Vishy bhai, dekh lo... thoda kum karo na?* (Vishy bhai, see if you bring it down a notch).' I found it funny that someone as experienced in international cricket as Javed would impulsively ask this of me. But then again, that's human nature, and Javed has always been the eternal optimist.

In the end, after much deliberation, I banned Akhtar for two matches and fined him 75 per cent of his match fee. I thought it was just punishment, neither too harsh nor too light, never mind Javed's exhortation.

Otherwise, I can't remember conducting too many hearings during my five-year tenure. I have had the odd word with a player flirting with the line, I have spoken to a manager or two at the end of a day's play, cautioning him to tell his players not to go overboard, but there wasn't any serious incident beyond the one involving Akhtar.

There was, though, one bizarre development in Harare that same November after which my already high regard for Brian Lara shot up several notches.

We were at the Harare Sports Club for the first of two Tests between Zimbabwe and West Indies, led by Heath Streak and Lara, respectively. Zimbabwe batted first and declared with more than 500 on the board, Streak making a brilliant hundred batting at No. 8. West Indies had just about started their reply when the second day ended prematurely due to bad light.

We had pencilled in an earlier than normal start on the third day to make up for time lost, and I was at the ground along with the umpiring team as the pitch was being rolled. The players were having nets inside the ground when all of a sudden, a ball struck by Trevor Gripper, the Zimbabwe opener, invaded the pitch in front of the roller.

Unaware of the intruder, the operator continued rolling the pitch. To his great shock, he realised that he had rolled over the ball, which was now stuck in the pitch. The only way to get the ball out was to dig into the surface, but how do you do so and not cause significant damage?

We were in the middle of perplexed looks and furious head-scratching when Ray Price came to our rescue. The left-arm spinner was the nephew of famous Zimbabwean golfer Nick Price. To our great fortune, because Nick used to play and practise at the Royal Harare Golf Club adjoining the Sports Club, Ray had connections that could help sort out the mess.

Golf courses have augers, machines used to make holes in the ground or on wood. The position of the hole on each of the 18 greens is changed on all four days of competition, which means not only must you have the capability to make a hole, but also fill one.

Obviously, before we could proceed further, I needed to speak to Lara. His was the visiting side as well as the batting team staring at a 500-plus total. Additionally, the dent had occurred at just short of a length to a left-hander from the southern end of the ground and the West Indians had five left-hand batsmen in the top seven, the skipper included. No matter how well Operation Hole Fill went, there could still be assistance from a greenish surface for the bowlers when they hit that patch. Zimbabwe had a mountain of runs and a top-class seam attack, so Lara would have been well within his rights to express his apprehensions.

Without a moment's hesitation, he told me, 'Go ahead with it, let's get on with the game.'

It was a fabulous gesture that warmed my heart. I was full of appreciation for Lara and his thought processes. So out came the auger and Robin Brown, the groundsman at the Sports Club who had previously opened for Zimbabwe, got down to work. Within minutes, the pitch looked good as new. The offending ball, which had made an inch-deep hole, was carefully plucked out. Then, using the portion of the pitch behind the stumps, Brown filled up the hole, cleaned the area and rolled it in to make it as close in appearance to the adjoining area as he could. The surface looked in fine fettle, though it was impossible to miss the fresh patch. Again, Lara could have at least protested if he so wanted, but he didn't say a single word. I had been a huge admirer of his batting all these years, now I became a fan of the person too. It's been so long now, I can confess I was both happy and relieved when West Indies hung on to clinch a thrilling draw on the final day, the last-wicket pair batting out more than 30 minutes to stave off defeat.

◆

Not long after venturing into match refereeing, I took charge as chairman of the KSCA Academy when it came into existence in 2000. The KSCA Academy is the first cricket academy to have been put in place by a state association, and our objective was not just to identify and hone talent, but also take the game beyond Bangalore and to the hinterland. With Kiri as the director, we embarked on a plan to set up academies in most of the major cities in the state: Hubli, Shimoga and Mysore. Brijesh kicked off this ambitious project when he was the secretary of the association, and when Javagal Srinath succeeded him in 2010 and Anil Kumble became the president, we went beyond the bigger cities to deeper inside Karnataka. Over time, that process started to yield results and more and more players from outside Bangalore, not just from the big cities but even remote places, started to break through into the big league.

It was that which prompted the conception of the Karnataka Premier League in August 2009, a franchise-based Twenty20 league tournament along the lines of the IPL. The tournament was the brainchild of Brijesh and Srikantadatta Narasimharaja Wadiyar, the KSCA president and a scion of the Mysore royal family. Karnataka's representation in the IPL has grown by the year, which speaks to the vibrancy of the processes put in place by the KSCA.

I forayed, perhaps not wholeheartedly, into administration too. Having served as vice-president, I contested for the post of president in 2007 against Wadiyar. I thought my cricketing abilities would see me through, but I was mistaken. Wadiyar's background and his popularity worked in his favour, perhaps royalty helped him come through too. What his father and forefathers had done for the state of Mysore as it existed then is amazing, they have left a fabulous legacy behind.

I met Wadiyar's father, Sri Jayachamarajendra Wadiyar, at his palace to seek his blessings before we embarked on our tour of England in 1974. He put his arm around my shoulder and said, 'I have been to Lord's, it's a fantastic ground. I hope you do well there.' Little did I know then that that was the last time I'd meet him.

Long before I got into the governing council of the IPL, I had a stint at the National Cricket Academy as a consultant, another thoroughly enjoyable outing that put me in proximity with a host of promising young batsmen: Shikhar Dhawan, Murali Vijay, S. Badrinath and Abhishek Nayar. Most were 19–20 years old then and I was keen to share my learnings with them. I had always wanted to give something back to cricket and cricketers, and I got several wonderful opportunities to do so. I tried to give back whatever knowledge I had picked up. I don't know to what extent I succeeded, but it is satisfying knowing that I gave it my all, just like I did with bat for club, state and country.

◆

This brings me back to golf, the game I love the most after cricket. One of the very few regrets I carry is that I didn't take to golf until 1995, when I was 46. I wish I had listened to Pras nearly 20 years earlier and started playing it then; not to make a career out of it, but just for the enjoyment it has given me in the last quarter of a century. I am very happy to have played cricket for the length and at the level I did. That's my life, my career. But golf, now, that's unbelievably fulfilling.

I needed an outlet once I was left out of the Test team, so I turned to billiards and snooker in 1983. The KSCA had recently acquired a new table, and I picked up a cue just for the heck of it, to keep myself occupied. I realized I had a 'feel' for snooker, and soon I was hooked to the 15-red game. It became a part of my everyday routine, and my enthusiasm rubbed off on Sudhakar Rao, B. Vijayakrishna, Raghu and Jayaprakash.

I thought snooker was my greatest addiction—I don't think of cricket as an addiction, needless to say—but that was only until I swapped the green baize for the greens of a golf course.

It's not as if once you have played a sport at the highest level, like we did in cricket, you can't approach another discipline with the same seriousness. There are so many cricketers worldwide who are avid golfers. Kapil, for instance, became a single handicapper in no time, which again just goes to show what a naturally gifted all-round sportsperson he is. Such great batsmen as Lara and Ricky Ponting take a round of golf as seriously now as they did a Test match innings in their prime.

I now understand that golf is anything but an old man's game. You can start playing at any stage, you can enjoy recreational golf as much as when playing it professionally. Like any other game, you need to put in hours of hard work. Even that doesn't guarantee success because such fickle factors as the wind, the lie and the slightest twitch can bring disastrous consequences. It's a tough game mentally, one of the few sports, like shooting, where you are competing with yourself, not reacting to what someone else does. It's helped me make a host of friends, expanded my social circle and exposed me to a wider populace I would otherwise never have crossed paths with.

Sometimes, I have found the little stationary white ball more vexing than the heavier red ball hurled at me in anger by a mean fast bowler. It's not an easy sport if you take to it in your 40s without having played any other sport. But if you have been a sportsperson at any level, you almost instinctively have that ball sense. Once you get a hang of golf, you feel focusing on anything else is a waste of time.

Until a few years back, I used to ring my doctor friends to invite them to a round of golf. They'd blanch when I said the full 18 rounds would take four hours. 'No time, I am too busy,' they used to brush me off. Now, the same doctors call me up asking if I am free the following afternoon for 18 holes. I chuckle to myself—welcome to the club.

◆

I embarked on my latest adventure in 2018 when Star Sports kindly invited me to do Kannada commentary during the IPL. I get as nervous before a stint as I did before going out to bat or entering a selection committee meeting but it's 'good nerves', as I call it. I'd marvelled at those who'd commentate on games, at their fluency and their command over the language. But my fellow commentators instantly put me at ease. We have conversations rather than commentating on the game alone, and I love engaging my younger colleagues in cricketing discussions. It took me a little time to get used to pausing when the ball is about to be bowled, to pick up the thread soon after, to think on my feet and come up with peppy, snappy comments. But now, I feel comfortable in the knowledge that I have picked up the metaphorical bat and started my next big innings.

I am glad Star Sports has facilitated this platform through which I can give back to the game I have lived and loved my whole life. I'd love to use this opportunity to share my knowledge as an 'expert', and hope to continue giving back to the game in some form or the other.

26

A PACK FULL OF ACES

Every generation of cricketers believes it played in the golden era of the sport. That's understandable because the best reference point is the one that actively involves you. The jury will always be out on whether the sport was in a better space then, or is more vibrant, inclusive and popular now. What I can say with certainty is that I was fortunate to play with and against some of the greatest athletes to have graced our planet. Not only are they all extraordinary cricketers, they are wonderful human beings too.

When I sat down to compile the list of my peers and contemporaries who influenced me immeasurably, it ran into dozens and dozens. Within the contours of this exercise, it was an unmanageable bunching; after my most challenging examination, I arrived at this wondrous collection of superstars that I consider the greatest among the plethora of greats I encountered during my two-decade playing career.

THE SPIN QUARTET

These three words bring an immediate smile, conjuring visions of mesmeric performances that left some of the finest batsmen in the world clueless and bemused. Chandra, Pras, Bishan and Venkat exemplified the best of cricket. They were magicians who tricked you in broad daylight, with magic in their fingers and wrists and an astute brain which was the precursor to the profusion of data and analytics prevalent now.

All four had made their Test debut well before me, and had established themselves as household names in our country while spreading panic and uncertainty in the opposition ranks. To see them in operation was phenomenal. Their control was rare, their command over basics exemplary. They loved bowling, they relished the thrill of setting batsmen up, the gleam in their eye at the successful culmination of a cunning plan indicative of the pleasure they derived from the process, not merely the outcome (words I have picked up in the last 15 years or so, I must confess).

To me, Chandra is a match-winner without parallel. His rise from club cricket to the international stage was meteoric, almost unprecedented all those years back. As he played more, he became more rounded and versatile; towards the later part of his career, he gave the ball more air too, another sign that he didn't believe the learning process ever stopped. When he got his line and length right, he was practically unplayable, a terror to any batting line-up anywhere in the world. I was lucky enough to witness first-hand the mayhem he unleashed on batsmen. Even when they felt they knew what was coming out of his right hand, they were powerless to tackle it. He was as consistently prolific in the cold of England and New Zealand as in the heat of Australia and the Caribbean. I don't need to say much, really. His record speaks for itself—58 Tests, 242 wickets.

Pras is by a mile the best off spinner I have seen. Period. I don't think anyone can lay claim to being nearly as good, apart from, probably, Venkat. Pras and I being from the same state, I didn't play him much except in the nets. Instead, from the safety of being on the same side of the fence, I saw him plot dismissals, systematically dismantle defences and game plans, and do it with a panache unique to him. Venkat and I had numerous face-offs in the Ranji Trophy and I can't say with certainty that I ever drove him through the covers. I'd put Pras ahead of Venkat because he had more variety, he could coax batsmen out of their comfort zone in so many different ways. Venkat was very steady, keeping things tight because of his height. He was a supreme competitor who never gave an inch. His spinning compatriots applauded good shots from the batsmen even if they were at the receiving end. Venkat, I can assure you, didn't fall in that category.

Bishan, of course, was poetry in motion, beautiful to watch. He literally had no run-up, just a short walk of a couple of steps, but when the ball came out of his hand, it was as if he had it on a string. His flight was an event on its own, luring the batsman into complacency. Then, the ball would dip without warning and you could see the panic in the eyes of the batsman. From lining himself up for a big stroke, he was reduced to trying to prevent himself from being embarrassed.

Apart from their jaw-dropping skills, what captivated me was the way they carried themselves, on and off the field. They embraced youngsters who broke into the team, immediately made them feel at home, and exuded a warmth and affection which was both genuine and heartfelt. It was a great lesson for guys like me, somewhat overawed by the big stage, to be guided through the early days of uncertainty and nerves by these legends. Obviously, I had a great relationship with Chandra and Pras even before my India debut, and our bond grew stronger once we started playing for the country. We are all in regular touch, exchanging stories, lapsing into nostalgia and pulling each other's legs. Much has changed in our respective lives, and yet the important things remain the same.

The relationship between the four champions is unique. In some ways, they were competing with each other for wickets, but they revelled in the other man's success because they were true lovers and connoisseurs of the sport, first and foremost. Some of Bishan's fastest sprints have been when Chandra has got a wicket. I marvel at their friendship, at how close they are to each other six decades on.

SUNIL GAVASKAR

What else can I say about Sunil that I haven't before? As a cricketer, he is in a league of his own. To continue to maintain the standards he did at the highest level for 16 years, match in and match out, is surreal. Apart from a few instances, he always opened the batting, and uncomplainingly carried the team on his shoulders from his first Test in 1971 to his last in 1987.

Sunil the batsman never ceased to surprise me with his powers of concentration. I have never seen him lose concentration, be it whether 10 minutes are left for stumps or at the very start of his innings after a long stint in the field. I don't know how he acquired that enviable character trait. He took nothing for granted, and his preparation was a lesson in meticulousness.

I had played against Sunil a few times before he made the Indian team, a year and a half after me, at the Moin-ud-Dowlah Gold Cup Tournament in Hyderabad and in the Ranji Trophy. His focus was unmatched and his confidence sky-high. I expected nerves, if nothing else, when he made the next step up, but he was unfazed by the challenges of international cricket. There was no change in his approach or attitude, except for the fact that he was forced to cut out some strokes because from the time he announced his arrival in Port of Spain, he became the bulwark of the Indian batting.

The unbelievable array of strokes was pared down. There was not a shot in the book he couldn't play with aplomb, but given the fragility of our middle order, Sunil had to be selective in his choice of strokes because he had to perforce lend the solidity we desperately craved. That being said, whenever an opportunity presented itself, he pounced on it. He didn't try to manufacture strokes, but he also didn't get so obsessed with occupation of the crease that he became ultra-defensive. His greatness lies in the wonderful balance he seemed to strike so effortlessly between watchfulness and stroke-production.

It's often been pointed out that Sunil and I didn't have too many big partnerships in Test cricket. My counter is that the first time we batted together in Tests, in Georgetown in 1971, we had a century stand, which showed we could have partnerships when the stage demanded.

Sunil was my roomie at the start of the tour, and I pulled rank more than once, I am happy to admit. I remember asking him to make me coffee at seven every morning but only waking up at 9.30 to drink it. 'If you are going to drink coffee only at 9.30, why do you want me to make it at seven?' he'd ask, irritated. I'd smile sweetly and tell him, 'I love cold coffee!'

I am sure that daily routine must have infuriated him, but I wasn't done yet. I am not a prankster as such, but when it came to Sunil, I couldn't help myself. Sunil was very particular about the clothes he wore, no matter whether we went out or not. One evening, I watched with great interest as he methodically ironed a shirt, hung it neatly and went for a shower. He stepped out of the washroom to be greeted by the sight of me sporting his lovely shirt, striking a pose and asking,

'How does this look on me?' I am sure it took him his famed powers of restraint to keep himself in check.

At the end of the first Test, Sunil moved out of my room. I was thinking, surely these couldn't have been the reasons for him to opt for a different roommate!

Perhaps I am exaggerating, but I felt very early in our careers that we might have a long partnership away from the game. Sure enough, we became brothers-in-law in a few years' time. We meet as often as our schedules permit; Sunil is the busier one with his various media commitments, and while we don't talk a lot of cricket, we intuitively know what the other person is thinking. There is a lot of give and take: I do most of the talking, needless to say, because that's the level of comfort we have slipped into over the last 50 years.

Sunil is understated and self-contained, quietly going about helping needy sportspersons in whatever way he can. He doesn't make a song and dance of it, which is typical Sunil. The CHAMPS Foundation is his way of expressing his gratitude to the many superstars of Indian sport who have fallen on hard times. He started off by trying to make life slightly easier for other embattled cricketers, and has subsequently brought achievers from other disciplines under his fold. I salute him for his generosity and selflessness. The hallmark of a true champ.

KAPIL DEV

Kapil is the baby in this group because he debuted much later than we all did. From the beginning, it was obvious that he wouldn't be content with merely playing cricket, he was in for the long haul, he wanted to make a name for himself, he wanted to make his family and his country proud. It's little wonder that he scaled the heights he did. For an Indian fast bowler to hold the record for the most Test wickets isn't something anyone would have even imagined till the start of the 1990s.

Kapil was an unpolished gem on the tour to Pakistan in 1978, but emerged as the inspiration for generations of cricketers from non-traditional centres. I initially thought he was predominantly a bowler, but it didn't take me long to change my mind and class him in the all-rounder category. He struck the ball beautifully and, with experience and maturity, started to think like a batsman as well.

Kapil had oodles of natural ability, but he didn't rest on his laurels. He worked really hard to keep himself fit, to hone his craft. He didn't miss a single Test due to injury or fitness issues, remarkable in itself but magnified by the fact that he played more than half his cricket on unresponsive surfaces in India and often single-handedly manned the bowling troops.

Blessed with a lovely action which facilitated swing away from the right-hand batsman, he also developed the in-swinger that made him an even more potent force. He was express when he burst on the scene and bowled really quickly early on. Indeed, until Javagal Srinath towards the end of the 1980s, I hadn't faced a faster Indian bowler, but even though he was forced to compromise on pace, he hardly lost his efficacy because he mastered other skill-sets. A wonderful athlete who moved gracefully on the field, Kapil was three cricketers rolled into one. His place in the pantheon was secured when he inspired the country to the 1983 World Cup title, a development that changed the face of Indian cricket and is primarily responsible for where the sport is in India now. Few have done as much for their sport in their country.

Most importantly for me, Kapil is a lovely person with no hang-ups. What you see is what you get, he says what's in his heart. He doesn't hide his feelings or embrace diplomacy, which means he has stayed true to character despite all his achievements. He is an avid golfer and a great story-teller who guarantees there will never be a dull moment when he is around.

As I write this, I realize, again, what a bonus it was for me to have played Test cricket for India alongside these legends, great gentlemen and cricketers who enriched the sport beyond words.

SIR GARRY SOBERS AND ROHAN KANHAI

From my tennis-ball days, these two names had grabbed my imagination. I knew their scores, I followed their fortunes whenever West Indies played. To see their names in the papers gave me almost as much of a thrill as seeing my own.

Not for a second had I, however, envisioned sharing a cricket field with Sir Garry and Rohan. As destiny would have it, my first overseas tour was to the Caribbean, and there were these two legends in flesh and blood, men who I could now shake hands with.

I was kicking myself for my belated entry into the 1971 Test series due to my cussed knee injury. Under Jai's tutelage, I had observed these two giants keenly during the first two Tests, and when I took guard in Guyana for the first time in a Test in the West Indies, up against me was Sir Garry, the greatest all-rounder the game has seen.

His first ball was a gentle full-toss, on leg and middle. Grateful for the gift, I flicked it through mid wicket for four. Relief!

Years later, I asked Sir Garry if he remembered that ball. 'I do, I do,' he replied with a grin. 'Full-toss despatched through mid wicket.' He paused for a second and added, 'I just wanted you to feel good, to get off the mark as soon as possible.' My mouth fell open. Sir Garry wasn't joking; he had meant to bowl that ball, he had meant for me to move past the dreaded duck. I mean, who does that?

Sir Garry was the captain of the side, Rohan was still a key member. Then, I remembered that the skipper had made his Test debut in 1954, Rohan in 1957. That, so many years on, they were still playing, entertaining and performing alone testified to their greatness and commitment.

Nothing had prepared me for the show Rohan put on during the first two Tests that I missed. He was at least as accomplished a batsman as Sir Garry, if not more gifted. But what left a lasting impression was how he would talk at length about batsmanship, how he would offer nuggets of advice and warning even when we were in the middle, trying to score runs against his team. Sunil, Ekki and I were the biggest beneficiaries of his wisdom and willingness to help without being asked. I can't thank Rohan enough for his guidance on that tour; our Indian connection cemented our friendship, but it was cricket that catalysed our bond.

Sir Garry and Rohan were professional in their approach, but cricket wasn't a job to them. They enjoyed showcasing their skills, and they played the game in the manner in which it should be, all of which played a huge part in influencing how I viewed cricket, in how I carried myself. They influenced not merely West Indian cricket, but youngsters far and wide.

Both of them are extremely proud individuals who believe in letting their cricket speak for them. I have had the privilege of listening to exhilarating stories about their deeds. On West Indies's tour of India in 1958–59, leg spinner Subhash Gupte had dismissed Rohan thrice in a row when he came out to bat in the third Test in Calcutta. Legend has it that when Rohan arrived at the crease early on the first day of the game, someone told Subhash within Rohan's earshot, 'Here comes your bunny.' The 'bunny' put on quite a show: 42 fours, his highest Test score of 256.

Sunil was picked, as part of the World XI including Rohan and Sir Garry, to tour Australia in 1971–72 to play five 'Test' matches. On his return, I bombarded him with questions. I wanted to know what he had seen, I wanted to hear about his experiences and the time spent sharing a dressing room with these great men.

Sunil made a brief reference to Dennis Lillee, 'He is quick, really quick. That's it.' It wasn't until years later that I realized what he had meant.

Lillee took eight wickets in the first innings of the second 'Test' in Perth as the World XI were shot out for 59 and forced to follow-on. They lost Farokh early, which brought Rohan to join Sunil. It seems after Sunil tried to play a couple of shots, Rohan went up to him and said, 'Just hold your end up, I will look after the runs.' He proceeded to score 118, an innings Sunil rates as one of the greatest he has seen.

Three weeks later, Sunil was privileged to witness another masterpiece from close quarters. Sir Garry had made a mere 68 runs in five innings when the series moved to Sydney for the third 'Test'. After his first-innings duck, tongues started wagging and the media went to town suggesting he was no longer interested in cricket, that golf had taken precedence in his list of priorities, that he was a spent force. Sir Garry, Sunil says, never uttered a word, but there was an unmistakable glint in his eye. He went out and smashed 254 in the second innings, leading Sir Don Bradman to call it the greatest innings ever played in Australia. Sir Garry was 35, the tearaway Lillee a sprightly 22. What can you even say?

SIR VIV RICHARDS

Unquestionably the greatest batsman I have played against, Sir Viv was a force of nature, a destroyer when he chose to be, which was often. All my life, I have seen just two cricketers whose very walk to the batting crease indicated their supreme self-confidence—Sir Viv and Sir Garry. Whether they were coming off a duck or a 180, and whether the score read 25 or 275, they breezed in like they owned the stage, like the bowlers were there merely for their entertainment.

Sir Viv's body language suggested he didn't mind facing any bowler. Truth to tell, he didn't, really. I was transfixed by his approach to batting. He wanted to stamp his authority on bowlers of all kinds on any pitch anywhere in the world. He began his career that way, and he sustained that aggression and swag till his final appearance.

A handy off spinner and an outstanding fielder, if Sir Viv isn't spoken of as a genuine all-rounder, it's primarily because his exploits with the bat eclipsed all else. He was, however, the quintessential team man who was the first to congratulate the bowler when he got a wicket, no matter where he was fielding. He was very passionate about West Indian cricket, and made no attempt to disguise or temper that. Playing for West Indies, alongside his mates, meant the world to him, and he always put team ahead of himself.

Sir Viv didn't play for personal milestones, he played to win. I remember Michael Holding once telling me that he didn't care for his own scores. 'He wasn't bothered about scoring 200s, he wanted to win matches. Once he made sure he had put West Indies in an unbeatable position, he would often lose concentration.' Despite his aggressive approach, he finished with an average of over 50, and when he wanted to, he could showcase a different side to his batting, like during his eight-hour 291 against England.

Sir Viv and I became thick friends over time, and when we meet even now, we talk about his batting against spin and Bishan in particular. Sir Viv would lunge forward in exaggerated defence for two deliveries, and pretend-advance down the track to the third. Mid-stride, Bishan would change tack and bowl a quicker, slightly shorter ball. By now,

Sir Viv had started to rock back and would invariably cut him through point. After that, he would turn in my direction with a little half-smile, as if to tell me, 'Did you see what I did there?' That twinkle in his eye is unforgettable, a beautiful expression of child-like delight and tremendous pride in outfoxing a quality opponent. I would respond with a half-smile of my own, mindful that anything else wouldn't amuse Bishan one bit.

Sir Viv was an amazing batsman for whom I have the greatest admiration. There was something about England that set him off, and while the English team didn't enjoy being flogged mercilessly, the cricket world couldn't have enough of Sir Viv versus the Englishmen.

KISS OF LIFE

First things first. Anyone who says he likes playing fast bowling isn't being honest. I have seen Sir Viv tear the best attacks to shreds, but not even he has said so. Then why would mere mortals?

I had had little experience of playing searing pace until my first overseas visit. Graham McKenzie was brisk in my debut series, the fastest I had played till then, but he wasn't an out-and-out pace bowler, not when I faced him at least. He was broad-shouldered and had a strong upper body, so he bowled what is called a 'heavy ball'.

It wasn't until I landed in the Caribbean that I encountered raw pace. Mind you, the pace attack in 1971 wasn't the most fearsome, but it was enough of a window to what lay ahead. I didn't even know bowlers could bowl this fast. Over the next decade, I came across some real quick bowlers who challenged my technique and my courage. I'd never expected to stand up to that examination because, let's face it, we had no quick bowlers back home until Kapil arrived. But once in the middle, I found to my pleasant surprise that while I didn't like being peppered, I actually enjoyed trying to first keep these big men at arm's length, and gradually get on top of them.

Was I afraid of fast bowling? No, not really, I don't think 'afraid' is the right word. But that apprehension was always there, the fear that you might get hit, that the hard red ball could do serious damage. I don't mean to crib and complain, but the fact is there were no helmets, very little protection. If you misjudged the length or top-edged the ball on to your face/head, you can imagine the consequences.

But you can't keep playing with fear. If you don't leave fear behind, you will freeze. I told myself, if you get hit, big deal. You get hit, you tackle it then. No point worrying about it all the time. It's a bit like driving on the highway. You can't not get on to the highway because you fear an accident. If it happens, it happens.

I have held the view that to play great spinners on a turning track, you need impeccable technique and artistry to survive and thrive. And that against great fast bowlers, you need a solid technique to go with loads of courage and bravery. If you have one and not the other, then you are doomed to fail. Today, we see players getting hit on their helmet almost every Test, but they are ready to face the next ball. I can't imagine that happening 45 years back, for instance.

The helmet has become an integral part of one's cricketing gear, as it should. Once you get used to the helmet, you can't play without it. Apart from the leg guards, I was accustomed to wearing a thigh pad reasonably early in my career, and no matter what, I always sported one thereafter. That was all we had. I am glad today's cricketers have access to greater, more advanced protective equipment.

I can state with honesty that I have never been hit on my face or head by a fast bowler. There were a few close shaves, as is inevitable. The first came in my maiden away series, in Bridgetown. I was batting on maybe 14 or 15, just before an interval, when Vanburn Holder unleashed a short ball. I went under, sure the ball would sail over me, but luckily, I didn't take my eyes off it. It didn't climb as much as it should have, and zeroed in on my face at pace. When it was but inches away, I slumped to the ground, the right hand holding the bat handle, the left on the pitch for balance. As my backside thudded into the turf, I could feel my heart pounding. Sir Garry whispered from the slip cordon, 'Almost like Nari.' I was too shaken up to understand what he was saying.

Within minutes, as we broke for tea, Sir Garry walked up to me and said, 'Good that you were watching the ball, thank God nothing happened. You do know that something similar happened to Nari, right?' Sir Garry was talking about Nari Contractor, the captain on the 1962 tour whose career ended when he lost sight of a Charlie Griffith ball in a first-class game, was hit on the back of his skull and nearly lost his life.

That night, when I closed my eyes, I could see the Holder ball coming at me. I sat up, bolt upright, refusing to close my eyes. I didn't sleep that whole night; Holder didn't kill my sleep only that night, it was the first of several sleepless nights.

The other close shave, quite literally, was in my first Test as captain, against Pakistan in Calcutta in 1980. A short ball from Imran brushed the top of my head and went through to the keeper. It wasn't a hit, just minimal contact as it breezed over me. I continued batting and spent the night at hospital where I was under observation, but that was as bad as it got.

Ironically enough, the only time I have been hit in the face while batting was at practice, and by a left-arm spinner at that. We were having nets on a bad surface at the Chinnaswamy Stadium, when Raghuram Bhat got the ball to turn and bounce alarmingly from a spot. I went forward, and bang! It nailed just above the bridge of the nose, between the eyebrows. There was a cut, with blood oozing out. I looked quizzically at him, as if to ask, 'What have you done to me?' I saw the panic on his face and realized he was more shaken up than I was. I still proudly wear that little badge on my forehead as the outcome of friendly fire.

THE SPEED DEMONS

Without a doubt, Michael Holding was consistently the quickest pace bowler I came up against in international cricket. Numerous others were nearly as quick as Michael, but for sustained hostility, he had no equal.

Michael was the classic, classical fast bowler, all rhythm and smoothness. Even as a batsman waiting for him to unleash thunderbolts, you couldn't help but admire his wondrous run-up. It was as if he didn't want to disturb the grass beneath him as his legs ate up ground at great pace. He was a 100-metre sprinter earlier, which explained the lovely run-up.

Unlike Colin Croft, you could see Michael clearly all the way from when he left the top of his bowling mark, till he passed the umpire and let it rip. That didn't guarantee that you could still clearly see the ball, or play it with supreme authority all the time. His short one was a nasty piece of work, slippery and skidding through and forcing the batsman to get into awkward positions.

Andy Roberts, of course, was the master. I faced him more than I did any of the other West Indian quicks, and sometimes when I sit back and think, I really wonder if I actually played and made runs against the likes of Michael and Andy. It all feels so unreal now. For us to chase down 404 against West Indies in the Caribbean, it was quite an accomplishment. It speaks to the grit and character of the batsmen. With the luxury of post-retirement wisdom, I can state without hesitation that I don't know how I played these men, beyond that it came naturally to me, aided by technique and courage. Batsmen of eras past showed us the way, and we learnt from them and tried to show batsmen of the next generation how it is done. It's for history to decide how that worked out.

I have the greatest regard for Malcolm Marshall, though I didn't play much against him. I only faced him in a couple of Tests in his debut series in 1978–79 when his pace was negated by his rawness and docile surfaces. Before long, he established himself as one of the greatest fast bowlers of all time. Croft was tricky because he sprang out from behind the umpire at the last instant, while Joel Garner was a champion whose height made him even more dangerous.

It would have been nice to against play Lillee and Thommo bowling in tandem at their peak. I am not being blasé, it's one of those things you wish for knowing it will never happen. I had heard stories about them long before my first tour of Australia, in 1977–78. How a short ball from Thommo during the series against England in 1970–71 took off from just short of a length, soared over Rod Marsh's head and crashed into the sightscreen.

When you hear things like that, you wonder, 'My God, how will I play bowling of that quality?' I realized later that when you are out there in the middle, it's an entirely different feeling. Listening to tales of their pace and exploits, I was curious about how I would measure up. That I am here to talk about it is by itself an accomplishment.

I was a great believer in visualization on the eve of a Test match.

Our brain was the only data base, so the night before the game, I would lie in bed picturing how specific bowlers in the opposition would run in, how they would load and how they would release the ball. It wasn't so much about what positions I got into rather than embracing the frame of mind that would enable me to move seamlessly into a match situation. Of course, more often than not, I didn't straightaway face a Thommo or an Imran, but they would soon arrive at the bowling crease, wouldn't they?

One of the early pieces of advice I got was to watch the ball into the wicketkeeper's gloves once it is past me, so that I could gauge the nature of the pitch and the pace of the bowler. Where the wicketkeeper gathers the ball is a pointer to the character of the surface. In the West Indies in 1971, every time I turned back, I saw Deryck Murray leaping to collect it high above his head. I was getting a pain in my neck. I knew where the ball would land up anyway, so why bother? Midway through the series, I stopped checking. That routine was history.

Even though he had to shoulder a heavy workload in 1977–78 with Lillee and other key men away playing World Series Cricket (WSC), Thommo bowled superbly throughout the five Tests, and was particularly pacy in the Sydney Test. When we next toured Australia in 1980–81, Lillee was not the express paceman he once was, but he was still more than a handful who had added more cunning and nous, while Len Pascoe was seriously quick.

Among the others who left me in awe were fast-bowling all-rounders Sir Ian Botham, Imran Khan and Sir Richard Hadlee and Englishman Bob Willis, a genuine paceman. All truly, truly great. Botham was rapid in his early days of Test cricket; he was also a very good swing bowler with the outswinger as his patent. He was versatile, willing to experiment and dole out rubbish balls from time to time in order to buy wickets. He had the unbelievable knack of getting wickets which, allied with his uninhibited ball-striking and wonderful hands in the slip cordon, elevated him to a unique category. After Sir Garry, he and Kapil are the best all-rounders in my estimation.

Imran and Sir Richard were bowlers first and all-rounders next. Imran started off predominantly as an inswing bowler but later on added the outswinger to his armoury, and he could make things happen. Sir Richard was always on the money, making the batsman play and therefore putting him in a position to make mistakes. He challenged both the outside and the inside edges by getting the ball to seam in or out, while with the new ball, he was a champion exponent of outswing.

Willis, with his height, was a very awkward customer. Even in India, he was quite a handful, especially at Chepauk where he relished the bounce. To bound in for 90 matches like he did, without compromising on intensity or pace, was a monumental effort. He was worth 325 Test wickets and more, an amazing performer who struck a wonderful alliance with Sir Ian.

If I had the luxury, I would have included a hundred other names in this exercise. Suffice to say that few men appealed to the aesthete in me more than these aforementioned gentlemen.

27

LATER-DAY TITANS

The legacy of Indian cricket has been kept afloat by a string of top-notch performers who have not merely entertained and enchanted, but also taken the country to great heights. That list is long and illustrious. I have spoken about several superstars I was fortunate to play with. After my playing days, my compulsive cricket-watching in various capacities allowed me the luxury of appreciating later-day stalwarts who have wowed the world with their creativity and authority.

Given obvious constraints, I have chosen a group of 10 Indians I'd travel miles to pay and watch in Test cricket. Each brought a special set of skills to the table. Several of them played in what is referred to as the Golden Generation of Indian cricket, a generation that set the tone for the current health of the sport in our country. Here is my pick, in the chronological order of their Test debuts.

MOHAMMAD AZHARUDDIN

The only one in this set against whom I played at the first-class level, Azhar was a magician who used his bat like a wand. His wristiness touched an instant chord in me, and I loved watching him take the ball from outside off and flick it anywhere from mid on to long leg, depending on his mood. It's not as if he didn't have many strokes on the off side, he had everything. But when he played on the on-side with his wrists coming to the fore, it was other-wordly. His wrists were so supple and flexible, and he made shot-making look ridiculously easy. Mind you, those weren't easy strokes to master because you were looking to keep the ball down, not hit in the air. When you play such strokes, you have to be in total control, and Azhar had that control.

I especially loved how he neutralized the spinners even on raging turners. Because of his wrists and because of how he used the crease, he would manoeuvre the ball into gaps with such regularity that you had to marvel at his control. He would shape to play a forward defensive stroke but turn the bat-face at the last instant to pick up ones and twos and keep the board ticking over. That was so beautiful to watch. I also thoroughly enjoyed how he would get on top of the ball and drive off either foot against the faster bowlers. He was extremely difficult to set fields to because he played the angles that so few did. When in full cry, Azhar made the best bowlers in the world appear ordinary, and left the opposition captain looking helpless. That he hardly bludgeoned the ball added to his appeal. In so many ways, he was my kind of batsman.

I remember reading about how one small adjustment to his grip, suggested by Zaheer Abbas on India's tour of Pakistan in 1989, made a huge difference to his batting. While the change in grip was not pronounced, it is to Azhar's credit that he made the adjustment very quickly, and went on to have a successful career for more than a decade thereafter. From his first Test to his last, he never sacrificed grace or elegance, he never made ugly runs. As much as anything else, that delighted me.

While issues with his back and the responsibilities of captaincy forced him to stop bowling, Azhar was a brilliant all-round fielder all the way through, no matter where he was positioned. His catching, especially in the slips, was stunning, and the way he glided across the turf made for riveting viewing. He had very uncanny anticipation, which is why he was there in the right place at the right time, and therefore didn't have to dive around frenetically. That's the greatness of any fielder, anticipation is the key. I am sure his eyesight helped there, and in his batting also: it was a combination of the eyes and the hands, he was just excellent, excellent. If I haven't mentioned that he worked very hard to make the most difficult things appear straightforward, it's only because it is too obvious to need reiterating.

SACHIN TENDULKAR

I enjoyed playing with Sunny Gavaskar, I enjoyed batting with Dilip Vengsarkar. If I could, I would love to have batted with Azhar. And, needless to say, Sachin as well.

When I think of what Sachin has accomplished, I am in awe. To maintain high standards at the top level for nearly a quarter of a century, and that too after having started so young and quickly established himself as the premier batsman in his country, is an extraordinary achievement that speaks volumes of his commitment. I haven't seen a more driven cricketer than Sachin.

Right from his days as a baby-faced 16-year-old, you could make out that there was something special about this young man. You could sense he would go on to scale unprecedented heights, his appetite for runs was insatiable and his focus for one who should have been out with his friends bunking classes and running off to movies was fierce.

Sachin started off wanting to be a fast bowler, but destiny had other plans. World cricket owes a big thanks to Dennis Lillee for quickly scuttling Sachin's fast-bowling aspirations, and he immediately found his calling in a different discipline. That's why, in so many ways, I am convinced he is God's gift to cricket. I believe God sent him to play cricket, and primarily to bat.

I can't begin to imagine what must have been going through his mind when he made his Test debut in a high-pressure series, across the border in Pakistan, who had a formidable bowling attack at the time. He stood up to the challenge like a seasoned veteran, making it clear right at the beginning that he was the real deal. I remember him getting hit on his face by Waqar Younis, reluctantly agreeing to receive treatment, and then smashing the next ball for four. That's when I knew he would go a long, long way.

Sachin owns almost every record there is, but the beauty is that he didn't chase records, they started chasing him from very early as he made runs in all parts of the world. In his first two years in international cricket, he narrowly missed out on a century in New Zealand, and made hundreds in England and Australia.

I don't think anyone, Sachin included, would have bargained for the numbers he ended up with. I mean, who can even predict that someone will finish his career with 100 international hundreds? Amazing, absolutely amazing. I honestly can't see that record being surpassed anytime soon. It's really hard to describe the magnitude of his accomplishment. Across sporting disciplines, that is perhaps the ultimate achievement, yet, to me what he has created is more than even ultimate.

Sunil getting to 10,000 Test runs was phenomenal for world cricket. He set the benchmark, he showed the rest that it was possible to reach that milestone. He is the cricketing equivalent of Sir Edmund Hillary, the New Zealander who was the first to scale Mount Everest. Within a couple of years of his Test career, it was taken for granted that it was a question of when rather than whether Sachin would follow Sunil into that club. For him to finish with nearly 16,000 Test runs, phew! It is testament to his grit, determination, fitness, hunger and the ability to keep his head on his shoulders.

Sachin's stroke-making was so mellifluous that it often overshadowed other aspects of his batting. He was a wonderful technician. Technique personified, if you ask me. He played close to his body, very tight, and presented the full face of the bat, you could see just how straight it was. From a paragon of supreme orthodoxy, Sachin embraced a few cute shots later in his career because the demands of the IPL dictated so, but you could see that a lot of thought and effort had gone into mastering those strokes. It went to show that even after 20 years of international cricket, he was willing to learn and improve, he was eager to adapt to the changed dynamics of white-ball batting. Sachin was very good at deconstructing bowlers and, like Sunil, had the knack of picking up length that was bit quicker than most of the other top batsmen, qualities you find in only the greatest of the great.

For someone to play 200 Test matches and 463 one-dayers is phenomenal. Just imagine the guy's fitness levels, which contributed to his endurance and longevity. He had issues with tennis elbow, with the sesamoid bone before that, and with his groin and back, but they were wear-and-tear rather than fitness-related problems, which are bound to crop up when you have such a long career.

Sachin's presence was so commanding that it automatically created a massive importance around his wicket. Very quickly, he realized that his was the most important wicket in the Indian team. Till his final game, he made sure he retained his focus and didn't throw his wicket away, and even in his last encounters, the opposition felt the job was incomplete until they got him out. Like all true champion sportspersons, he didn't allow the pressure of expectations to affect him because once you get out there in the middle, you get into the zone. You set everything aside and focus on what you are doing, what you are supposed to do. I don't think the fans or the critics affected him one bit. In any case, he was his biggest critic.

Sachin wasn't a bad bowler at all, especially when he delivered leg spin. That he could do anything on the field was even more evident when he switched effortlessly from medium-pace to spin, or from leg spin to off spin in the same over, depending on whether he was bowling to a right-hander or a left-hander. He loved getting wickets as much as sculpting hundreds, and was a magnificent fielder to boot.

Just about the only area where he didn't enjoy as much success was during his two stints as the Indian captain. Maybe I am wrong, but I got the sense that he didn't really enjoy captaincy. But make no mistake, Sachin will go down in history as one of the best sportspersons ever across disciplines. He played cricket the way it should be played, and showed the others too how it should be played.

The aura that accompanied him, I don't think it will surround too many others. The chant of 'Sachin Sachin' still rings in my ears, so many years after his retirement. He is a truly great, great sportsperson. There was a reason why he was treated practically as a God in India.

ANIL KUMBLE

During my playing days, I considered B.S. Chandrasekhar the ultimate match-winner, no two ways about it. Chandra won so many matches on his own, including most famously at The Oval in 1971 to secure our first series win in England. I can say without hesitation that the greatest match-winner since I stopped playing is Anil, and I don't say it only because he finished with 619 Test wickets or because he is from Karnataka.

Fred Trueman was the first bowler to reach the wonderful milestone of 300 Test wickets. For a paceman to achieve that in that era was a grand feat. I remember reading that when he finished his career with 307 wickets, he was asked if he thought anyone could break his record. He said something along the lines of, 'Probably yes, but whoever does will be bloody tired.' Now we are talking about someone with more than 600 wickets, it is unbelievable.

I genuinely dislike comparisons between players, be it from the same era or across generations, but it is difficult not to put Chandra and Anil in the same bracket, Anil readily comes to mind after Chandra. Again, when I say 'after Chandra', I do so because Anil came into the game after Chandra had retired. Who is to say what Anil would have done had he bowled in Chandra's era, or what the latter would have ended up with if he played at the time when Anil did.

Anil's biggest weapon was his control, his accuracy. It always gets my goat when people say he wasn't a big turner of the ball. How does it matter? It's about getting the job done, isn't it? And I know few bowlers who have got the job better than this studious-looking engineer from Bengaluru. I feel if he had the advantage of Umpire Decision Review System (UDRS) during his career, he would have finished with a lot more wickets in his bag because of his lines of operation.

I have seen so many batsmen trying to play him off the back foot. The moment the batsman went back, you knew that was the end of his stint, Anil was that kind of a bowler. He was very aggressive for a spinner, he never gave an inch to any batsman nor did he ask for any. He had the attitude of a fast bowler, was fully aware of what he was capable of, and knew not only his game inside out but also the games and mindsets of the batsmen he bowled to.

He kept finding chinks in their technique and exploited them relentlessly, and with time, he developed plenty of variety. That is bound to happen; being a spinner, you always mature a little later. He started to give the ball more air and because of his control, that made him even more dangerous. He came up with two googlies which fetched him a lot of success, but even as he became a more rounded bowler, he never sacrificed his core strength, which was his line.

Very shrewd and always giving it his 100 per cent, one of my favourite memories is of Anil coming on to bowl in Antigua with his broken jaw strapped up, and getting Brian Lara's wicket on the 2002 tour. That showcased his competitiveness and his commitment, not to mention his propensity to put the team before self. I don't think any other spinner can beat his competitiveness.

In his brief stint at the helm of the team, Anil did an excellent job, most notably on the tour of Australia in 2007–08 when he handled explosive situations with the composure and authority of a statesman. Then again, he wasn't the kind of player who needed a title to take up additional responsibility. After all, during his long and illustrious career, he was always the leader of the Indian bowling pack.

He was a more than handy bat and his Test hundred at The Oval in 2007 is something he cherishes as much as his huge haul of wickets. His crowning glory was taking all 10 Pakistani wickets in the second innings of the Kotla Test in 1999. Only three bowlers have managed that in nearly 150 years in Test cricket. It's a matter of great pride for all of us that one of those three is an Indian.

At the time of writing, he has the most five-wicket hauls in a Test innings by an Indian bowler, another feather in his overcrowded cap. That shows his consistency as a bowler, even though consistency for a leg spinner is not easy to master. Anil was Jumbo in every sense of the word: a jumbo personality with an aggressiveness second to none.

JAVAGAL SRINATH

As I was winding down my career, I kept hearing about a tall, wiry lad from Mysuru who had a whippy action and was frightfully quick. Several of those who talked about this lad were people whose word I trusted implicitly, but even so, I was unprepared for what lay in store in my only encounter against Srinath, at what was then the KSCA 'B' ground.

It was a KSCA league fixture between SBI and Srinath's team, and it wasn't long before he had my number. In my brief stay at the crease before he clean bowled me, I saw for myself how quick he was. He had a beautiful run-up and an awkward, high-arm action. His natural loading and alignment prompted him to primarily bring the ball into the right-handers, and with his pace and the height from which he released the ball, he was a particularly difficult customer to negotiate.

I was witness to Srinath's progression once I became the chairman of the state selection committee, and watched him in a fair few representative matches. That one knock against him, right at the end of my career and at the very beginning of his, had convinced me that he would have a long innings with the national team, all other things being equal. As I observed him more often and more closely, I knew it was just a matter of time before he made the cut.

Kapil Dev was an out-and-out fast bowler at the start of his career, and I played against him at his sharpest, both in domestic cricket and at the Indian nets. I am not exaggerating when I say that Srinath was a shade sharper than Kapil, that he is the fastest Indian bowler I have encountered.

It was a little unfortunate that early in his career, he missed out on so much international cricket due to exigencies of team balance, but the more he played, the more complete he became. With time, while he didn't necessarily consistently get the ball to go away from the right-hander, he got it to straighten from an angle, which brought the outside edge into play quite regularly. It came as no surprise to me that he went on to play for the country for nearly a dozen years with great distinction. He became a highly respected bowler in world cricket, flying the flag of Indian fast bowling and tasting success both overseas where the conditions were to his liking, and in India where he toiled manfully and exploited variable bounce in the fourth innings of Tests with devastating results.

All through his career, on bouncy decks overseas and more docile surfaces at home, he made the top batsmen hop. He hit the deck hard, and because he is naturally intelligent, a lot of thinking went into his bowling. He didn't just run in and bowl fast, he worked batsmen out.

Bowling fast is hard work, and Srinath never compromised on effort. We know of so many who reach the top, and then try to stay there without putting in the necessary effort. But even after establishing himself as a serious force and becoming a permanent member of the Indian team, Srinath kept trying to improve every single day.

There is no doubt Kapil changed the dynamics of Indian bowling. Till his advent, spin was the dominant weapon from a little before our time. I played alongside Madan Lal and Karsan Ghavri, good bowlers who did what was asked of them, but I am sure even they won't call themselves world-class fast bowlers. Kapil inspired a lot of people to want to bowl quick. Several pace bowlers came into the picture after Kapil started playing for India. Srinath was among those inspired by Kapil, but you could make out straightaway that he was different compared to the other young bowlers who charged in and tried to blast batsmen out.

Once he became a senior in the team, Srinath started mentoring newcomers like Zaheer Khan and Ashish Nehra. I am delighted that he followed in my footsteps and has been a highly regarded ICC match referee for many years now, a stint he seems to be enjoying as much as he did bowling fast for the country and picking up more than 550 international wickets.

SOURAV GANGULY

I was a selector when Sourav was picked for the Indian ODI team in 1991–92, and the chairman of selectors when we named him for the tour of England in 1996. Our decision, which generated plenty of heat and debate, stood vindicated when he made hundreds in his first two Tests and announced his arrival on the world stage emphatically.

Sourav has to be among the finest left-handers to have played for India. He was very graceful through the off side, and was a destroyer of spin with his twinkle-toed approach and sweet timing that carried the ball well over the boundary ropes. He had a great eye, and even though he didn't move his feet a lot, he seldom hit the ball in the air unless he wanted to. His cover-driving, and generally driving through the off, was out of the top drawer, and he played with such ease, grace and effortlessness that you could watch him bat all day long.

Once he moved up to open the batting in one-day cricket, he became a more free-stroking player in Test cricket too, hitting over the top without inhibition or fear. Sourav was the kind of player who never struggled to score runs. When he did make big runs, he scored them with imperial authority.

Beneath that sinuous grace was a steely resolve. He had a great run in his last two years in Test cricket when he fought his way back into the team after being dropped. I believe the final stanza of his career was as exhilarating as the first couple of years, when he hardly put a foot wrong in Test cricket.

As fine a batsman as he was—in limited-overs cricket, he is among the all-time greats—Sourav's greatest contribution to Indian cricket was as captain. He took over from Sachin in early 2000 at a difficult time for the sport in the country, but it didn't take him long to win back the trust and adoration of the fans. Sourav was a terrific student of the game, very shrewd, and he knew how to get the best out of his team. A lot of youngsters who subsequently went on to big things were hand-picked and nurtured by Sourav, who was a master motivator and who instilled the belief in the team that they were second to none.

They call him the Prince, and that shows in the way he carries himself. Just as the Nawab was in a league of his own, so is the Prince of Kolkata.

RAHUL DRAVID

The first thing that struck me about Rahul was his eyes. The hunger in them, the desire to do something, the desperation to not just chase his ambition but also fulfil it. It wasn't overt or overstated, but it was there. Unmistakably.

This boy had been making waves in junior cricket, and I couldn't but notice the admiration and respect with which those who had seen him bat spoke of him. That piqued my curiosity; the more they talked about his technique, the more eager I was to see him in action.

It didn't take me long to realize that my friends and fellow cricketers weren't exaggerating. I was impressed with his correctness, technique and temperament. Everything about Rahul was so controlled, until you reached the eyes and noticed the raging fire in them. He was full of determination, his face told you, if you paused to listen, how hungry he was to excel in what he was doing. That determination was to be his calling card during a fabulous career that lasted 16 years. As he played longer, he became as much a part of the limited-overs firmament as the red-ball set-up. Even though these variants placed additional, sometimes even unfamiliar, demands, the quality of his batting and his fierce determination never changed.

His mantra was to occupy the crease and play according to the merit of the ball. And work hard. Day after day. He was the kind of person who derived a lot of confidence from working hard. When he got out, he wasn't the sort to sit back and brood. He would get into the nets and work on rectifying whatever problems he might have identified. Not many people possess that quality. Basically, when you get out, you think, you think, and you think some more. But this guy, he would think, and then go the nets and work, work and work. Nobody is perfect, but identifying and working on one's shortcomings makes a lot of difference to your mindset. It also takes a lot of courage to do what he did, to keep working on his technique. It takes a lot out of you, especially when you have tasted success at the international level, which is why not many people do that. It takes so much energy out of you, and the vast majority prefers to preserve that energy for matches, not practice. In my opinion, for the length of his international career, he was technically the soundest batsman in world cricket. He got runs everywhere, and it's not like he had a short career. He played more than 150 Test matches and as I said, no compromise: work, work and work harder. He was a very astute thinker, and analysed the game perfectly.

Thinking came naturally to him, and that obviously helped him when he became the captain in 2005. He was able to get what he wanted out of his team-mates, and in conjunction with his bowlers, was able to identify and exploit the weaknesses of the opposition batsmen, key factors that helped him emulate Ajit Wadekar and lead the team to series wins in the Caribbean and England.

Rahul was the ultimate team man who never knew how to say no. Even though he didn't enjoy opening the batting in Tests, he still put his hand up when the team required him. When he was asked to keep wicket in ODIs to help with the balance of the 11, not only did he take up the challenge, but he worked his backside off to ensure he didn't let the bowlers down. He might have kept at school, but to stand up to quality bowlers at the international level after many years of not donning the big gloves is no easy task. He approached wicketkeeping with customary diligence, and it was no surprise that his work behind the stumps was exemplary.

As if all this wasn't enough, Rahul was an outstanding catcher close-in, to pacers and spinners alike. I am not saying he didn't put down any, but I don't actually remember him dropping too many. He made magnificent catches appear straightforward because he worked so hard at practice. I mean, to hold 210 catches in Test cricket, unreal!

All told, a tremendous package who, thankfully, is still actively involved in cricket. He did great work with the India Under-19 and 'A' sides, contributing to the growth of several youngsters and with many more in the pipeline. As the head of cricket at the National Cricket Academy and now as the national head coach, Rahul is the definition of giving back to the game.

V.V.S. LAXMAN

Like most top batsmen from the south of India, Laxman was an excellent player off the back foot because he was brought up on matting wickets. Consequently, not only did he have time to play his shots, but he also used his wrists superbly to keep the ball down, much like his Hyderabadi predecessor Azhar. I know Laxman played in an era different to mine, and started his international career more than a decade after Azhar, but in his formative years, a lot of his batting was on matting. That pretty much moulds your approach, and it stays with you for the rest of your career, no matter where you play and what the conditions are. Of course, in order to be successful on a consistent basis, adaptability is the key, and Laxman adjusted to situations and conditions a lot better than most.

Laxman used to be a bit nervous in the initial stages, which can happen to the best in the business. I am not saying he was always a nervy starter, but in some ways, he was like me because I didn't feel comfortable until I got my first run, a legacy of my duck on Test debut.

But after he played out a few deliveries, what I call the genuineness of the batsman would come into play.

Laxman had all the shots in the book, and he played all of them so beautifully because he had lots of time, again a lot like Azhar. He used the crease very well, and because he was blessed with a little more time, he was such a fantastic puller of the short ball off the front foot. I used to marvel at the pace at which the ball raced off his bat even though he hardly tried to hit it. I loved watching him bat, it was such a grand treat. He cut an imperial figure at the batting crease, and whenever he made a substantial contribution, you could rest assured that it would have been entirely struggle-free.

I thoroughly enjoyed his 281 in Kolkata, one of the greatest Test innings of all time. He put on a masterclass against the very potent leg spin of Shane Warne, driving one ball through the covers and whipping the next through mid wicket even though both pitched at the exact same spot. His wrists were both supple and steely, and he could find the narrowest of gaps with a little twirl of his exceptional wrists at the very last fraction.

A series of tall scores in Test cricket to go with that monumental 281 reiterated not just his class but the skill to fuse style with substance. He has triple-hundreds in first-class cricket as well. I admired the fact that he played the game on his own terms. It must have taken so much guts to inform the selectors in 2000 that he was done with opening the batting in Tests when the Indian middle order was packed. To follow that up with a string of hundreds and double-hundreds, and break open the door to the middle order, was a statement of intent with few parallels.

Over time, Laxman became adept at batting with the tail. Even though he relished the No. 3 position, he batted at No. 5 or No. 6 for most of his career, which makes his contributions more noteworthy. You know there aren't too many accomplished batsmen to follow, but Laxman was able to coax and cajole his partners to play above themselves. When, as a tail-ender, you know that the specialist batsman has so much confidence in you, it does wonders for your thinking. Laxman enjoyed being in such positions, and he showed faith in the tail. In those situations, the opposition knew he was a crucial figure, but he seldom threw his wicket away because he knew that would open up both ends. He assessed which player could handle the pressure and the situation, and who had the technique to survive in which conditions, all ingredients of an excellent cricket brain.

I can't recall too many other batsmen winning so many matches off their own bat. That was largely because of his strength of conviction that as long as he was there, he could do it for the team. The opposition would be worried, because they knew that if Laxman was still at the crease, the runs would come. He wouldn't just potter around, he'd make time in the middle count. Because of the ease of his batting, the strokes he played and the ability to find the gaps, he would almost creep up on you. And because he played the ball on its merit, he was largely risk-free even though his stroke-making was exhilarating.

Like Rahul, Laxman worked very hard on his catching in the slips, where any lapse in concentration can be disastrous. He wanted to be involved in the action because otherwise, fielding the whole day can become a drudge. Rahul and V.V.S., they spared no effort at practice, which is why they were so reliable in match situations.

Now, Laxman has followed the Rahul path and become the Head of Cricket at the NCA. Quite clearly, Indian cricket is on to a good thing.

VIRENDER SEHWAG

Watching a domestic 50-over game from the Diamond Box at the Chinnaswamy Stadium, I was astonished to see a stocky right-handed opening batsman attack the cricket ball like he hated its sight. I thought his hell-for-leather approach was too good to last, but even though he came hard at every ball, he was connecting most of them sweetly, off the middle of the blade. I was wondering who he was when Madan Lal, my former teammate, sauntered up and said, 'Keep an eye on this guy Sehwag.'

I'd be less than honest if I said I took Madan seriously. I mean, why was this guy trying to smash every ball? The target was modest, there was so much time to get the job done, but no, he kept hammering away. I had never seen Sehwag bat before, and I thought Madan's words was a classic case of someone talking up a batsman from their own state, even when Madan earnestly informed me that that's how 'Viru' batted, and with great success back home in Delhi.

I am happy I was proved wrong, that my scepticism turned out to be without basis. Sehwag brought such joy with his unbridled shot-making and uncomplicated approach that sometimes, just sometimes, I envied him a little.

A lot of players change their approach when they graduate from first-class to international cricket. They feel compelled to conform, almost, so they try to become something they are not. Sehwag was different. He didn't try to change anything, either when he started playing Test cricket or when he was thrust into the role of an opener. I shudder to think what might have happened had either his early coaches, or the Indian team management, asked him to tone down his aggression. Surely, the results would have been disastrous?

I am not sure Sehwag worked on his game as much as some of his contemporaries in the Indian team, but then again, he was a unique player who became better and better and who matured almost on his own. His hand-eye coordination was simply unbelievable; I saw such coordination and instincts in a player for the first time since the maverick, Srikkanth.

At my first sighting, I did feel Sehwag was a gifted player, but I wasn't a fan of what I thought were the undue risks he was taking. But Madan knew what he was talking about. Just as I had witnessed the growth of Anil, Srinath and Rahul from close quarters, Madan had seen Sehwag for a long time, and his words turned out to be prophetic.

The more I saw Sehwag play, the more I marvelled at how simple he kept things. He continued to play his strokes fearlessly, but it was impossible to miss the steadiness of his head, the secret to his success, if you like. Even when I saw him play in Raipur in March 2021, that still head was such a feature of his batting, as steady as it was when he was at his prime. Neither that, nor his style of batting, changed over time. If the first ball of a Test match was there to be hit, he would oblige. He thought nothing to going from 99 to three-figures with a six, and I don't know if anyone else would have even contemplated hitting a six to become his country's first triple-centurion! I have been asked if I ever expected Sehwag to be the first from India to score a Test 300. My answer is simple, you don't expect anyone to get a triple because it is not an everyday occurrence. After all, only 31 triples have been scored in Test history, and it's remarkable that Sehwag is one of only four players to boast two 300-plus scores.

A lot of people had questions about his technique, even I had my doubts when I first saw him. I remember having a conversation with Rohan Kanhai about Sir Viv Richards, where he said, 'He's a very good player, he has got a beautiful eye and has great coordination between eye and hand. But he is young now, let's see how long he can carry on like this.' Look where Sir Viv finished up! Likewise, people had their doubts about Sehwag, but look at what he achieved. What a tremendous career he had!

His approach was so simple: anything in his arc would disappear. But you can't survive and have a long, successful career merely by throwing your bat around. He knew what he was doing, he knew what worked for him. Sehwag had a wide range of strokes, even though he played away from his body quite a lot. He had the control despite his approach. He was pretty much left to his own devices all the time, I don't think many tried to teach him or change the way he batted. Credit to all his coaches who recognized the kind of player he was and let him be. That helped his way of playing because if you make a batsman curb his shots, it can so easily affect the entire thinking of his batsmanship.

M.S. DHONI

M.S. Dhoni had played senior representative cricket for Bihar and East Zone for more than four years, but I knew little about him until I got a call from Sandeep Patil. Sandy was the India 'A' coach during the tri-series in Nairobi in August 2004, when Dhoni provided the first glimpses of his wondrous ball-striking with blistering knocks at the top of the order against the 'A' teams of Kenya and Pakistan.

Sandy spoke highly of his young ward's promise, adding that he was a little unorthodox. When I first saw Dhoni, I thought to myself, 'He isn't just a *little* unorthodox, Sandy!'

To play for as long as he did, and with the success he enjoyed, despite remaining true to his core character, is one of Dhoni's greatest strengths. Like Sehwag, he didn't change his style too much, but he kept improving by making subtle adjustments that came with experience and a greater understanding of his game.

Dhoni has the not unjustified reputation of being a dasher, but he knew exactly what he was doing. Like all driven achievers, he wanted to be the best version of himself every single day, which is why it is no surprise that he excelled as a batsman, a wicketkeeper who changed the dynamics behind the stumps, and a leader who won everything there is to win.

Somewhat of an unexpected selection as captain for the inaugural World T20 in South Africa in 2007, Dhoni marshalled a relatively inexperienced team superbly to take them all the way to the title. That was to kick off the legend of Dhoni the captain. Over time, he led India to the 50-over World Cup as well as the Champions Trophy crowns, and was in command when the team rose to the No. 1 rankings in Test cricket for the first time, in December 2009.

In so many ways, Dhoni became the inspiration for cricketers from the hinterlands. He was proud of his Ranchi roots, and each of his successes became a stepping stone for players from the non-traditional centres, who now were convinced if they possessed the skills, consistency and ambition, nothing could prevent them from reaching their goals. Dhoni's contribution to Indian cricket in that regard is as significant as his glittering deeds on the park.

While Dhoni's one-day coups have earned him just plaudits, he was a very good Test batsman too. You have to be if you are to score a double-hundred, among other things. Even in Test cricket, he could switch gears effortlessly, but he was a veritable giant in the limited-overs formats who elevated finishing an innings to rarefied levels. At his prime, he would literally intimidate the bowlers into committing mistakes. The margin for error in the final stages of a chase was so miniscule and Dhoni's heavy bat so punishing that even the best bowlers lost the battle in the mind long before they hesitantly ran in and copped severe punishment.

The label Captain Cool summed him up beautifully. I have never seen him ruffled on the field, a wonderful trait to possess when 10 other men are looking to you for guidance and reassurance. He knew how to maximize his resources, be it for India or in the IPL, where he took Chennai Super Kings to dizzying heights. How he managed to stay unruffled while playing at the highest level for so long will remain a mystery. It is common for skippers to get frustrated from time to time when things aren't going their way, and I am sure Dhoni did as well because he too is human, but nothing showed on his face or in his actions. Extraordinary.

I have been told he didn't work a lot on his keeping. I am sure whatever he did, he did so quietly, in the background, though because he had confidence in himself, he knew his limitations as well as he did his strengths. Without outwardly being so, Dhoni was authoritative and in total command.

He is very high on my list of the greatest all-rounders in cricket history. Make no mistake, he was a true all-rounder: captain, keeper and batsman. In all these facets, he did a marvellous job. I have been a huge admirer of his fitness and how, even until a couple of years back, he was so quick between the wickets. Only in recent times in the IPL have I seen him struggle physically, but you expect that, considering he is 40 and only plays from IPL to IPL. All told, he has done a tremendous job for India. Truly a gifted athlete, and one of the all-time greats of Indian cricket.

VIRAT KOHLI

At a young age, almost by himself, Virat realized that he needed to change himself as an athlete if he was to touch great heights as a batsman. That awareness is a remarkable trait to possess. His physical transformation has been stunning, and because he is such a fit individual, it gives him a massive edge over other equally skilled batsmen.

Virat not just plays all three formats but captained the country in all of them as well until recently, apart from leading his IPL franchise. All of this is bound to make huge demands on his mind, but his healthy body, as much as anything else, enables him to meet those challenges effortlessly.

His fitness keeps him fresh at the end of each day, and at the beginning of the next. Even if he has batted an entire day, you won't suspect that by just looking at him the following day when he walks out to resume his innings. He never looks tired, and is always seeking ways to keep the game moving forward, whether it is through resplendent ball-striking or electric running between the wickets. And that's not just once in a while. His energy is unbelievably striking, and when he takes fresh guard, he is fresh as a daisy.

Virat is beautifully balanced when playing his shots, which is why even if he goes with his hands more than his feet while driving through the off side, he is still able to keep the ball down. The higher the quality of the bowling he is confronted with, the more he seems to enjoy getting on top of the attack. That's been his plus point, he doesn't want to concede the upper hand to the bowler. His response to a poor tour of England in 2014 was breathtaking. In so many ways, that tour contributed to making him the player he is today. For the last seven years, he has been the most dominant batsman in the world, and not merely in one format.

Because he works so hard, Virat expected the same from his colleagues in terms of effort. It is impossible for the rest not to be inspired by their captain's approach, you could see that they wanted to give their all to him and to the team. He didn't demand of his men what he didn't do. And when he did ask them to get out of their comfort zones, they responded readily because of the high standards he had set.

He is the classic example of correct, orthodox batting translating to handsome, heavy and quick runs even in T20 cricket. With strong basics, you can hold your own in the shortest format, as I have mentioned more than once. When you have that base covered, you can play your strokes freely, you can hit over the top, but you don't necessarily have to play fancy strokes. Chances are that if you attempt 10 fancy strokes, only three of them will come off and you could be dismissed the other seven times. If, on the other hand, you play with the full blade, it is more than likely that you will be able to execute properly seven out of 10 times. That's something Virat appears to have worked out very well. Why take a risk unless you have to?

So much has been spoken about Virat's aggression but to me, it shows how involved he is and how much he wants to win. Sometimes, he overdoes it, especially when he hurls the ball to the keeper's gloves even though the batsmen have no interest in running. He loves to set an example in the hope that the rest will be equally focussed and hungry for victory. But I don't think he is a very aggressive person off the field. He has what is called white-line fever which, when channelled, is a lovely quality in a competitive sportsperson. India's most successful Test captain with 40 wins in 68 matches when he stepped down in January 2022, Virat has left his successor with an exciting, talented and motivated bunch.

28

HUMAN BEING FIRST, CRICKETER NEXT

I am not sure when it was, but the first time I saw my name in the newspaper, a jolt of electricity shot through my body. I experienced a thrill I didn't know was possible. It was heady and intoxicating; I wanted to see my name in the headlines on a regular basis.

The entire process fascinated me, I must admit. Here I was, playing an obscure schools' match in some remote part of the city, so how did the newspaper reporters know about this? How did they know who had performed in which match? Where did they get the information from? I had numerous questions but no answers, largely because I asked these questions of myself.

I hadn't been big on reading newspapers until that point. But from then on, every time I played a match, I'd scan the papers the next morning to see if I found a mention. One particular day, I was very disappointed that I had been ignored. My older brother, who had watched my sudden interest in newspapers with mounting curiosity, asked me what was bothering me.

'I thought they would carry my score. I played really well yesterday.'
'How much did you make?'
'I am not sure. Maybe 15 or 16, I batted beautifully.'

With a chuckle, he told me, 'That's not enough to merit being reported. You have to score at least 30 runs or take two wickets. Otherwise, they will run out of space, won't they?'

That was an eye-opener; I understood that to be recognized, I had to perform. If I wanted to see my name in print, I had to score big. I loved reading my name, so now I had an added incentive to keep performing.

I never took a newspaper to my family or my friends and proudly boasted that my name had been carried. I derived satisfaction from being recognized; even today, when I see my name on print, I feel electrified. Honest.

◆

As I have mentioned previously, cricket and I were a natural fit. From the time I first held a bat, I had no time for anything else: not another sport, not academics. I was too young to know what I wanted, or how to go about things, but I knew I'd play for the country. How? Wish I had the answer.

My first reality check came when I was not picked for the state schools' team. I sat down and asked myself if I knew where I was headed. I thought my life in cricket was over even before it had begun, but I wasn't unaware that academics wasn't my cup of tea simply because I had no interest in studies. I had no choice but to pursue cricket if I wanted to make a name for myself, if I wanted to be successful, if I wanted to have a career (not that there was a career to be had out of cricket then). It was a very happy coincidence that I would be pursuing something I loved deeply.

Simply put, cricket is my everything. It's my life, it's made me what I am. I love the game so much that even today, I set my alarm clock to 4.30 a.m. when India are playing in Australia to catch every ball of every Test match. I might not necessarily enjoy all the formats, but because it is my sport, I watch any and every live cricket on television. Whenever I can, I go in person to the Chinnaswamy Stadium; I talk and joke around, but I never take my eyes off the ball, literally.

Few people outside of my immediate circle had heard of me when I made my debut for Mysore in the Ranji Trophy. All that changed within one day. On the first day of the match against Andhra in Vijayawada, I was unbeaten on 200-plus. When I woke up the next morning, I was delighted to see my name figuring prominently in the local papers. As I walked into the ground, my senses acutely sharp, I could hear people whispering my name. Wow, so this is what being recognized entails! I could live with this, for sure.

Between that game and my India debut, when I was frolicking with my friends on the streets of Bangalore, I'd try to gauge if others on the road recognized me. I didn't think of myself as a celebrity, but I'd look from the corner of my eye to see if any of the people we passed on the road identified me, mentioned my name. If they did, I'd inwardly be delighted. Perhaps that's how it was for my other contemporaries too, I don't know. I can only speak for myself.

I had been entranced from the beginning by the attention famous people get, by the appreciation for not just their craft but also their conduct. My shining example was Dr Rajkumar, the great Kannada and south Indian actor who captivated me with his presence and charisma. He was my first non-cricketing hero. Even now, when I hear of the reverence and affection with which people talk about him, my heart is filled with joy. The legacy he left behind is celebrated not only in Karnataka, but across the country; it's an unbelievable legacy of kindness, warmth and love.

I'd watch his movies by myself, if I had to. He lorded the screen, just like Mr N.T. Rama Rao and Mr Sivaji Ganesan did. When I looked around, I'd see the awe on people's faces as they watched them perform. We all knew we were seeing masters at work.

I wanted to be like them. I wanted to entertain people, I wanted their appreciation. Compared to Dr Rajkumar, I have achieved little, I am aware. But I craved people's appreciation. Being recognized was a huge boost. It gave one the confidence that people are following your progress, so you must give something back to them as well.

◆

As is inevitable during a long career, there was plenty of criticism of my batting. That was fine, I made my peace with it very early on. If I expected to be praised when I did well, then it was natural that I should be prepared for flak when I let the team down. I realized that on my debut itself; the same Kanpur crowd that hurled matkas at me after I was dismissed for zero in the first innings gave me a rousing reception when I walked back after making 137 in the second. My conviction that fame and recognition were linked directly and only to success was further firmed up.

I am huge on friendships, as anyone who knows me will agree. At various stages of my life, I had different groups of thick friends. I have lost touch with many, but so many are still very good mates with whom I communicate on a daily basis. Cricket has encouraged me to forge these relationships, to form bonds that might not have been possible otherwise.

Raghu (B. Raghunath) is my closest buddy, we know each other from the time we played tennis-ball cricket as teenagers. We weren't teammates then—we lived in different localities and often played against each other—but we organically gravitated towards each other. He was already with SBI when I joined the bank, and we spent more than 35 years as colleagues. I know Raghu will always have my back, just as he knows that I am with him every step of the way.

My wife has been my constant companion for all these years and has been supportive of me every step of the way. For this, I feel blessed. Further, I believe it's important for a family to be friends too and for this to happen, it is necessary to have a good understanding of one another and to be able to share the good and especially the bad. I have never sought to impose a strict pecking order at home and have always strived to be just as approachable as a husband/father as I was a cricketer/coach. I don't expect Kavita to conduct herself in a particular way because she is married to me, or for Daivik to remember that he is my son when he goes out in public. Likewise, they are happy for me to be me.

I am also an inveterate lover of dogs, we have had a dog from the time I can remember. Various breeds: Doberman, Labrador, Lhasa Apso. I remember as a young boy, if I found a puppy on the streets who was playful and clearly uncared for, I would pick it up very gently and take it home with me. I'd take great care to ensure that the owners of our house were kept in the dark because they frowned upon tenants owning pets. I even recall my mother getting mildly cross with me for constantly bringing home a new furry little friend, yet her heart of gold would not allow her to let it go without giving it a bellyful of food. Once she had fed the little one, she'd firmly tell me to take it back to where I had found it. I couldn't argue with her logic, 'Its mother will be missing it, won't she, Vishwa?'

Now we have a frisky fella called Alaska, a Siberian Husky who is the apple of our eyes. One look at him, and all my tensions disappear. He has taken it up upon himself to religiously give me adorable little licks as 'good mornings' and 'good nights', all the while keeping his sky-blue eyes firmly fixed on me. From all my furry friends, I have learnt the power of unconditional love—the kind of love that is pure and untethered, much like how all my dogs lived their lives and were a big part of mine.

◆

Having said that, I am not averse to starting a little fire from time to time. I can be a bit short-tempered when I want to be, sometimes I deliberately instigate arguments. I believe when you argue a little, you learn a lot of things so long as you are not emotionally involved in the process. Especially in a bar, the truth comes tumbling out when discussions get heated. You learn a little bit about exactly what the other person thinks of you!

The one thing I can say with complete certainty is that I have not changed as a person. I am what I have always been: it's a bit like my batting. With experience, I customized my game according to situations without changing my inherent technique. Likewise in life, I have remained the same: it was never Young Vishwanath, Great Vishwanath, Greater Vishwanath. It is just Vishy, plain and simple. You can't be someone today, and someone else totally different tomorrow just because you have become slightly famous. What does that say about you?

People sometimes refer to me as a celebrity. If that's the case, I am contented. I consider myself fortunate to have the love and affection of so many. If, owing to my so-called celebrity status, I am able to help friends in need, or support good causes, then why not? In my view, being in the public eye has more plusses than minuses. I'd like to think I have never misused or abused the esteem in which people hold me.

If there's one thing that puts me off, it's dishonesty and double standards. I don't like people who say something to your face, then say the exact opposite behind your back. I don't claim to be Harischandra, but I can keep my hand on my heart and swear that I haven't done so. Don't tell me I'm a nice person, and then go to someone else and say something different because there is a very good chance that someone else could be my friend. Why indulge in such whataboutery?

I don't claim to be the perfect human being. Far from it. I am sure I have hurt people, but what I do know is that I have never done so knowingly. I don't want to hurt anyone because I don't like being hurt. You must be with others how you expect others to be with you. That's my philosophy. I believe you don't have to achieve anything in life, just being a good person is an achievement in itself.

That's what I want to be remembered as: a nice person, maybe a good batsman too. Sport, any sport, teaches you how to be a good human being if you are willing to learn. Why just sport, every walk of life comes with the same lessons. Cricket has taught me things I might not have learnt otherwise. Like gentleness. Don't taunt the bowler, enjoy your batting. When you apply those learnings to life, the world invariably becomes a better place.

Cricket's life lessons have made me the person I am, warts and all. I will be eternally indebted to the sport I love for giving me my identity, and to the Almighty for giving me cricket, above all else.

ACKNOWLEDGEMENTS

I'd like to thank all those who helped give shape and substance to this book.

First, my family and especially Daivik, who has been my pillar of support all through this emotional journey that took me back to the very start.

Kapish Mehra and his team at Rupa Publications, who made this exercise become a reality.

Deccan Herald, who generously threw open their photo library and allowed me to dive into their excellent collection.

The Hindu, who readily agreed to let me use their images, an offer I could not avail.

To Kaushik, who broke down all my inhibitions and has patiently spent countless hours transforming my life story into this book, which is long due and has finally come to fruition.

And finally, all my friends, fans, teammates and lovers of our great game, for whose affection I will be eternally grateful.